Books are to be returned on or before
the last date below.

Nationalism, Violence and Democracy

Also by Ludger Mees

DOCUMENTOS PARA LA HISTORIA DEL NACIONALISMO VASCO: De los Fueros a nuestros días (*with S. de Pablo and J.L. de la Granja*)

EL MEDOC ALAVES EN EL ORIGEN DEL VINO DE CALIDAD DE RIOJA

EL PENDULO PATRIOTICO: Historia del Partido Nacionalista Vasco, I: 1895–1936 (*with S. de Pablo and J.A. Rodríguez Ranz*)

EL PENDULO PATRIOTICO: Historia del Partido Nacionalista Vasco, II, 1936–1979 (*with S. de Pablo and J.A. Rodríguez Ranz*)

ENTRE NACION Y CLASE: El Nacionalismo Vasco y su base social en perspectiva comparativa

EUSKOEUROPA

NACIONALISMO VASCO, MOVIMIENTO OBRERO Y CUESTION SOCIAL, 1903–1923

Nationalism, Violence and Democracy

The Basque Clash of Identities

Ludger Mees
University of the Basque Country
Bilbao
Spain

First published 2003 by
PALGRAVE MACMILLAN
Houndmills, Basingstoke, Hampshire RG21 6XS and
175 Fifth Avenue, New York, N.Y. 10010
Companies and representatives throughout the world

PALGRAVE MACMILLAN is the global academic imprint of the Palgrave Macmillan division of St. Martin's Press, LLC and of Palgrave Macmillan Ltd. Macmillan® is a registered trademark in the United States, United Kingdom and other countries. Palgrave is a registered trademark in the European Union and other countries.

ISBN 1–4039–0265–8

This book is printed on paper suitable for recycling and made from fully managed and sustained forest sources.

A catalogue record for this book is available from the British Library.

Library of Congress Cataloging-in-Publication Data
Mees, Ludger.
    Nationalism, violence, and democracy : the Basque clash of identities /
Ludger Mees.
        p. cm.
    Includes bibliographical references and index.
    ISBN 1–4039–0265–8 (cloth)
    1. Nationalism–Spain–Paâs Vasco–History. 2. Paâs Vasco
(Spain)–History–Autonomy and independence movements. 3. Political
violence–Spain–Paâs Vasco–History–20th century. 4. Democracy–Spain–Paâs
Vasco–History–20th century. I. Title.

DP302.B53M374 2003
320.54'089'992–dc21   2003044170

10   9   8   7   6   5   4   3   2   1
12   11   10   09   08   07   06   05   04   03

Printed and bound in Great Britain by
Antony Rowe Ltd, Chippenham and Eastbourne

For my sons Oier and Jan, now German-Basque youngsters and later, hopefully, also citizens of the world

Contents

List of Tables

List of Graphs

Acknowledgements

This book would have been impossible without the cooperation and help of different friends and colleagues. I would like to mention firstly the members of our research project 'Coming out of Violence: the Problems of Building Peace' hosted at INCORE and sponsored by UNESCO's Culture of Peace Programme and the Central Community Relations Unit of the Northern Irish Government. During the two years of our common research, the project managers, John Darby and Roger Mac Ginty, as well as the co-researchers Pierre du Toit, Tamar Hermann, David Newman and Paikiasothy Saravanamuttu were helpful by providing crucial comparative insights concerning their own cases of conflict and violence. Moreover, they all proved their academic collegiality and expertise within an atmosphere of real cross-cultural friendship, and this combination was what made our project so very gratifying and productive.

Special thanks are due to Alison Howson at Palgrave, who gave me the opportunity to reconsider and finally redo my initial book proposal, when the breakdown of the ceasefire and the new information published afterwards made this reconsideration necessary.

I am also grateful to Bill Mac Alevey, who did a great job in cleaning up the impurities of my written English, which suffers from the linguistic confusion produced in the mind of a German scholar whose daily work and life develops among permanent language shifts from Spanish to Basque, German and English or vice versa.

Finally, a special mention for my friend and colleague Pierre du Toit from the University of Stellenbosch in South Africa. As an expert on ethnic violence and peace processes, he took the time to read carefully and comment on the complete manuscript. I really appreciated his remarks and reflections, trying to incorporate them into the text as far as possible. However, it goes without saying, that all the hypothetical deficiencies of this book are exclusively mine.

Last, but not least, I need to mention my wife Begoña. She sponsored this book both by excusing me temporarily from housework and by restoring my energies with intriguing dishes from the Basque cuisine. Mila esker, zuri ere!

List of Abbreviations

ADEGI	Asociación de Empresarios de Gipuzkoa
AP	Alianza Popular
BAC	Basque Autonomous Community
CCOO	Comisiones Obreras
EA	Eusko Alkartasuna
EE	Euskadiko Ezkerra
EH	Euskal Herritarrok
EHNE	Euskal Herriko Nekazarien Elkartea
EIA	Euskal Iraultzarako Alderdia
ELA–SOV	Eusko Langileen Alkartasuna–Solidaridad de Obreros Vascos
ETA-p.m.	ETA político-militar
ETA	Euskadi 'ta Askatasuna
ETA-m	ETA militar
EU	European Union
GAL	Grupos Antiterroristas de Liberación
GDP	Gross Domestic Product
HB	Herri Batasuna
IK	Ipartarrak
INCORE	Initiative on Conflict Resolution and Ethnicity
IRA	Irish Republican Army
IU	Izquierda Unida
KAS	Koordinadora Abertzale Socialista
LAB	Langile Abertzaleen Batzordeak
LOAPA	Ley Orgánica para la Armonización del Proceso Autonómico
MLNV	Movimiento para la Liberación Nacional Vasca
PNV	Partido Nacionalista Vasco
PP	Partido Popular
PSE–EE	Partido Socialista de Euskadi–Euskadiko Ezkerra
PSOE	Partido Socialista Obrero Español
SDLP	Social Democratic and Labour Party
SF	Sinn Féin
UCD	Unión de Centro Democrático
UGT	Unión General de Trabajadores
UPN	Unión del Pueblo Navarro
UPV–EHU	Universidad del País Vasco–Euskal Herriko Unibertsitatea

It is always wrong to explain the nature of a country by simply referring to the character of its inhabitants, since an inhabitant of a country has at least nine characters or identities: a professional, a national, a state, a class, a geographic, a sexual, a conscious, an unconscious and maybe also a private character (...). Yet, there is still one more character, that of his fantasy, that allows him all but one thing: to take the previous nine too seriously.

Robert Musil, *The Man Without Qualities*, 1930

1
Introduction: the History of This Book

This book has been written despite an initially mistaken hypothesis and an adverse socio-political context. This is probably not the most attractive way of presenting a new publication, because it might provoke reasonable doubts concerning the intellectual ability of the author, who instead of commenting on his own errors should rather underline the correctness and validity of his hypothesis and arguments. Yet, the particular history of this book should be mentioned for two reasons: firstly, because it has influenced its content, and secondly, because it is a good example of the complicated relationship between (social) science and politics and of the problem of how to ensure a minimum of scientific objectivity and rigour in the work of an academic, if his or her research is carried out under the more or less direct impact of politics.

The origin of this book stems from an international research project concerning the management of peace processes conducted under the auspices of the Initiative on Conflict Resolution and Ethnicity (INCORE) at the University of Ulster between 1996 and 1998. While working on the Basque case analysing the evolution of violent nationalism and its political wing, I became more and more convinced of the increasing necessity and willingness of radical nationalists to embark upon a peaceful settlement of the conflict and in doing so to follow the example of other protracted ethnic conflicts, which during the 1990s had entered a phase of de-escalation. All the doubts concerning my hypothesis vanished in March 1998, when the Basque President Ardanza issued his official peace proposal and then, finally, in summer of the same year, when the ETA paramilitaries called the first unconditional and indefinite ceasefire in the organization's history.

This academic certainty collapsed together with the calling off of the ceasefire in the winter of 1999. The decision to take up arms again and, in January 2000, to continue killing took me – and most of the political and academic observers – completely by surprise. I was unable to understand why ETA had returned to armed struggle despite the manifest unpopularity and political ineffectiveness of terrorism. Why had it not seized the opportunity that arose in the summer of 1998, when thanks to the pro-nationalist *entente* the radical nationalists' political power had reached a historical peak since the foundation of ETA in 1959? My bewilderment increased over the following months, when it became evident that the cancellation of the ceasefire did not mean a simple return to a prior strategy, but a historically new intensification of violence by a radical extension of the targeted collectives. For the first time since I came to the Basque Country, terrorism became a very personal experience: ETA killed the Basque businessman Joxe Mari Korta. Korta, a nationalist, who felt more comfortable speaking Basque than Spanish, was very popular as a sponsor of Basque cultural and sporting activities. During the research for this book I interviewed Korta as President of ADEGI, the Association of Employers in the province of Gipuzkoa. Later, we discovered our common hobby of cycling and met on several occasions to practise our favourite sport and, incidentally, discuss and resolve the world's and, particularly, the Basques' problems. Joxe Mari was sentenced to death by ETA and executed by a car bomb due to his refusal to pay the revolutionary tax demanded by the paramilitaries.

At the same time ETA started campaigning against non-nationalist university teachers. In my own faculty, a bomb was placed in a lift with the intention of killing one of my colleagues in the Department of Politics. Fortunately, the bomb's detonator failed when the terrorist tried to activate it by remote control, and my colleague escaped with her life. Ever since, she and other colleagues, whose names were found on the lists of potential victims drawn up by ETA commandos, have to go everywhere on the campus (and elsewhere) under the protection of bodyguards. The university, usually a forum of democracy and peaceful exchange of ideas, has become a new target of paramilitary violence and it is not at all clear if there is any limit to this violence. I myself became aware of this situation when I received phone-calls after publishing political comments in the Basque daily papers. These were no anonymous phone-calls with threats, but calls from friends who, after assessing their full agreement with the thesis of the article, invited me to take more care and to apply a kind of auto-censorship in my public comments, 'You know, just in case ...'.

As a consequence of this new situation after calling the ceasefire off, the reader might understand that I felt unable to continue working on the book about the Basque peace process. My hypothesis of the probable end of ETA violence had failed and there was no longer any 'peace process'. Furthermore, my personal involuntary involvement in the conflict was provoking an emotional reaction, which pushed me to the conclusion that for the moment I was unable to maintain a minimum of rational distance between my object of research and myself, which is an indispensable precondition for any scientific work.

I needed several months to overcome this intellectual and emotional block. This was possible for three reasons. Firstly, the human being's capacity for adapting to the most extreme circumstances is well known, and this is exactly what has happened: if after the collapse of the ceasefire the unexpected return and intensification of violence had produced a real shock effect, now violence has unfortunately recovered its place in the daily lives of people living in the Basque Country, who continue protesting and mobilizing, but also trying to live their lives and to do business as usual or, in my case, to reflect and write about the problem of nationalism and violence. Secondly, many friends and colleagues in the Basque Country, in Spain and abroad convinced me that after the abortion of the peace process a book about the Basque conflict, its roots and frustrated settlements was even more important than it was during the truce. And thirdly, after revising the chapters written before the breakdown of the ceasefire and contrasting the text with new political and academic information, I came to the conclusion that notwithstanding my mistaken hypothesis concerning the probable early ending of ethnic violence by a Basque peace process, the main arguments, which this hypothesis was based upon, apparently remained valid. In other words, if it was the growing unpopularity of the armed struggle, which – together with the police successes against the underground group and other factors – pushed the paramilitaries towards the ceasefire of 1998, in post-ceasefire *Euskadi* plenty of evidence can be found to prove that this situation, which led to the truce, has not changed at all. Obviously, if this analysis were correct, any book about the Basque conflict necessarily had to tackle the reasons for the continuance of violence despite the evident, growing loss of ETA's popularity. While reading and thinking about this question, I became more and more convinced that the correct answer to this question required an analytical separation of what we might consider the political conflict on the one hand, and the problem of violence on the other, since the latter has achieved a proper dimension and can no longer be understood as a mere derivation of a deeper political conflict. Therefore, in my opinion it was no longer possible to maintain the original concept of the book focused especially on the (frustrated) peace process. The new book I had in mind had to be based upon a broader approach dealing with the historical evolution of Basque nationalism since the nineteenth century, in order to explain this particular transformation of a political contention about identities and self-determination into a conflict with two dimensions obviously linked to, but at the same time autonomous of one another. I am grateful to Palgrave Macmillan and the anonymous readers for having accepted this new proposal for a modified book, as well as the circumstances which impeded the completion of the original proposal.

Hence, this book deals with three issues with capital importance not only in the Basque Country, but also in other places in the world affected by the consequences of ethnic conflict. It analyses firstly the rise and evolution of Basque **nationalism** as a political and social cross-class movement within the particular context of a weak Spanish nation-state. Secondly, the genesis and development of **political violence** will be explained. Finally, the third focus will be on **democracy**. I shall consider the opportunities created by democratic politics to facilitate progress towards a conflict settlement, paying special attention to the limits and obstacles on the way, including the problem of the persistence of violence. These problems will be discussed against the background of the political process leading to the pro-nationalist *entente* and the ceasefire of the summer of 1998, which was the most serious attempt to create the conditions for a democratic accommodation of the contention since the restoration of democracy in Spain. In the final part of the book, drawing on a comparison of this frustrated Basque peace process with the Northern Irish one, I shall consider the errors committed, the lost opportunities and the causes for the return of terrorist violence, which – as I shall argue – cannot be found within the common theoretical explanations of political violence in the Basque Country. In this book, the concept of political violence is used in a broad sense, as 'acts of disruption, destruction, injury whose purpose, choice of targets or victims, surrounding circumstances, implementation, and/or effects have political significance, that is, tend to modify the behaviour of others in a bargaining situation that has consequences for the social system'.[1] Historically, political violence has adopted different forms of expression (food riots, Luddism, land occupations, violent demonstrations, revolutions, and so on), with terrorism being one of those expressions. Terrorism means the 'systematic use of murder, injury and destruction or the threat of such acts for political ends'.[2] It is at the same time a 'strategy of communication', since the main goal of terrorist organizations is not a particular act of killing or destruction, but the transmission of a political message to society or certain sectors of it.[3] However, terrorist groups with a long life-cycle like the Basque ETA tend to put more emphasis on the means ('armed struggle') than on the ends (political message or goals). In the Basque case, this evolution produced an increasing typological separation between violent nationalism and its democratic predecessor, which emerged at the end of the nineteenth century.

2
Why It Began: a Strong Periphery within a Weak State

Spain (...) is a case of early state-building where the political, social and cultural integration of its territorial components – nation-building – was not fully accomplished.

Juan Linz[1]

The historical roots of what is commonly called the Basque problem do not coincide with the year 1959, when the radical nationalist underground organization Euskadi 'ta Askatasuna (ETA, Basque Country and Freedom) was founded. Basque nationalism is now more than 100 years old and its radical, violent wing cannot be regarded as the predominant feature of that history, which started in 1895 when Sabino Arana Goiri founded the first cell of the Basque Nationalist Party, the Partido Nacionalista Vasco (PNV). This party is now, together with the Partido Socialista Obrero Español (PSOE), the oldest active party in the political system of the Spanish state.

An analysis of the shape of Basque nationalism, however, cannot be reduced to the history of the PNV. Basque nationalism emerged much earlier than Sabino Arana's appearance on the political stage. The sociologist Juan Linz was one of the first scholars to point out the relationship between the rise of peripheral – Basque, Catalan, Galician – nationalist mobilization and the particularities of the processes of state- and nation-building in Spain. Indeed, any attempt to explain the successful mobilization of not- or even anti-Spanish nationalism in those three peripheral regions of the Iberian Peninsula has to be put into a broader analytical framework based on a lack of synchronization between state- and nation-building in Spain.

In the historiography, Spain is usually regarded as one of the 'old established states like (...) Britain and France'. In his excellent study on *Staat und Nation in der europäischen Geschichte*, Hagen Schulze holds that even in the sixteenth century in Spain there was a 'similar high level of state and cultural nationalization as in the case of its traditional enemy England'. Another Spanish scholar counts Spain among the 'two or three oldest and – in terms of territory – best defined "nations" of Europe'.[2]

5

In fact, the origins of the modern Spanish state date back to the fifteenth century, when the future 'Catholic Monarchs' Isabel and Fernando prepared with their marriage (1469) the unification of Castile and Aragón, the two most powerful monarchies of the peninsula. The end of the Reconquista with the conquest of Granada (1492), the obligatory baptism of the remaining Muslims and the expulsion of the Jews were other stepping-stones on the road to cultural and ethnic homogenization of the new state. The motor for this process of unification was the Catholic Church, whose agents did not hesitate to make use of their most efficient instrument in their struggle against dissidents and contenders: the Inquisition. The cultural homogenization was accompanied by attempts to fix territorial unity. The Treaty of the Pyrenees (1659) fixed the border with France. Less than a decade later, Portugal was definitively separated from the rest of the Monarchy. Having lost its territories in Italy and the Netherlands owing to the Peace Treaty of Utrecht (1713), Spain carried out what Jover has called a 'peninsularization' of the state.[3] Finally, his victory in the War of Succession (1701–15) permitted Felipe V to abolish the institutions and traditional rights of self-government in the territories of the former Kingdom of Aragón (Aragón, Valencia, Catalonia, Mallorca) and thus to proceed towards the administrative centralization of the state. This policy of Felipe V has been characterized as a 'decisive step forward in the construction of the Spanish nation'.[4]

Was the *ancien régime* Spanish monarchy already a modern state *avant la lettre*, which – following Max Weber's classic definition – is an organization, whose administrative staff successfully claims the monopoly of the legitimate use of physical force within a given territory? Was it even a precocious nation, in the sense of a mutually binding community, that due to its members' historically multiple relationship in terms of language, culture, religion and politics had become conscious of its common interests and destiny?[5] There can be no doubt about the early origins of Spanish state-building. Yet, recent historiography has also revealed the remarkable deficit of this process with its important costs for nation-building, which Linz already referred to in 1973. The debate has focused specially on the nineteenth century and the weakness of the liberal bourgeoisie. In comparison with other European states of that period and in allusion to the controversial discussion about the distinctive features of contemporary German history on its way to modernity, Spanish development has been described as a 'particular way' towards the building of the modern nation-state.[6] It was a special way, because just at the moment when other states had started fulfilling Weber's criteria, completing the process of state-building with far-reaching political efforts to achieve the 'nationalization of the masses'[7] and, during the last decades of the century, entering a new phase of extreme nationalist agitation in the era of imperialism, Spanish history took exactly the opposite direction. Spain mutated from being the most influential colonial power in the world into a nearly bankrupt third- or fourth-class state with tremendous internal problems of legitimacy, identity, penetration and participation.[8] After the loss of most of the Latin-American colonies in 1824, and challenged in three civil wars (1833–39; 1846–49; 1872–76) by the strong neo-absolutist movement of Carlism, even after the definitive military victory over that movement in 1874, Spanish liberalism was not able to come to terms with its problems. The liberal bourgeoisie, in other cases the promoter of state- and nation-building, was fragile and instead of constituting a 'national class', it was territorially fragmented. Politics depended much more on military and royal interventionism than on parliamentary decisions. The participation of the citizens, formally granted by the institution of universal male suffrage since the elections of 1890, was strongly devalued by a broad network of paternal relationships reaching from the Ministry of the Interior to the local *caciques*, who would make sure that the correct votes were cast in the elections according to the decisions previously taken in Madrid. The vehicles of national integration and cohesion which were more or less successful elsewhere did not fulfil their function at all in nineteenth-century Spain. Public education was a victim of the chronic lack of funding of the public budget, a situation that was exploited by a powerful anti-liberal ally of Carlist neo-absolutism, namely the Catholic Church and its educational institutions. The new 'national' army was at least until the second decade of the twentieth century not at all 'national'. It was a class organization representing those sectors of the society unable to pay the amount necessary to secure release from compulsory military service. Until 1898 there was no external enemy and there were no national symbols to create and represent the imaginary community of the Spanish nation. In other words, in liberal Spain it was not, as nationalists frequently argue, the aggressive imperialist attitude of Spanish nationalism but its weakness which permitted the durability of regional and local particularisms.

One of these was the Basque local particularism. During the *ancien régime*, the Basque provinces, which in the War of Succession had fought on the side of Felipe V, conserved – though formally linked to the Spanish monarchy – a broad political and financial self-determination, as well as a differentiated particular culture. Hence, their inhabitants constituted an ethnic community in the sense of Anthony D. Smith, which during the nineteenth century would be gradually transformed into a politically mobilized nation.[9] In 1876, after the liberal victory in the last Carlist War and due to the Basque support of the traditionalists, the status of self-government was definitively abolished. This drastic measure provoked the opposition even of the Basque liberals, who proposed a reform and an updating of the traditional laws, the '*Fueros*', but not their abolition. '*Fuerismo*', i.e. the huge social movement which was started with the aim of recovering the lost freedoms of the Basque people, can be considered a more culturally than politically successful proto-nationalist movement, which stimulated the shaping of a Basque national consciousness which, nonetheless, was not yet completely incompatible with a Spanish identity.[10]

This broad proto-nationalist movement, whose sentiments were shared by the remnants of the militarily defeated Carlists, created a hostile political and social atmosphere towards the central government in which nationalism could emerge. Moreover, at the end of the 1890s, and after the pathetic debacle in the naval war against the United States and the loss of the last colonies (Cuba, Puerto Rico, the Philippines), the Spanish political and intellectual elites had descended into a deep crisis of identity, as a consequence of the shocking contrast between European imperialist glory and Spanish decay and disaster. At the end of the century, 'doubt was cast on the Spanish nation'.[11] Both in Catalonia and in the Basque provinces this *fin-de-siècle* crisis coincided with the apogee of an alternative nationalist movement, the Basques being openly anti-Spanish and separatist. This Basque nationalist radicalism was the answer to the challenge of an also radical and disruptive process of socio-economic modernization that first affected the province of Bizkaia.[12] Since the 1880s when Bizkaian society was turned upside-down by rapid industrialization and violent class struggle, the public space for relatively moderate ideologies like those of Fuerismo or even Carlismo was getting narrower and narrower, opening the doors to radical thinking and movements like nationalism or socialism.

3
How It Began: the Evolution of Basque Nationalism until the Civil War (1876–1939)

Like other nationalist movements, Basque nationalism was in its origins a phenomenon closely linked to modern, urban, bourgeois, industrial society. It emerged in Bilbao at the end of the nineteenth century within the context of rapid economic growth, massive immigration and violent social turmoil. Its first followers were recruited among sectors of the traditional urban, lower middle classes, who saw themselves as victims of modernization, displaced from the centre to the periphery of society and under pressure both from the socialist labour movement and from the small clan of the politically and economically leading elite of the financial and industrial oligarchy.

The founder of the Basque Nationalist Party was Sabino Arana Goiri.[1] In 1895, when establishing the first cell of what later would be the Partido Nacionalista Vasco (PNV), Arana was a 30-year-old former law student, who during his studies at Barcelona University had spent more time learning the Basque language and history than the subjects he was taught by his lecturers. He was the eighth son of a well-off, Catholic family with Carlist leanings from Bilbao, his father being a small shipbuilder forced into exile due to his active and financial support for Carlism during the last war. Sabino and his elder brother Luis, who some years after Sabino's death in 1903 became the party's leader, grew up and were educated in a strongly philo-Carlist tradition. The political decline of Carlism and the radicalizing impact of industrialization, which was producing a complete transformation of his hometown, Bilbao, created a growing gap between Arana and Carlism. Both his reading of Basque history and then, finally, a long conversation on Easter Sunday 1882 with his brother, who had already broken with Carlism, were what ignited his new political, nationalist philosophy.

This philosophy, however, was not at all an invention *ex nihilo*. In fact, Sabino Arana Goiri, the founder of the Basque Nationalist Party, did little more than draw radical conclusions from the fuerist and Carlist programmes, interpreting Basque history not in terms of autonomy, but as complete independence from the Spanish state. In his discourse he mixed well-known elements from the Carlist tradition, such as extreme Catholicism, agrarian romanticism or the moralizing rejection of all 'exotic' and 'anti-Basque' ingredients of the new, modern world like industry, capitalism and secularization, together with other ideas borrowed from traditional social Catholicism (harmony of classes; anti-socialism with – in the case of Arana – racist implications against the immigrant workers). But Arana even shared some issues with socialist or republican politicians, such as the call for a crusade against the patronage system and the anti-democratic power structures of the Restoration monarchy.

The solution to all the problems and the way to never-ending happiness for the Basques, in the eyes of Sabino Arana, would come through the reaffirmation of their own history, culture and race, the consequent expulsion of everything considered external to that tradition and the recuperation of the old independence by restoration of the *Fueros*. This attractive message was embedded, as we shall see below, in the daily work of creating a nationalist history with deep mythological implications, as well as the nationalist symbols such as the flag, the anthem or the national festivities, all together with a purification of the Basque language by means of the elimination of all Roman influence and the invention of neologisms supposed to be totally Basque in their origins like the word 'Euzkadi' for the Basque territory.

As a defensive means of protest articulated by the petty bourgeoisie against the consequences of the process of modernization, Sabino Arana's nationalism was initially quite similar to what Charles Tilly calls 'reactive collective actions' 'against someone [big business; socialism; and the Spanish state] who had unjustly deprived, or tried to deprive, a local population of a precious resource [its independence, customs, morale, religion, and its language]'.[2] But even during Arana's lifetime this type of collective action, which in Tilly's model is more linked to the pre-revolutionary society than to the end of the nineteenth century, was altered by the mobilization of new social layers predominantly among the local, native working class, the growing new middle classes and those sectors of the industrial and commercial bourgeoisie not integrated into the oligarchy of leading industrial monarchists. Without abandoning completely its reactive character, Basque nationalism became increasingly 'proactive', expressing 'group claims which [had] not previously been exercised'.[3] Obviously, beyond the common claim of a new distribution of political power in order to protect Basque identity and culture, each of the different layers that made up Basque nationalism as a cross-class social movement had its particular group interest and it was this complex mixture of different interests and aims that explains the internal contradictions and the on occasions erratic political strategy of Basque nationalism very nearly from its beginnings.[4] The fluctuation between radical essentialism and moderate pragmatism, between secessionist separatism and regional autonomism, between reactive defence and proactive claims has been compared to a 'patriotic pendulum' that never stopped swinging from one side to the other.[5] These contradictions are visible even within Sabino Arana's political biography. When in 1898 a sector of the liberal fuerist bourgeoisie joined the party, Arana shifted from a position of radical intransigence to an attitude of more realistic pragmatism. The first fruit of this new cooperation between the radical popular sector and the new moderate bourgeois wing of nationalism was the election of Arana as a deputy in the regional parliament of the province of Bizkaia in 1898, when the Spanish state entered its severest crisis since conservative liberalism had become the new power elite. As deputy, Arana unsuccessfully proposed bills demanding regional autonomy within the Spanish state, an attitude that did not really coalesce with his initial anti-Spanish separatism. The overwhelming reality of capitalist industrialization forced him to accept the new situation. By investing money in several new enterprises, he even tried to benefit from the possibilities of becoming rich offered by the booming industry in and around the gold-fever city of Bilbao. If in earlier years Sabino Arana had pleaded for isolation from the modern world as the only means of protecting and recovering the Basque identity, now he recognized clearly that the Basque language, *euskara*, would be condemned to disappear, unless the nationalists managed to put both industry and the economy at the service of its language and culture. Only a year before his death in 1903, the charismatic founder of the PNV astonished his followers by suggesting, in a press article, the idea of renouncing national politics in order to design a new non-anti-Spanish regionalist strategy leading to Basque freedom. Nevertheless, by the time of Sabino Arana's death, the spectacular shift in the party leader's strategic reasoning, which in the historiography is normally referred to as the 'Spanish evolution' ('evolución españolista'), was embellished by other radical, separatist statements, which left the nationalist programme and strategy in total confusion. His political legacy contained both arguments in favour of moderate autonomism and radical separatism. But since 1903 the situation had changed: with Arana, not only did the founder of the party and the movement disappear, but so did the charismatic referee, whom everyone had venerated and who was the only person able to keep all the different political, social and ideological interests united within Basque nationalism as well as loyal to the PNV. Thus, it was not surprising that after Arana's death political observers augured the split of the party and even its disappearance.

What really happened was exactly the opposite. During the twenty years between the death of the leader and the beginning of General Primo de Rivera's dictatorship, Basque nationalism passed through a period of slow but continuous expansion, reaching during the First World War the peak of this apogee and the characteristics of a real mass movement according to Hroch's model.[6] This success can be attributed to several reasons. The first was, of course, the structural context. No social movement can be reduced to the magic invention of a certain ideologist, however strong and popular his charisma might be. Nationalism in the Basque Country was the product of the confluence of different factors like ethnic and politic particularism, a pre-nationalist conscience, weak Spanish nation-building, the deficit of parliamentarian democracy and participation, socio-economic modernization and the decay of traditional political options like *Carlismo* or *fuerismo*. At the beginning of the twentieth century, no remarkable changes in this context had been produced.[7] Moreover, as we have seen, the crisis following the disaster of 1898 had opened up new opportunities for political contenders of the Restoration monarchy. The Basque society, especially Bizkaia, absorbed the impact of industrialization, urbanization and immigration. The most significant symbol of Basque ethnic particularism, *Euskara* – a language divided into several dialects, without an outstanding literary tradition or a standardized grammar – experienced a dramatic acceleration of its historical decay since the Middle Ages. The language of the modern world was Spanish and even in Basque-speaking families it was quite normal to educate their sons, who had to get on in their careers, in Spanish and to transmit the native language only to their daughters, whose most important challenge in their life was to find a well-off husband. There are no precise statistical figures for the regional and local distribution of the Bascophone population at the beginning of the twentieth century, but due to the massive language-desertion by the locals and the waves of immigration into the new industrial areas it can be taken for granted that in Bilbao and its industrial hinterland *Euskara* had been reduced to an absolutely marginal and residual position. Liberal Basque intellectuals like the philosopher Miguel de Unamuno considered it a relic of the Middle Ages and an obstacle to human progress, inviting in 1901 the Basque people to 'bury it with honour' and to speak Spanish. In his famous speech, Unamuno did nothing else than repeat more controversially what Wilhelm von Humboldt, after his visit to the Basque Country and his studies of the local language, had prophesied about a century before: the 'ruin of Basque nationality, and even of its language within a short time'. When Humboldt visited the Basque Country, the situation of the language was not yet so bad, at least from a quantitative point of view. Years after Humboldt's trip, another famous linguist, Louis-Lucien Bonaparte, Napoleon I's nephew, published what would become the first more or less reliable statistic concerning the percentage of the Basque-speaking population during the nineteenth century. According to Bonaparte's figures of the 1860s and the updated version presented by Velasco at the end of the 1870s, more than a half of all Spanish and French Basques were *euskaldunak*, that is, Bascophone. The province of Gipuzkoa was nearly completely Basque-speaking (96.43 per cent) and in Bizkaia the *euskaldunak* counted for more than 80 per cent of the total population. The implantation of the language was less in the French part of the country (64.62 per cent) and only a minority phenomenon in Navarre (20 per cent) and Alava (9.96 per cent).[8]

Once the process of industrialization had started, the dramatic decay of the Basque language was a reality of everyday life. Owing to the strong diglossia situation with respect to the dominant Spanish language, Unamuno's invitation to bury *Euskara* was no longer a malicious joke of a vain intellectual, because the language had indeed entered an agonizing phase, reflected also by the fact that many of the first nationalists had already lost their language when they joined the movement. Sabino Arana taught himself. His brother Luis, during many years the chairman of the party, did not, though. A language that was in such a situation of absolute inferiority could not serve as a core value around which national identity and the cohesion of the nationalist movement could be constructed. It is for this reason that Sabino Arana, despite all his linguistic efforts, put race at the centre of his definition of the Basque nation, giving it a clear priority over language. Consequently, citizens who wanted to become members of the party had to prove their Basque origins by demonstrating that their first four surnames, later only one of the four,[9] were etymologically Basque. Thus, Basque nationalism conserved a strong objectivistic, primordialist and even an undemocratic element for a long time, since if a person's belonging to a nation depended on race, there was no possibility of non-natives joining. If it depended on language, however – and this was the case in the Catalan and the Galician movements – nation membership could be acquired by learning. This characteristic of orthodox Basque nationalism was not altered until the rise of leftist, radical, nationalism in the 1960s, when some of the new ETA ideologists started criticizing the racial ingredient of Basque nationalism and the abandonment of the language by the traditional leaders.

Besides the persistence of the contextual structure favourable to the apogee of nationalism, another reason to take into account in order to understand the movement's expansive cycle after Sabino Arana's death was the efficient mobilization of organizational resources committed by Arana's successors. Since the publications of McCarthy and Zald, the importance of the Social Movement Organizations for the articulation of grievances and the mobilization of discontent in modern societies is a widely accepted fact.[10] In the case of Basque nationalism, the organization started in 1904 with the formation of the local cells of the party. From that moment on, in only a few years the PNV became one of the most modern political parties of Spain, breaking with the traditional and still predominant politics of notables and building up a democratic internal structure based on the principles of elective bottom–top democracy and the incompatibility of party and public offices.[11] The first official programme or the PNV, passed by the party's National Assembly in 1906, remained valid until post-Francoist times. Its principal achievement was its ambiguity, since it formulated the 'recovery of the *fueros*' as the party's supreme political aim, without specifying if this meant independence or autonomy. Ever since then, both tendencies have coexisted within the PNV. But the effort of organization did not only affect the party. From its very beginnings, Basque nationalism was keen to create an image of the movement as a national community that went beyond the limits of party politics, which due to corruption and electoral manipulation had a very bad reputation in Restoration Spain. The change of the party's official name from Partido Nacionalista Vasco into Comunión Nacionalista Vasca (Baque Nationalist Community) in 1913 was the consequence of this philosophy.[12] Step by step, this community was built up as a broad network of formal and informal organizations and initiatives covering not only the area of politics, but also those of culture and leisure. Until the Civil War, the list of different groups and activities organized within Basque nationalism was very large, including youth groups, the organization of the nationalist Emakume Abertzale Batza (whose membership was female), traditional dance, theatre and football groups, groups for the Basque language and history, as well as special unions for fishermen, peasants, employees and industrial workers.[13]

In fact, one of the most spectacular and singular proofs of nationalist success in the Basque Country was the foundation of a nationalist worker union Eusko Langileen Alkartasuna–Solidaridad de Obreros Vascos (ELA–SOV) in 1911. In Catalonia, the control of the nationalist movement by regional big business, since the foundation of the conservative Lliga Regionalista de Catalunya in 1901, was an important obstacle to the penetration of nationalist ideology into the working-class and the mostly anarcho-syndicalist orientated labour movement. In the Basque case, on the other hand, the bourgeoisie remained loyal to the Bourbon monarchy and Spanish nationalism was radically opposed to the Basque movement. In these circumstances, a local worker was not necessarily forced to give up his class consciousness if he wanted to join the nationalists, because the social cleavage reinforced the political one. This was the basis of the growth of the nationalist union ELA.[14] At the beginning of General Primo de Rivera's dictatorship in 1923, the union already reached a similar degree of affiliation to that of the socialist Unión General de Trabajadores (UGT), which had been – together with the political party Partido Socialista Obrero Español (PSOE) – the pioneer of worker mobilization in the industrial areas around Bilbao since the first general strike in 1890. During the first years, and despite its organic independence, ELA was a conservative and defensive organization, a kind of friendly society more concerned with providing different social services to its members (insurance policies in case of illness, death, accidents or unemployment) than with participating in social conflicts by strikes or negotiations. The radical anti-socialism of Basque orthodox nationalism and the absolute lack of sensibility toward the national question shown by the socialist leaders blocked the progress of ELA to the left and towards a more autonomous position with respect to the party. Only from 1917/18, when the PNV became an attractive party for sectors of the business world, while at the same time inflation cut wages and more and more conflicts between nationalist workers and nationalist employers arose, did ELA start a progress that converted the organization into a real labour union still close to the party, but no longer willing to evade conflicts with the party and the employers.

On the other hand, because of the strength of the union, the PNV leaders were keen to maintain a fluent relationship with the union, especially in times of elections. During the Second Republic, two outstanding spokesmen of the union, its president Robles Aranguiz and De la Torre, another member of the directing board, were elected deputies to the Spanish parliament in the lists of the PNV. Both PNV and ELA kept up their traditional anti-socialism, and in this sense Eric Hobsbawm's statement about Basque nationalism and its success in 'isolating and eventually practically eliminating the traditional working-class socialist movements'[15] is correct, but only if we add the fact that this very attitude, in correspondence with the insensibility and even the repulse of Basque particularism by the socialists, also permitted the mobilization of many autochthonous workers within the nationalist movement. The Basque example is further proof of the heterogeneous character of nationalism, which cannot simply be reduced to an invention of the bourgeoisie, since there is no 'determinate link between class and territory but a variety of relationships according to economic and political circumstances'.[16]

The explanation of nationalist success in the Basque Country after the death of its founder Sabino Arana is attributed to one more crucial factor: the invention and celebration of a huge symbolic microcosm that facilitated the shape and the consolidation of nationalist identity, the differentiation from other out-groups and the internal cohesion of the movement. Like other nationalisms, Basque nationalism was also in part an 'imagined community'[17] based on a history that had been reinterpreted, if not invented by Sabino Arana according to predetermined political interests. Arana was a politician and not an historian, and thus in his task of inventing the tradition there was not much room for academic skill and scientific exactness.[18] In his most important political-historical study, *Bizkaia: for its Independence* he drew a dramatic picture of the heroic medieval inhabitants of that Basque territory resisting on the battlefield several foreign (Castilian) aggressions, as well as the betrayal of some evil Basques who had sold their soul to the aggressor, until finally in 1839 the Spanish government put and end to Basque independence after the liberal victory in the first Carlist War. From this moment on, the decay of the nation, its traditions, its culture and its religion started, the race ran the risk of disappearing in the turmoil of history. In Arana's political discourse, expressed even in his two plays, the obscure reality of the present was contrasted with the Golden Age when the *Fueros* were still the shield protecting Basque freedom and granting the people's happiness. For Arana and his followers, the *Fueros* acquired the character of a highly mythologized totem, which had to be reconquered, if the misery of everyday life was to be overcome. Nobody really cared about what the *Fueros* had been and how their hypothetic re-establishment within the framework of modern society could be carried out. This vague and emotionally overloaded ambiguity in the nationalist comprehension of the old foral system turned out to be a useful instrument for the internal cohesion of the party, which after the death of its founder, was for some years on the point of splitting thanks to the crude struggle between the two opposite wings of moderates and radicals for the control of the party. This danger of a split was avoided in 1906, when the first PNV programme defined – as we have seen above – the restoration of the old *Fueros* as the supreme political aim of Basque nationalism.

Once they had created their own tradition and history as the basis for the legitimacy of the political project, and after initiating the mobilization of organizational resources to channel the protest against grievances, it became necessary to invent symbols both for external differentiation and for the internal integration of the movement. Once again it was Sabino Arana who laid the groundwork in this field. First, he invented the neologism *Euzkadi* as a geographical denomination for the Basque Country. Rejecting the more traditional name of *Euskal Herria*, which in Basque literally meant 'the people possessing *Euskara*', Arana chose a biologically inspired definition of the Basque nation, attributing the meaning of 'the land inhabited by the Basque race' to the new word. This excluded all immigrants and their descendants, whereas all members of that broad native Basque majority who had lost their language were included. Arana submitted the language itself to a radical process of purification. The founder of the PNV demanded the elimination of all words or expressions with Castilian roots and their substitution with neologisms, which in his opinion were clearly Basque in origin. This ideologically motivated, artificial linguistic intervention provoked the criticism of most of the philologists of the time. Instead of helping, it hindered the normalization and standardization of the language, a task that was not carried out until the 1960s.

More successful were Arana's efforts to design the nation's flag and the composition of its anthem. The colours of the flag, the *ikurriña*, namely white and green crosses on a red background, were chosen as symbolic expressions of the two crucial issues in the PNV's official slogan 'God and the Old Laws'.[19] The first appearance of the *ikurriña* in public was in 1894, when the first nationalist centre, the Euzkeldun Batzokija, was inaugurated. It became more and more popular. During Sabino's lifetime, it was not very clear if the flag was supposed to be the flag of the whole nation, or only that of the province of Bizkaia. Notwithstanding these ideological disputes, *de facto* the *ikurriña* soon became the symbol of Basque nationalism in general. Having been declared the official flag of *Euskadi* in 1936 by the nationalist president José Antonio Aguirre's multi-party coalition, the *ikurriña* subsequently was transformed from a political to an institutional symbol. After

Franco's death and the re-establishment of Basque autonomy, the regional parliament confirmed the decision of 1936, proclaiming the *ikurriña* the official flag of the Autonomous Community of the Basque Country. Something similar happened to the anthem 'Gora ta Gora', composed during Arana's first imprisonment in 1895. Today it is the official anthem of the autonomous *Euskadi*, even if among the deputies of the regional parliament a strong minority of non-nationalists voted to back the alternative, more traditional and prejudice-free 'Gernikako Arbola', written in the 1850s by the popular Basque bard and troubadour Iparraguirre.

Finally, *Euskadi*, along with its symbols and the movement for the recovery of lost national freedom, needed occasions for the public display of grievances and claims. The nation had to be celebrated. Besides other minor festivities, like St Andrew's Day on 30 November ('the Battle of Arrigorriaga') or the annual masses on the anniversary of Sabino's death (25 November 1903), the nationalists first celebrated in 1932 what still today is celebrated as the 'Day of the Fatherland' (*Aberri Eguna*). This festival is yet another example of the close relationship between nationalism and religion highlighted by scholars like Anthony D. Smith and which is discussed below. The event that is commemorated on this day is Sabino Arana's conversion to nationalism, which in his own words happened on Easter Sunday 1882 in a discussion with his elder brother Luis, who had already abandoned the traditionalist ideology of Carlism in order to become the first nationalist. The synchronization in time of this political *revelation* with one of the major feast-days in the Catholic religion, strengthened the emotional and symbolic implications of Basque nationalism. For Sabino Arana's followers there was no doubt that the resurrection of the nation would come just like Christ's resurrection had come after a long period of suffering and pain. Contrary to what occurred with the anthem and the flag, in the post-Francoist autonomous Basque Country no political majority could be found to back the nationalist proposal to declare the *Aberri Eguna* the official holiday of the Autonomous Community of the Basque Country.

Before autonomy was granted Basque nationalism had to cross a long political desert marked by both the unwillingness of the Spanish governments to meet the demands of the nationalists and the nationalists' inability to win sufficient majorities or to define their relationship with the Spanish state. In contrast with Catalan nationalism, Basque nationalism was from its very beginnings a much more defensive project, whose leaders were not too concerned about the state or about the role the Basque Country should play in (or out of) Spain (or France). During the first decade of the twentieth century, even participating in the elections to the Spanish parliament was considered politically incorrect, since the Cortes and the government in Madrid were seen as the business of Spaniards, and not of Basques. Nonetheless, these ideas did not lead to the elaboration of a stringent separatist policy, because the expansion of nationalism into the middle and upper layers of society strengthened the position of those among the followers of Sabino Arana, whose professional interests made them reluctant to support separatist adventures. Consequently, nationalist policy towards Spain was inhibited, since it failed to formulate its own position in relation to the state.[20]

This calculated ambiguity was in response to a strategy of anti-nationalist stonewalling by the central government. The leading elites of the Restoration monarchy were too weak to design a policy of integration towards any of the challengers of the system (republicans, socialists, anarchists, peripheral nationalists). Any regionalization of the state via the establishment of autonomies had to be rejected, since it was regarded as a new threat to the power of the traditional elites and as a danger to the survival of the Spanish nation. This was the bitter experience the Basque nationalists underwent during their first campaign for regional autonomy (1917–19). At that time, the party had reached its electoral zenith, winning its first majority in the provincial parliament of Bizkaia, all the mandates to the Spanish Cortes except one being from the same province, as well as another two deputies from the provinces of Gipuzkoa and of Navarre. Encouraged by these splendid results and by the nationalist euphoria all over Europe at the end of the First World War, the Basque nationalists made their first serious attempt to overcome their traditional ambiguity, concentrating and focusing their strategy on one major aim: the achievement of a regional autonomy within the Spanish state, which was 'sold' to the radical sectors of the movement as the first step in the restoration of the *Fueros* and thus, as a milestone towards independence. At the same time, Basque nationalism performed a conservative and moderate shift in its discourse, which now emphasized the party's image as a tough defender of law and order and, moreover, as a possible ally of the monarchy. Within a political and social context characterized by the most important crisis of the Spanish political system since 1898, this offer was more than a meaningless rhetorical gesture. Yet, the hope that this strategy would erode the Spanish government's centralism and produce political benefit in the form of regional autonomy, finally turned out to be nothing but a naive illusion. Once the survival of the system was guaranteed and the elites had overcome the shock, the hand the nationalists had stretched to the state and its government was answered with a resounding blow: the autonomy project was buried and nationalism once again was persecuted by political and juridical means. Frustration and repression boosted radicalism within the party, which split in 1921. Two years later, the military dictatorship installed and headed by Primo de Rivera aimed at cleaning Spain of all separatist and anarchist spots. Both nationalist parties were condemned to political ostracism, until in 1930/31 new expectations were raised with the fall of the dictatorship and the monarchy, followed by the proclamation of the Second Republic. Yet the new leftist government's mistrust of the conservative and

ultra-catholic, reunified[21] Basque nationalism caused another postpone-
ment of regional autonomy, which finally was agreed between the government of the Popular Front and the PNV in October 1936. Previously, a new
generation of leaders had pushed the party from the right to the Christian
Democrat centrist position, guaranteeing their allegiance to the Republic as
well as the nationalists' determination to defend it against the fascist
elements in the army who had led their own putsch some months before.[22]

It was the PNV that controlled the first autonomous government of
Euskadi, presided over by José Antonio de Aguirre, its popular leader and
former soccer player for Athletic Club de Bilbao. This predominant position
was a consequence of the fact that the nationalists had made the implementation of autonomy their principal and virtually only political aim, having
designed their whole political strategy in accordance with this objective.
Thus, the unwillingness of the Carlists first and of the conservative republicans later to meet this demand of autonomy was the reason for the PNV's shift
to the centre and its alliance with the Popular Front, whose communist,
socialist and left-republican members had been the traditional ideological
enemies of conservative nationalism since the very foundation of the party.
This development and the new cooperation with political forces that only a
few years previously were being condemned as 'Spanish centralists' and 'the
enemies of religion' was carried out even at the risk that this new and
surprising orientation would provoke concern and protest among the nationalist rank-and-file. In fact, in the February elections of 1936 the party, now at
the centre of the party system, became the target of attacks from both the
right and from the left. Despite losing more than 30,000 votes and three
deputies, the PNV still remained the largest – but not hegemonic – political
party in the Basque provinces. At the beginning of the Civil War, the Basque
Country was, in political, cultural and ideological terms, more than ever a heterogeneous and pluralistic society. Nationalism was strong in the economically and socially mobilized areas in the two coastal provinces; it was weaker
where the structure of society had not been transformed and where the
cultural roots of Basque particularism, especially the language, was more
a reminiscence of history than a feature of everyday life.[23] But even in rural
areas with a strong ethnic tradition, which had not yet known the mobilizing impact of socio-economic modernization, as for example in the northern
part of Navarre or the interior of Gipuzkoa, nationalism had enormous
problems breaking down the dominant role of (Carlist or fundamentalist)
traditionalism. The result of the 1936 elections symbolizes quite well the
triangular polarization of Basque society, including Navarre: the PNV nationalists won nine deputies, the rightists eight and the leftist Popular Front seven.

This polarization also affected the progress of the Civil War in the Basque
Country. In the conservative provinces of Navarre and Alava, the fascist
uprising succeeded without major problems. Gipuzkoa, under the fire
also of Carlist paramilitaries from Navarre (the 'Requetés'), surrendered in

September 1936. Up until this moment, the PNV had adopted a clear, but not very active attitude in defence of the Republic. This situation changed when the PNV started negotiating with the new republican government headed by Largo Caballero.[24] The result was a stronger commitment from the PNV with the defence of the Republic, symbolized by the inclusion of the first nationalist, the Navarrese Manuel de Irujo, as minister in the Spanish government. A few days later, as already mentioned, the Cortes passed the Basque Autonomy bill, which enabled the formation of the first autonomous government under the presidency of the *Lehendakari* Aguirre in the historic town of Gernika, on 1 October 1936.

Basque autonomy was based on the dispositions fixed by a statute of autonomy, which in November 1933 had been voted by 84 per cent of the census in the provinces of Gipuzkoa, Bizkaia and Alava. Previously, owing to the defection of the Carlists and the lack of Basque consciousness among most of the socialists and republicans in the province, Navarre had opted out of the process towards Basque autonomy.[25] Ever since then, for Basque nationalists, who have always considered Navarre part of the historic Basque homeland, it has become something like a gaping wound. Its exclusion from the Basque autonomous region provoked frustration and sharp criticism even among PNV leaders such as the Navarrese minister Manuel Irujo. Later, this 'artificial' splitting up of the Basque fatherland by autonomy for only three of the four (seven, including the French parts) historic territories that nationalists considered their homeland became one of the strongest arguments of all radical nationalists opposed to autonomy. In recent years, as I will discuss below, the 'principle of territoriality', that is, the political and administrative rapprochement of the four Basque regions in Spanish and the three in French territory, has become one of the nationalists' core demands and one of the keys to a political solution to the problem of violence.

In October 1936, however, the *Lehendakari* Aguirre did not even control the three provinces that officially constituted the autonomous *Euskadi*,[26] since Alava and nearly all of Gipuzkoa were in the hands of the Francoists. Nevertheless, during the eight months preceding the conquest of Bilbao, Aguirre organized the free Basque region as a semi-independent state, even counting on its own army. The active military resistance of the Basque warriors ('Gudariak') and of the Popular Front militia was not enough to break the fascist offensive supported by Italian soldiers and German bombs, which in April 1937 destroyed the city of Gernika, the symbol of traditional Basque freedom. This dramatic event gave rise to Picasso's famous painting.[27] When Franco's troops captured Bilbao in June of the same year, autonomy was immediately abolished and a violent campaign of repression against the *provincias traidoras*, the 'traitor provinces', started. For Basque nationalism, this meant the beginning of a new era: the era of exile and clandestine struggle, which would last about 40 years.

4
Dictatorship and Exile: the Shape of the New Nationalism

After Franco's definitive victory in the Civil War in 1939,[1] any expression and symbol of Basque political or cultural particularism was brutally persecuted and the working capacity of the Basque government established in Paris was completely absorbed by the organization of different kinds of humanitarian aid for the thousands of refugees crossing the border. With the beginning of the Second World War, the panorama for the Basque nationalists – and in general all Basques opposed to Francoist fascism – became even darker. The Germans surprised President Aguirre on a family visit to Belgium. He escaped and disappeared for more than a year, before returning to the political stage after a long and dangerous odyssey with a changed identity.[2] The occupation of France forced the Basque government to leave Paris and establish itself in New York. But even during this period of desperation, Basque nationalism did not surrender and maintained an important level of activity with the foundation of the 'Basque National Council' in January 1941 in London.[3] Chaired by Manuel de Irujo, former PNV minister in the Spanish Republican government,[4] the Council was conceived as a temporary substitute for the Basque government, which due to the disappearance of its president and the German occupation of France was forced into political inactivity. Irujo's initiative was inspired by the example of other governments exiled in the London, and particularly the Polish one. The PNV politician and his party-fellows in London were convinced that the Western democracies would be victorious against Hitler, which would open the door to the overthrow of the fascist regime in Spain and the recovery of Basque freedom, even in the form of independence. This strategic calculation and his profound anti-fascist conviction gave Irujo access to high representatives at the Foreign Office and to the French Resistance, to whom he offered the help of the Basques in the struggle against Hitler. Thus, in the negotiations with de Gaulle, the formation of a Basque battalion, attached to the French Liberation Army was agreed. However, only a year after its inception, the battalion and its 300-odd Basque soldiers were once again obliged to demobilize, since Churchill feared that if the Basques were to fight against the Generalissimo's German and Italian allies, Franco might enter the war. Only later during the last phase of the war in April 1945, did the 'Battalion Gernika' consisting of about 200 Basque soldiers, now under the command of the reconstituted Basque government, participate in the last battles against the German army near La Rochelle.[5]

The defeat of fascism and the victory of the Allies suddenly turned depression into euphoria for the Basques. As President Aguirre emphasized on every possible occasion, it was only a question of time before Franco would be expelled by the western democracies, just like the other fascist regimes in Europe. For Aguirre there was no doubt that the Allies would pay for the solidarity shown and the services offered by the Basques during the world war not only in military terms. The Basque government had also organized a broad espionage network, supplying all kinds of political and military information to the British and American governments. Aguirre had still another point in his favour: he was the most popular and charismatic leader amongst all Spanish republican exiles[6] and the relative political homogeneity of his multi-party government contrasted sharply with the never-ending controversies and internal struggles that weakened the Republican government and undermined its political reputation in the western world. The excellent propagandistic result of the general strike organized in 1947 in the Basque provinces by the underground nationalist Resistance and workers' trade unions, as well as the active part played by the PNV in the foundation of the Christian Democratic International during 1947 and 1948, were both the culmination and, at the same time, the turning point of this phase of nationalist optimism.[7]

The beginning of the Cold War frustrated once again Basque expectations. In the new international context of bloc-confrontation the most dangerous enemy of western democracy was no longer fascism, but communism. The image of Franco, the anti-Communist *par excellence*, underwent a spectacular process of metamorphosis. The dictator ceased to be the gravedigger of democracy, obtaining a new reputation as freedom fighter against communism. Truman's decision to exclude Spain from the 'Marshall Plan' awoke the nationalist hope for a while.[8] The maintenance of the Basque espionage services after the end of the war, now with the aim of discovering all kinds of communist activities, was decided with the purpose of assuring American support in the struggle against Franco. One of the most active spies was Jesús Galíndez, the head of the Basque government's delegation in New York, who delivered about 18 monthly reports to the FBI, which – according to an internal FBI source – were considered of 'extraordinary value'.[9] The Americans paid by providing important funding for the Basque government's activities, but were not willing to meet the Basque demand for a more active role against Francoism. What happened was the very opposite. Already in November 1947, in a session of UNO, in which the Franco regime was condemned and possible sanctions were mentioned, the speaker of the American government had voted against this resolution, evidencing the beginning of a new policy towards the Spanish dictator. The treaty on military cooperation, signed in 1953 between the USA and Franco's Spain, underlined this new situation of western cooperation with the dictator. Thanks to this alteration in international relations, the Basques suddenly found themselves politically offside once again. Their anti-fascist tradition was still an honourable argument, but this argument had lost its entire political efficacy. The western powers, upon which President Aguirre and the Basque nationalists in exile had concentrated all their hopes, had changed allegiance and were no longer interested in the fate of a small and powerless nation like the Basques. The result of this displacement was a total vacuum in the politics of Basque nationalism, whose leaders were obliged to recognize that the whole strategy on which Aguirre had built his policy since the beginning of the Second World War, was nothing but an illusion. A last attempt to win the support of the western democracies for a strategy of isolation against Franco was the Basque nationalists' timid backing of the so-called 'monarchical solution' promoted by the socialist leader Indalecio Prieto. In March 1945, Juan of Bourbon, son of the last king Alfonso XIII and heir to the crown, had published his famous 'Manifesto of Lausanne', in which he defended the restoration of the monarchy as the only way to a real peace in Spain. This caused a deep rift in the relationship between Franco and Don Juan and, consequently, Prieto's political shift led to open confrontation with the republican government and a rapprochement with the monarchist groups in exile. The result was the pact between the Spanish socialists and the Confederation of Monarchical Forces, signed in Saint Jean de Luz in August 1948. Since both Prieto and the Spanish monarchists had quite good, fluent relations with the British Labour government headed by Attlee, who was presented by Prieto as one of the principal inspirers and guarantors of the socialist–monarchist *entente*, the latter was supposed to increase international pressure on Franco. Telesforo Monzón, one of the nationalist ministers in Aguirre's government, was the most prominent and passionate defender of the monarchist solution in the PNV. 'The Government of the Republic and everything moving in its orbit has finished for me. (…) If it's a question of throwing Franco out, today there is only one serious policy left, that is to support the monarchy.'[10] Despite a very controversial internal debate, the PNV followed Monzón's ideas without sharing his radical anti-republicanism and backed this new initiative by withdrawing its minister from the internationally more and more discredited republican government. Yet it very soon became evident, first, that it was impossible to unite such opposing forces as the socialists and monarchists in a compact, homogeneous alliance and, second, that the British government would not engage in any dubious international strategy against Francoism, if it was not clear what the feasible political alternative would be or what the political dividend of such a strategy for British politics would be at a time when anti-communism was the principal guideline of western foreign affairs. After the failure of Prieto's monarchist initiative and the break-up of the complete nationalist Resistance in the interior by Franco's police after the strike of 1951, the crisis of Basque nationalism was total. Joseba Rezola, the PNV head of the underground Junta of Resistance, put it very clearly at a secret meeting of the party's Political Commission: 'We are in a tremendous crisis of everything, including the party'. In the opinion of Rezola, this was a consequence of the fact that 'we used to believe that our things would be resolved by the foreign affairs ministries and hardly any effort by ourselves'.[11] The death of the Basque President in 1960 symbolized and increased even more the dramatic decay of traditional Basque nationalism.

One of the consequences of this crisis was a growing unrest among the young underground nationalists. The rapprochement between Franco and the USA had not produced any benefit for the Basque population, who continued to suffer cruel repression and were not even allowed to speak Basque in public. More and more members of the PNV underground youth organization felt increasingly uneasy with what they considered the deplorable passivity of the exiled nationalists, whose only contribution to the anti-Francoist struggle was apparently the publication of bombastic communiqués. This was the political background to the deepest and – in the long term – the most dramatic split in the historically quite homogeneous Basque nationalism which was germinating during the 1950s and came to fruition in 1959 with the foundation of a new underground organization, Euskadi 'ta Askatasuna (ETA, Basque Country and Freedom).[12]

As at the end of the nineteenth century when Basque nationalism emerged, it was again the impact of a crisis of modernization that accompanied this new transformation of the Basque political landscape and the expansion of radical nationalism in the 1960s and 1970s. The liberalization of the Spanish economy by the Opus Dei technocrats in the Spanish government generated spectacular economic growth now in each of the four Spanish-Basque provinces. Industrialization, class conflict, massive immigration, the marginalization of the Basque culture – especially the language, the introduction of new values and ideas through TV and tourism, political repression and the increasing erosion of traditional values and channels of socialization – were all factors which contributed to turning the pillars of Basque society upside-down, creating a new scenario which in Durkheimian terms has been described as a situation of anomie.[13]

There was an especially huge influx of non-Basque workers and employees, and, as a consequence, the growing pressure on the language – the core element of the traditional cultural particularism of the Basque people – which most contributed to generating this mood of desperation in everyday life. Between 1950 and 1980, the population of Bizkaia increased by about 80 per cent, while that of Gipuzkoa by nearly 70 per cent (see Table 4.1).[14]

Table 4.1   Demographic evolution of the Basque provinces

	1950	1960	1970	1975
Alava	118,000	139,000	204,000	238,000
Bizkaia	569,000	754,000	1,043,000	1,151,000
Gipuzkoa	374,000	478,000	631,000	683,000
Navarre	383,000	402,000	465,000	484,000

Table 4.2   Percentage of Basque speakers in 1868 and 1970

	1868	1970
Alava	12	9
Bizkaia	93	16
Gipuzkoa	100	44
Navarre	20	11

According to the census of 1970, about 30 per cent of the inhabitants of the four Basque provinces were born in other provinces of the Spanish state. In the most industrialized Basque region, that of Bizkaia, 36 per cent came from Spanish regions. In Bilbao and its industrial hinterland, for which we do not have exact data, the percentage was probably a lot higher. Immigration also had an impact on the family structure. In 1975, only half of all Basque citizens living in the four provinces had been born in families in which both father and mother were originally Basque.[15] It is obvious that this demographic evolution dramatically accelerated the historic decay of *Euskara*, the Basque language (see Table 4.2).

The answer to this deep crisis of Basque society was in the form of a new cycle of mobilization, encouraged by a timid political liberalization of the regime and the demonstrator-effect of other popular movements on the international scene (anti-colonialism, civil rights, Cuba, anti-Vietnam war, and so on).[16] The emergence of radical Basque nationalism was just one of the elements of this broader cycle of not entirely but predominantly nationalist mobilization, which had political, social and cultural ingredients, the foundation of the first *ikastolak*, i.e. private schools teaching in the Basque language being one of its most remarkable products, which years later would create a broad educational network within the Basque territories.

ETA, which was a creation of dissidents from the PNV youth organization and other nationalist students, was initially nothing more than a pure reaffirmation of the radical interpretation of the nationalist doctrine that had never really disappeared from the PNV discourse since the times of Sabino Arana. The founders of ETA rediscovered Arana's radical and separatist writings, which, in their opinion, had been betrayed by the moderate leadership living in comfortable exile. The radicals' discourse of 1921 had provoked the first important split in the PNV, which had been very similar to this one.

It was the violent repression against the first ETA activists in 1961, who were captured by the police, tortured and condemned to imprisonment for more than 25 years in some cases, which produced a radicalization of the underground nationalist organization. In 1963, Federico Krutwig, one of the most prominent ETA ideologists, published his book *Vasconia*, which symbolized the definitive rupture between new and old nationalism. For the first time since the establishment of the Basque government, a Basque nationalist publicly and very controversially criticized the autonomous government, its representatives and the political party that controlled it. Krutwig did not even spare Jesús María Leizaola, José Antonio Aguirre's successor, the new president of the government since 1960, from his caustic criticism:

> In reality, Mr Leizaola is nothing but a collaborator with the Basque people's enemies, who works for free. (...) This Basque government cannot be much more than a stinking dead body, a rotten organ (...) that should disappear as soon as possible.

Krutwig reserved a special comment for the fact that Leizaola, who spoke the Basque language perfectly just as his wife did, did not educate his children in *Euskara*, but in Spanish. For Krutwig this meant converting 'one's own children into instruments in the service of anti-Basque repression'. Such kind of 'high treason' committed by a 'false nationalist' would have been punished in other countries of Central Europe by 'forcing the man to kneel down and then shooting him in the neck. Here, on the contrary, we still considered this man the president of the Basque people's national government, from which we very naively thought it would bring independence to our fatherland.'[17]

The book represented the first positive review of Marxist thought in the history of Basque nationalism, presenting a highly explosive ideological cocktail mixed with references to Sabino Arana, Marx, Proudhon, Bakunin, Lenin, Mao, Ho-Tschi-Min, Clausewitz and European ethnolinguists like Guy Héraud. One of the central conclusions drawn from his analysis was the comparison of the Basque Country with a Third World colony. The only way of breaking the oppression and the dependence on the (Spanish and French) metropolis was by carrying out Mao's strategy of action–repression–action.

The Franco regime seemed to be keen to supply some kind of realistic basis to Krutwig's not very convincing comparison between a highly industrialized and developed European region and a backward, agrarian, Third World country. From a total of eleven states of emergency, which the regime declared between 1956 and 1975, ten were applied in Bizkaia and/or

Gipuzkoa. That means that the citizens of these two Basque provinces had to live during this period of nearly five years in a continuous situation of military occupation, suffering from corresponding high levels of imprisonment.[18] Moreover, in the international context the reference to anticolonialism had a certain logic: between 1956 and 1968, just when Krutwig's book had been written, published and discussed, 49 new states were founded. The year ETA was born, 1959, was the year of the Cuban Revolution, too. The war in Algeria, the death of Che Guevara and the war in Vietnam were other important events which might explain why a leading, radical nationalist in the Basque Country was able to recognize in his own nation the mirror of anticolonialism and why this analysis, together with the propositions concerning an adequate strategy of anticolonialist struggle, got such a remarkable response from Basque society, and not only from among radical nationalists.

Once *Vasconia* was published, there was no remaining possibility of reconciliation between the young dissidents and the traditional mainstream nationalists in exile, which since the death of President Aguirre in 1960 had lost its charismatic leader respected by Basque nationalists of all tendencies. His successor, Jesús María de Leizaola, did his best to remember the legitimacy of Basque self-government and to keep the tradition of his party alive, but he could not avoid the profound crisis of traditional nationalism which did not really have any inspiring answer to the question that thousands of young Basques – nationalists and non-nationalists alike – had in mind. Their daily exposure to repression provoked them to ask: 'What is to be done?'

The result of this crisis was a shift from the exterior to the interior in the activity of Basque nationalism. During the 1960s and 1970s the exiled nationalists of the PNV lost their capacity to mobilize. This now passed to ETA, which – despite the official criticism articulated by the PNV leaders – was considered with sympathy and pride by many nationalists, as the organization of lost, but brave and patriotic sons. The huge mobilization against the Burgos trial (1970), including general strikes, was the best visible demonstration of this shift in the history of Basque nationalism.

At the time of the Burgos trial, ETA had already put into practice the thesis published by Krutwig. Since its Fifth Assembly in 1966, ETA organized its 'Military Front' in order to prepare for 'revolutionary war' against the Spanish enemy. Two years later, for the first time in the history of the group, members of the underground organization were killed. At a traffic control, one of the policemen was shot dead. In the subsequent persecution the *etarra* Txabi Etxebarrieta was killed by the police. A few weeks later, another commando killed a policeman, Melitón Manzanas, who was known for torturing prisoners. The step from nationalist radicalism to political violence had been taken and the tradition of peaceful mobilization that characterized both the PNV and the early ETA was in ruins. Why did this happen in the Basque Country, and why didn't it happen in the other historic regions of fringe nationalism within the Spanish state, that is, Catalonia and Galicia? Both territories counted, just like the Basque Country, on strong nationalist movements. In neither case did the Franco regime allow any kind of public nationalist activity, and because of the crude repression it is probable that violent resistance would have aroused the sympathy of huge parts of the population. However, neither in Catalonia nor in Galicia was the political strategy of the nationalist movements seriously challenged by a dynamic and popular armed group like ETA in the Basque Country.[19] How then do we explain the shift of Basque nationalism towards violence and away from peaceful protest after seventy years? Although the literature on this issue is quite sparse, and despite the very small number of studies that analyse the phenomenon of political violence in the Basque Country from a comparative perspective, some hypotheses might be formulated:

1. ETA violence seen as lower-class   Based on different theories of 'lower-class violence', the German sociologist Peter Waldmann explains the shift towards violent forms of protest in the Basque provinces as a consequence of a major change in the social structure of the nationalist movements. He argues that in cases of extreme danger for the survival of the ethnic group the middle and upper classes are likely to lose control of the nationalist movement to the benefit of the lower social classes. According to Waldmann, this is what happened in Northern Ireland and the Basque Country. As empirical proof of his thesis he presents a biographical analysis of a sample of ETA prisoners, among which those belonging to lower social classes form a significant majority. More recent studies based on much larger and more representative samples draw the same conclusion concerning the recruitment of Basque prisoners among the lower layers of society.[20]

2. The tradition of violence   It would be an interesting task for anthropologists to see whether the fact that during the nineteenth century the Basques had been much more directly involved in never-ending warfare (the wars against France, the Carlist wars) than any other people in Spain has produced any kind of mental heritage, which – understood as a kind of *longue-durée* structure as explained in the works of the French historian Fernand Braudel – is not exposed to short-term historical changes, and is transferred from one generation to another. The consequence would be the durability of features fixed in the mental structure or patterns of social behaviour like the worship of the warrior or the predisposition for resolving conflicts by the use of force.

3. The weakness of culture   Comparing the   Basque and the Catalan cases, Conversi has underlined the role of culture as a major difference between both movements, especially that of language, which remained a 'core value' of cultural nationalism. Catalan was (and is) spoken by a huge majority of the population and its defence had a mobilizing effect even among non-nationalist Catalans or Spanish immigrants, who could learn it quite easily thanks to the Roman roots of the language. Thus, language

became a core value of nationalism, which – as a result of its deep-rooted tradition within society – it was impossible even for Franco to eliminate. Consequently, during the dictatorship, culture and language became important vehicles of nationalist mobilization in times in which political protest was outlawed. On the other hand, in the Basque case autochthonous culture and language were in a much worse position. *Euskara* was spoken only by a minority and it is very much harder to learn than Catalan. Furthermore, most Basque intellectuals and writers since the end of the nineteenth century scorned it as a rural relic useless in the modern world. Hence, Sabino Arana did not define culture and language as a core value of the nation and the movement, but rather religion and race. In his own and his successors' discourse, language had no integrating or proactive function, but a separating and a reactive one: it was one of the last remaining obstacles for the penetration of all the Spanish evils that were corrupting the Basque traditions and customs. In other words, we can concur with Conversi that 'the lack of a robust cultural nationalism and shared cultural elements meant that regeneration had to be carried out by other means'.[21] In Arana's nationalism the recovery of real national identity was to be achieved by the defence of religion and race. When these traditional values became jeopardized during the second wave of modernization since the 1960s, others had to be put into their place. In ETA's discourse and strategy, it was armed struggle that filled this vacuum.

4. Radical answers to radical challenges   Radicalism produces radicalism. In the Basque Country, this happened in two ways. First, the effects of industrialization, urbanization and immigration in a small territory like the Basque region with a weak traditional culture, were much more menacing and dangerous for the survival of the affected ethnic group than the same processes in larger areas like Catalonia and Galicia, where modernization was much more concentrated on different spots and autochthonous culture was stronger and wealthier. The second argument is related to the degree of repression. Even without reliable comparative studies, the small size of the Spanish-Basque population and the available data concerning the intensity of repression (detentions, tortures, police violence, states of emergency, aggression against *Euskara*) suggest that the level of state repression was higher in the Basque provinces than in any other region of the state and that the percentage of Basques directly and personally affected by these repressive measures was proportionally much higher than that of Catalans or Gallegos. This leads us to the following conclusion established by one of the most prominent experts in ethnic conflict and violence, a conclusion that could be perfectly valid for the case of ETA:

> The more violence is used by political authorities, the greater the likelihood that challengers will respond with increased violence. However, state authorities that have used extreme force, such as massacres, torture, and genocide, to subdue challengers are also less likely to be openly challenged, either because groups cannot organize open

resistance or they fear the consequences of doing so. Thus, the more extreme force is used, the less likely the chances for open rebellion. A curvilinear relationship thus exists between state violence and the extent and level of violence of political action taken by the challengers. Clandestine movements that use terrorism and guerrilla warfare are typically responses to situations in which government authorities have used deadly force in dealing with challengers.[22]

The introduction of new values, ideas and strategies in the nationalist movement, however, did not only produce the split between ETA and the PNV. It enabled the emergence of the armed wing of Basque nationalism, but at the same time it set the stage for never-ending controversies and splits inside ETA itself as well. To summarize, without considering the more subjective or accidental factors, the discussion developed about two major problems linked to one another: the relationship between class and nation or social emancipation and national liberation on the one hand, and between politics and violence or mass mobilization and the 'armed vanguard' on the other. Contrary to other terrorist groups acting in Europe during the 1970s and 1980s, one of the characteristic differences of ETA consisted in the fact that the Basque group was always much more nationalist than extreme leftist. Different attempts to convert ETA into a revolutionary leftist party open to class coalitions with other leftist groups, which was the aim of 'ETA-Berri' (1966) or 'ETA-VI' (1970), failed. The gradual sidelining of all those activists backing the predominance of the political struggle over the military, together with the propagandistic and mobilizing effects of spectacular acts of violence (in 1973 Franco's designated successor, the hard-liner Admiral Carrero Blanco, was killed by a bomb), enabled the 'Military Front' of ETA, that is, those who handled the arms and believed in the central importance of armed struggle, even in the foreseeable new context of a parliamentarian democracy, to keep absolute control of the organization. In this militarist conception of ETA there was not even space for those who, without renouncing the necessity for the armed struggle as such, tried to reduce the apparently absolute independence of the Military Front by linking its activities more closely to the decisions of the organization's political leadership as 'ETA político-militar' (ETA p-m) proposed in 1974. On the threshold of democracy, ETA was divided into two competing groups. ETA p-m continued, after a final particularly bloody offensive, its approach to parliamentary activity giving rise to a political party (EIA), a leftist coalition (Euskadiko Ezkerra) and finally in 1982, after negotiations with the government, to its own dissolution.[23] From that moment on, it was ETA-militar, which amalgamated all the elements of radical Basque nationalism, who still believed in the legitimacy and necessity of armed struggle and aimed at a total break with Francoism as the only valid strategy for Basque independence.

5
The Transition to Democracy and the Basque Problem

Since the late 1970s, the processes of transformation, which brought to an end dictatorial regimes and initiated the construction and consolidation of democracy, have become one of the favourite subjects for research among social scientists. Interest in this problem has increased even more since the collapse of the Soviet bloc and the wave of popular mobilization against communism. In the context of this debate, the Spanish example is generally considered a paradigmatic model for the successful and peaceful establishment of a democratic state after a relatively brief period of transition. The process started with the death of the dictator on 20 November 1975, or even some months earlier when the news concerning Franco's grave illness was known, and it ended with a large consensus backing the new Constitution, as manifested by the Spanish population in the referendum held in December 1978. Thus, in a little more than three years, Spain managed to overcome nearly forty years of dictatorship by carrying out an 'ideal type of a negotiated transition', which set the conditions for the following 'successful and relatively unproblematic consolidation of democracy'.[1] In comparison with other successful southern European transitions to democracy (Portugal, Greece), Spain has been ranked highest, 'since it has been able to resolve problems which were slightly more difficult faster and more efficiently'.[2]

Indeed, from a general point of view and within the analytical framework of comparative history and politics, there cannot be any doubt about this optimistic interpretation of the Spanish road to democracy. There are several factors which might explain this success. First of all, Spanish democracy was a product of a negotiated transition carried out by the soft-liners of the Francoist regime and the most relevant forces of the democratic opposition. It was the consequence of a 'transition through transaction',[3] in which both parts managed to marginalize their radical and intransigent opponents and to renounce extreme claims. This was possible because during the last 15 years of Francoism, the changes produced within society went along with an evolution of the regime towards a less monolithic bloc made up of different groups of elites, among which authoritarian and traditionalist hardliners (the bunker) worked hand in hand with other, more open-minded and flexible technocrats. Thus, when Franco died, reformist elites were already available within the regime. These elites, led by Adolfo Suárez, the former Minister of the Movimiento, were able to convince the democratic opposition of their willingness to establish democracy. The democratic parties, including communists and most of the peripheral nationalists, accepted these reformist dissidents of the regime as partners in the negotiations. Thus, the process of legitimacy transfer was controlled by the reformist elites and the democratic parties, who mobilized their followers as a means of pressure and backing their positions in the negotiations, but never as an instrument to question and challenge the process of negotiation itself.

Secondly, the transition was possible and necessary because the second wave of social and economic modernization, encouraged by the government's Opus Dei technocrats since the end of the 1950s, had shaped a strong civil society, inspired by western democratic values and cultural patterns of behaviour, which sooner or later had to come into conflict with the authoritarian, backward and repressive structure of the regime.

A third and no less important factor was the role of the young king Juan Carlos as a guardian of the peaceful transfer of legitimacy from the authoritarian regime to the new democracy. In 1969, Juan Carlos had taken the very controversial decision to accept the 'Law of Succession' which declared him the legitimate heir of the Spanish crown to the detriment of his father Juan, known for his democratic convictions. Only in 1977, before the first democratic elections were organized, did Don Juan abdicate his right to be the new Spanish king. After the dictator's death, however, the hopes of those who expected the young king to be the saviour of the fragile dictatorship were destroyed. The loyalty of the right-wing politicians and army officers to the King impeded on several occasions an openly anti-democratic rebellion or even a military putsch, especially when in the spring of 1977 President Adolfo Suárez legalized the Spanish Communist Party by decree in flat contradiction to the previous decision of the Supreme Court opposed to its legalization. This commitment to democracy bore fruit not only for Spanish society, but also for the monarchy. The Republic had abolished the monarchy in 1931; it had been restored by a dictatorial decision. Juan Carlos as king won a level of popularity and legitimacy for his dynasty never before reached in Spanish contemporary history.[4]

Within this context, the necessary favourable conditions for a transition to democracy were laid. The different steps of this process are well known and need only be briefly mentioned here. After the dictator's death, King Juan Carlos assumed his function as the new head of state, maintaining the government under Arias Navarro, which thus immediately cast doubt on his democratic aspirations among the parties of the opposition. However, soon Arias's incapacity and unwillingness to introduce even minor changes to the system and the resulting increase of popular protest, in the form of a wave of strikes, provoked a growing political and personal distance between the king and his president, who had to present his resignation in July 1976. Against all predictions, Juan Carlos charged a young unknown politician with the formation of the new government: Adolfo Suárez, the former minister of the Movimiento in Arias's government. From this moment on, things started to change. Suárez' masterpiece was the 'Political Reform Bill', which was a polite invitation to the institutions of the regime to commit hara-kiri, since – among other points – it established the holding of free elections and a two-chamber parliamentary system. Suárez, with the support of the king, obtained a broad majority in the Francoist Cortes for this law, which in December 1976 was backed by nearly 95 per cent – with a participation of 77.4 per cent – of the voters in a referendum, in which the opposition had campaigned for the voters' abstention. Now the way was open for the legalization of the political parties (including the Communist Party), the trade unions and for the first democratic elections (15 June 1977), Suárez' Unión de Centro Democrático (UCD) being the winner. The UCD was a centre-right coalition formed by the moderate conservative opposition and some reformist personalities linked to the Franco regime. It was a party which had been created only in 1976 and moreover without a clear ideology. Its principal aim was to support the president's task and its social and ideological composition symbolized the very nature of the Spanish transition itself, which was moderate and the product of a pact, rather than a rupture.

The government and the new democratic Cortes had two main immediate tasks to tackle: the writing of a Constitution and the response to the claims for self-government put forward by the peripheral nationalists. In the autumn and winter of 1977, pre-autonomous institutions were created in Catalonia and in the Basque Country. During the following years, the government set up similar institutions in other Spanish regions, generalizing a process of regionalization, which would later be confirmed and guaranteed by the Constitution. After long-drawn-out negotiations between the members of a parliamentary commission created for that purpose and made up of the major political parties represented in the Cortes, a broad consensus was reached on the text, which was backed by 88 per cent of the voters in a referendum held in December 1978. The Constitution defines Spain as a constitutional monarchy and declares the 'indivisible unity of the Spanish nation', recognizing at the same time the existence of 'nationalities' and regions within the Spanish nation and their right to autonomy, as well as the co-official status of the regional languages. One of the most controversial articles of the new Magna Carta defines the army as the guardian of the Spanish nation's unity; for many observers this seemed a Francoist relic – a gift to placate the armed forces and thereby ensure their compliant acceptance of democracy.

Once the constitutional framework was set up, the process of regionalization could be completed. Due to the fact that both territories had already reached democratically legitimized autonomy with their own self-governing

institutions during the Second Republic, it was obvious that the first to negotiate their Statutes of Autonomy would be Catalonia and the Basque Country,
which were both approved by popular referenda in 1979. Today, Spain is
divided into a total of 17 'autonomous communities', many of which are
inventions *ex novo* without any historical roots.[5] Four years after Franco's
death, Spain was a constitutional monarchy; the armed forces had apparently
been placated and brought under civil control; an ambitious programme of
regionalization had avoided the disintegration of the state. In other words,
the complex transition towards democracy had been carried out with success
and the new democratic system had entered a phase of consolidation.

This is the optimistic story of the Spanish conquest of democracy.
However, if we tell this same story from the Basque point of view, the
narrative would be quite different, since for Basque nationalists – both moderates and radicals – the transition and the establishment of democracy do
not represent that successful paradigmatic model praised by so many analysts. There is an evident lack of synchronization between the development
of transition in the Basque Country and in the rest of Spain. Whereas at the
beginning of the 1980s democracy already had a solid foundation in the
state, 'within this one region [the Basque, L.M.] (...) democratic politics and
institutions were not consolidated at that time'.[6] The political and social situation of the Basque provinces during the years immediately before and
after Franco's death was different from any of the other territories of the
Spanish state. This circumstance has been described as the 'Basque peculiar-
ity' in the process of the transition, resulting from the 'lack of legitimacy of
the state' in that region.[7] In the rest of Spain, transition meant basically the
problem of transforming a dictatorial regime into a modern, liberal, parliamentary democracy upheld by a constitution. In regions like Catalonia and
Galicia, the establishment of democracy was regarded a first and necessary
step for the achievement of a second aim: the implementation of some kind
of self-government. In the Basque Country, however, instead of consecutive
steps and aims (democracy then self-government), policy-makers had to
deal with a sort of three-dimensional knot, in which each of the dimensions
was closely linked with the others. In other words, in *Euskadi* it was impossible to talk about democracy without talking at the same time about self-
government, violence being the third dimension and interloper in this
debate: that is, violence as an instrument used by the defenders of the dictatorship – including the anti-ETA terror commandos from the extreme right
– against the Basque (nationalist and non-nationalist) opposition, violence
as a consequence of the lack of democracy and self-government, and
violence as a means of political pressure and intimidation in the hands of
the 'armed vanguard' of ETA and its struggle for the national liberation
of the Basque nation. This overlapping of three crucial problems shaped
the scenario in the Basque provinces, characterized by 'radicalism,
the importance of emotions and the impossibility or difficulty to rationalize

the political debate'.[8] This was not exactly a favourable context for a gradual and negotiated transition to democracy.

In fact, despite the economic liberalization of the regime carried out by the Opus Dei technocrats in the government since the end of the 1950s, until the death of the dictator and even in the following years there was no alteration in the repressive strategy against Basque nationalism. Only two months before his death, Franco confirmed the death penalty on five political prisoners, two of whom were ETA activists, ignoring all the international protests. Later, during the presidency of Arias Navarro, but also under the new government presided over by Adolfo Suárez, the Spanish police acted in the Basque region as if nothing had changed. Brutality in the repression of demonstrations, torture and even cases of shop-looting resulted in the protest of international observers like Amnesty International. One of the most dramatic incidents took place in March 1976, when the police shot dead five workers on strike. The partial pardons and amnesties for political prisoners, including ETA activists, were not enough to calm the climate of unrest and mobilization. The prohibition of the celebration of the nationalist 'Day of the Fatherland', the *Aberri Eguna* in 1976 and 1977, were other symbolic gestures that in the eyes of many Basque citizens seemed to demonstrate that nothing, or very little, had changed since November 1975.

ETA was one of those who did not cast any doubt on this interpretation. Since the famous Burgos trial in 1970, in which eight of the 16 ETA prisoners had been sentenced to death, the sentence later commuted to life imprisonment, ETA had accelerated its development as a clandestine underground group, in which the military logic of armed struggle dominated any kind of political reasoning. The success of spectacular attacks like the bomb in December 1973 which killed the then President of the Government, the hardline Francoist Admiral Carrero Blanco, helped to increase the prestige of the military front within the organization. Both the competition of the two ETAs (militar and político-militar) for the control of radical nationalism – the result of a split produced a few months before the beginning of the Burgos trial – and the spiral attack–repression–attack made the years of the transition the most violent period since the genesis of the paramilitary organization to date. In fact, the Basque paramilitaries tried to interfere in each of the crucial moments of the transition and the early democratic consolidation with a spectacular intensification of its violent activity. Since the first fatal attack in 1968 until 1977, there had never been more than a maximum of 20 mortally wounded ETA victims in a year (1974). During the three following years, when the stepping-stones to democracy and Basque autonomy had been fixed (1978: the Referendum on the Constitution; 1979: the Referendum on the Basque Autonomy Statute and the second elections to the Spanish parliament; 1980: the first elections to the regional Basque parliament) the figures register the total number of persons killed by ETA as 240. In the following years, this death rate dropped down to an average of 30 to 40 victims per year.

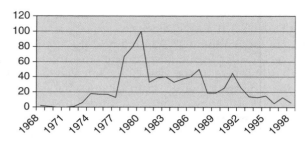

Graph 5.1   Number of killings by ETA
Sources: http://www.covite.org and http://www.avt.org.

The impact of radicalism, popular mobilization and violence converted the PNV into the only agency able to re-establish a climate of calm and normality in the Basque Country, and this was basically for two reasons. First, the party had an historical profile of Christian Democrat moderation, in which the utopia of independence went hand in hand with a pragmatic flexibility in daily political life. The party did not need too much time to overcome its long crisis in exile. The PNV national conference held in March 1977 in Pamplona, the first organized since 1933, as well as the good results in the general elections of the same year (28.8 per cent of the votes in the three provinces excluding Navarre), did great credit to the PNV as the old and new political axis of Basque politics and as an indispensable partner in negotiations with any central government. The second reason for the revaluation of the PNV was its relative proximity to ETA and the radical nationalist left. After all, ETA had been the result of a split within the PNV provoked not only by ideological differences, but also by the generation gap that divided the restless nationalist youth in the interior and the PNV veterans in exile, who seemed to have resigned themselves and settled down to a quiet life. In fact, for many years moderate nationalists regarded the ETA activists as the lost sons of the nationalist family, who, if they were doing wrong in performing acts of violence, did it because they were provoked by the repression as well as for patriotic purposes. Owing to this indulgence, the PNV was thought to maintain a certain level of influence within radical nationalism and ETA. Thus, for most of the political observers any strategy aimed at the normalization of Basque politics, which was essential for the success of the new Spanish democracy, had to pursue the PNV's integration into democratic consensus, the disappearance of the party's indulgence towards ETA and – consequently – the sidelining and, finally, the end of terrorism.

The PNV was conscious of this position of strength and tried to make political capital out of it during the years after Franco's death.[9] First proof of the party's influence, even before the above-mentioned National Conference of 1977 opened a new period of internal reorganization and political expansion, came as the result of the Referendum on the Political Reform in December 1976. Practically the complete democratic opposition had made a call for abstention given the suspicion and mistrust in a law that, instead of promoting the definitive 'rupture' with the dictatorship, put the power of decision-taking concerning the how and when of democracy at least partially into the hands of a Francoist institution, the Cortes, which had passed the law before it was submitted to a popular referendum. Whereas within the state only 23 per cent of the voters followed the instructions of opposition parties, in Gipuzkoa and Bizkaia, the most nationalist provinces, only 44.5 and 53.2 per cent of the voters participated in the referendum. In Alava (76 per cent) and Navarre (73 per cent), however, there was practically no difference from the Spanish average.[10]

The first discords between the PNV and the rest of the democratic opposition emerged only a few months later when preparatory work for the new Constitution started. The Constitution had to define the model of the future democratic state and therefore had a special relevance for all those peripheral nationalists, like the Basques, who demanded an end to the centralist structure of the state and the implementation of a system of self-government for their nation. On the other hand, it was foreseeable that this claim would provoke the resistance of the rightist and pro-Francoist groups and institutions, especially the army, educated since the Civil War in a spirit of Spanish nationalism as the supreme protector of the 'one single, great and indivisible' Spanish nation. One month before the general elections of June 1977, the PNV had signed the so-called 'Autonomous Compromise' together with the Basque socialists, communists, Christian democrats and other minor nationalist groups, announcing the will of the deputies and senators elected on the lists of these parties to work for the establishment of an autonomy which would 'recognize the political and administrative personality of *Euskadi*' and connect with the 'tradition of freedom and self-government of the Basque people, which can never be given up'. In any case, the text already included a reference to what was going to be the guideline of the PNV's strategy during the debate on the Constitution, stating that the future autonomy would 'by no means signify any renunciation of the political powers based on the complete restoration of the *Fueros*'.[11] Behind this statement we find the idea – with a long tradition in the Basque nationalist discourse – of a secular, original, and thus pre-constitutional Basque system of self-government granted by the *Fueros* and respected by the Spanish monarchs until the abolition of this system during the nineteenth century. Hence, for a Basque nationalist a constitution could only be accepted if it safeguarded these 'historic rights' of the Basque nation. This notion of the 'historic rights' as a reference to Basque self-government at the time of the *Fueros*, which was the centrepiece of PNV politics during the transition, recalls the party's situation in 1906 and shows how little the discourse had apparently changed in more than 70 years. In 1906, after Sabino Arana's death, the first political programme of the party was designed around exactly the same formula in order to permit the integration of moderates and radicals in the same party. Now, 70 years later, in a climate of socio-political mobilization and with a radical nationalist left prepared to compete with the PNV for hegemony in the nationalist movement, the party resorted once again to this old demand wrapped in the same ambiguous vagueness acceptable to both autonomists and separatists.

The elaboration of the constitutional project started in adverse conditions for the PNV. Like other minor parties of the Cortes, the Basque nationalists were excluded from the parliamentarian commission in charge of preparing the text.[12] The Catalan nationalist Miquel Roca was supposed to represent the interests of the Basques, but due to their political differences with that Catalan politician, the PNV did not accept this procedure, reducing its possibilities of participating in the process to informal encounters with the members of the commission and, later, to the presentation of amendments to the constitutional bill.

The result of the debate on the Constitution has already been described above. The PNV, even recognizing that 'from a global point of view, the Constitution may be a model of democracy', campaigned for abstention in the referendum, since the party 'could never give its voluntary adhesion to an Unitarian concept of state, which is not based on the free union and solidarity of the people that compose it'. Such a state was not 'constructed in a democratic manner from the bottom to the top', and the power given to the nationalities and regions was 'nothing but a simple act of delegation put into effect by the central power of the state itself'.[13] This concept was far from the nationalist idea of the 'historic rights', which, however, were mentioned – as a consequence of an amendment presented by the PNV and later modified and constitutionalized by the leading Spanish parties – in an additional clause of the Constitution. Similar arguments were used by the nationalist left, who rejected the very possibility of progress towards the freedom of the Basque nation by 'bureaucratic' negotiations with the reformist governments of the monarchy. Only a process of 'popular struggle' would ensure the 'democratic and national aspirations' of the Basques, 'undermining and destroying any formula aimed at the continuity of fascism and oligarchic power'.[14]

As far as the level of constitutional consensus is concerned, the result of the referendum made evident both a gap between the Basque Country and the rest of the Spanish state and a gap within the Basque region itself. In the four provinces the Constitution was voted by only 53.3 per cent of the census, whereas among the Spanish average the participation totalled 67 per cent. The Constitution was refused by nearly 22 per cent of Basque voters, in Spain only by 8 per cent. This percentage was even higher if we exclude the Navarre result and consider only the three provinces that would join later in the Autonomous Community of *Euskadi* (abstention 51.1;

no: 23.5 per cent). Compared to Catalonia, the other region with a strong nationalist movement, the Basque results were indeed remarkable. In Catalonia all parties in parliament had campaigned for a 'yes' vote. As a consequence, the abstention only reached 40 per cent, and the 'no' votes were no more than 7.8 per cent, that is, nearly a third of the Basque average, including Navarre.[15] This result was at least in part a consequence of the integration, as mentioned above, of a Catalan nationalist in the parliamentary commission which drafted the text of the Constitution. Basque nationalists had not been invited to participate in the drafting of the text and the high rates of abstention and no-votes in the most nationalist provinces on the coast were no surprise. On the other hand, the figures for Alava and Navarre, where nationalism was in a minority, do not differ that drastically from the Spanish average, as is the case in Gipuzkoa and in Bizkaia.

In contrast to the Spanish result, there was no majority for the new constitution in the Basque territories. The normative foundation upon which the new democracy was built had not been approved by the Basques. It is important to underline this fact, since during the following years the nationalist radical left and ETA converted this result of the constitutional referendum into one of their strongest arguments to prove the Spanish imposition of a centralist concept of state against the will of the Basques. This undemocratic imposition was considered a clear form of state violence, which provoked the popular violence of ETA as a legitimate means of response to the state's aggression against the Basque nation. In this discourse there was no place for a more realistic analysis of the referendum, because although it was true that there was no majority for the yes-votes, it was also true that only a minority of the voters had followed the call of radical nationalism (and extreme right-wing Spanish parties) to cast a no-vote.

Nevertheless, before the referendum was held and the results known, the government had decreed the first measures of a partial devolution, aiming at the restoration of the autonomy that the Basques had lost after Franco's

Table 5.1 Referendum on the Spanish Constitution (1978) (percentages)

Territories	Abstention	No
Alava	40.7	19.2
Bizkaia	56.1	21.6
Gipuzkoa	56.6	29.8
Navarre	33.4	17.0
Basque average	46.7	21.9
Spanish average	33.0	8.0

Sources: http://www.euskadi.net;Fusi/Palafox, p. 380; Linz et alii (1981), pp. 88–93.

conquest of the Basque Country in 1937. A pre-autonomous governmental institution had been established ('Consejo General Vasco') and a commission formed by the Basque political parties had drafted a first bill for a regional autonomy. Five days before the Constitution came into force as published in the *Boletín Oficial del Estado*, the Basque Assembly of parliamentarians approved by 28 votes, one abstention and none against, the text of the Basque Statute of Autonomy which would be sent to the Spanish Cortes in order to initiate the legal procedure for its ratification fixed by the Constitution. It was evident that the PNV could not share the argument of the radical nationalist left, according to which the only conclusion to draw from the constitutional referendum in the Basque provinces was the rejection of an autonomy that was a mere derivation of the Constitution. The PNV could not play this game of everything or nothing, because the process of autonomy had advanced too far and the PNV had been the protagonist and driving force in this process. The party's leaders also know very well the climate of popular support backing regional autonomy among the nationalist rank-and-file. The solution to the apparent contradiction between the attitude of passive rejection of the Constitution on the one hand, and the enthusiastic support of a regional autonomy based on this very Constitution on the other, was offered by an additional disposition to the text of the Statute. The function of that clause was to 'connect the Statute with the nationalist Utopia' in order to 'make evident that accepting the first did not mean renouncing the second'.[16] After being modified during the debate in parliament, the additional provision of the statute stated that 'the acceptance of the system autonomy established in this Statute does not imply that the Basque people waive the rights that as such may have accrued to them in virtue of their history'. The hypothetical updating of these rights has to be done 'in accordance with the stipulations of the legal system'.[17] Thus, the door was open for further steps towards a deepening of Basque self-government. Just as in previous situations (1917–19; the Second Republic), autonomy within the state could be sold as a provisional form of national freedom, to which others might follow. The traditional nationalist pendulum continued its movements between the celebration of radical nationalist essentials (independence) and the performance of a moderate step-by-step pragmatism in daily political business.[18]

The same argument about autonomy as a stepping-stone to a higher level of Basque self-determination in the future was applicable to another issue of an extremely symbolic and emotion-loaded dimension in the history of Basque nationalism: the exclusion of Navarre from Basque autonomy. In 1936, after the establishment of the first Basque autonomy, this same exclusion had provoked a turmoil of criticism and controversy especially among Basque nationalists from that province. During the Franco era, the unification of the four Basque territories in the Spanish state became one of the most popular demands of the nationalists, which was even looked upon with a certain sympathy by other political forces such as the Basque socialists.

However, in the 1977 elections in Navarre, parties attached to the Spanish right and centre-right had won the majority. These parties rejected integration into the Basque process of autonomy, opting for the construction of separate single-province autonomy. In order to neutralize the criticism formulated by the nationalist left (and shared by many moderate nationalists) that the autonomy negotiated with the successors of Franco would perpetuate the territorial division of the Basque nation, the PNV negotiated another additional clause to the text of the statute, which mentioned the possibility of Navarre's integration into the 'Autonomous Community of the Basque Country'. This possibility stood in accordance with a transitory disposition of the Constitution, where the consecutive steps of this process were fixed (decision of the Navarrese government; simple majority in a referendum; final majority vote in the Spanish Cortes).

Finally, after long and hard negotiations, carried out in an extremely tense climate produced by mass mobilization, violence and rumours about a military putsch, the text of the Basque Statute of Autonomy was agreed between president Adolfo Suárez and Carlos Garaikoetxea, president of the provisional pre-autonomous Basque government. According to this text, the three Basque provinces of Bizkaia, Gipuzkoa and Alava would constitute the Autonomous Community of the Basque Country, provided with their own regional parliament and government. A broad autonomy was guaranteed especially in the areas of education, taxation, communications and policing.

Finally, the PNV had found a solution to its internal conflict, the conflict between flexibility and pragmatism on the one hand, and dogmatism and extremism on the other, which basically was nothing other than Weber's famous bipolarity of a responsibility-guided ethic and that of a consciousness-guided one. Obviously, the same conflict affected and divided the nationalist left. Owing to the different amnesties, the legalization of the political parties and the perspectives of a Basque autonomy, a significant part of the nationalist left opted for a critical participation in the process of transition. Only a few months before the first elections of 1977, these groups – politically close to ETA político-militar – created the coalition Euskadiko Ezkerra (EE, 'The Left of the Basque Country'), which later took an active part in the preparatory work of the Statute of Autonomy. With hardly any time to organize the electoral campaign, EE won about 6 per cent of the votes, which meant one deputy and one senator, in the three provinces where the coalition ran for the elections (Alava, Gipuzkoa, Bizkaia). This was a surprisingly good result, since other radical nationalist groups, which criticized the reformist strategy of EE, had campaigned for a boycott to the elections and later for a 'no' in the referendum for the Constitution. These groups joined in 1978 to set up the coalition Herri Batasuna (HB, People's Union), close to ETA-militar. Thus, the split within the nationalist left, which had emerged during the 1970s within ETA's orbit of influence, had also produced its consequences for the new Basque party system.

The debate about autonomy deepened these differences between the radical and moderate nationalist left. Moreover, from a historical perspective it can be stated that this debate became the real watershed in the recent history of Basque nationalism. In the referendum on the Basque Statute of Autonomy, while PNV and EE – like all the other parties of the democratic opposition, as well as the governing UCD – asked their followers to vote 'yes', HB was, together with the rightist and philo-Francoist Alianza Popular of the former minister Fraga Iribarne, the only political force of importance in the Basque Country campaigning against autonomy. The main argument was that a nationalist could never accept autonomy based on a constitution rejected by the Basque people, which perpetuated the submission of *Euskadi* to the Spanish state and impeded the achievement of one of the principal nationalist aims: the unification of the seven (Spanish and French) Basque territories in an independent Basque state. Nevertheless, due to both the unpopularity of the anti-autonomy position and the wish to keep distance with the no-campaign carried out by the right-wing AP, even HB did not dare to vote 'no', calling for a boycott of the referendum. Finally, the figures indicate a participation of nearly 60 per cent, with more than a 90 per cent turnout of the voters, that is, 53 per cent of the census, in favour of the Statute of Autonomy. Obviously, it is difficult to determine the influence of the HB campaign among those who did not vote, but if we compare the Basque results with those in the referendum for the Catalan Statute of Autonomy, HB's influence seems to have been rather small. In fact, in Catalonia, where all politically relevant forces backed the autonomy, the results – including the level of participation – did not differ too much from the Basque ones.[19]

From this moment on, Basque nationalism was hopelessly divided. The main clash was not really about programmes. It was about procedures. In 1979, the majority had gambled on autonomy as a *modus vivendi* for a gradual realization of Basque self-government. The way to achieve this aim was that of building social and political majorities in the Basque Country and negotiating with Madrid. None of the moderate nationalist parties ruled out

Table 5.2   Referendum on the Basque Autonomy Statute (1979 (percentages))

	Bizkaia	Gipuzkoa	Alava	Total
Participation	59.0	59.9	63.2	59.8
Yes	90.8	91.9	83.7	90.2
No	4.9	4.1	9.1	5.2
Invalid	4.3	4.0	7.2	4.6
Abstention	41.0	40.1	36.8	40.2

Source: De Pablo/Granja/Mees, p. 159.

the achievement of complete Basque self-determination in the future. The ideological spectrum of this moderate nationalist bloc covered Christian democrats like the PNV, socialists like Euskadiko Ezkerra – which later in 1992/93 split and disappeared – or social democrats and separatists like Eusko Alkartasuna (EA), a party founded as a product of an internal conflict in the PNV between 1983 and 1986.

On the other fringe of Basque nationalism we find the organizations of the self-denominated 'Basque Movement for National Liberation', which includes HB, the labour union LAB and other political and cultural groups representing feminists, youth, ecologists, prisoners' relatives, and so on. ETA is considered the military vanguard of the movement.[20] The coordination of the movement was accomplished by the Koordinadora Abertzale Sozialista (KAS) (Patriotic Socialist Coordinating Council), a clandestine organization constituted in 1976 with a fairly unstable membership over the years, but including both ETA and HB. In the opinion of many observers it was KAS which, transmitting the instructions of ETA, defined and controlled the political strategy of the movement, including HB. All these groups rejected autonomy, refusing to cooperate in all the institutions linked directly or indirectly to the Spanish state. Ever since, they have shown a quite mono-lithic defence of all ETA activities with the argument that ETA and violence are nothing but understandable results of an unresolved political conflict between the Spanish (and French) state(s) and the Basque people. Since 1976 and until the appearance of ETA's so-called 'Democratic Alternative' in 1995, the following five demands of what has become known as the 'KAS Alternative' made up the only political programme supported by all the groups forming part of the Liberation Movement during many years:

1. Total amnesty.
2. Legalization of all political parties, including those whose programme includes the creation of an independent Basque state without having to reduce their statutes.
3. Expulsion from *Euskadi* of the Guardia Civil, the Policía Armada and the General Police Corps.
4. Improvement of the living and working conditions for the popular classes and especially for the working class, and satisfaction of their immediate social and economic aspirations as expressed by their repre-sentative associations.
5. An autonomy statute that, as a minimum, recognizes the national sover-eignty of *Euskadi*, authorizes *Euskara* as the principal official language of the country, provides for the Basque government control over all law enforcement authorities and all military units garrisoned in the Basque Country, and endows the Basque people with adequate power to adopt whatever political, economic or social structures they deem appropriate for their own progress and welfare.[21]

In March 1986, ETA introduced two major changes in point 5, petitioning for the integration of Navarre in the future Basque autonomy and the recognition of the Basque right of self-determination, 'including the right to the creation of their own independent state'.[22]

This state has not yet been created; instead, after the official approbation of autonomy, the three Basque provinces started a new process of limited nation-building with at least some results, which Sabino Arana would not even have dreamt of. The problem of violence, however, has continued during the current period of democracy.

6
Democracy, Autonomy and Violence

The establishment and consolidation of the new democracy in Spain as a consequence of the peaceful transition after Franco's death in 1975 was the background to a spectacular increase of Basque nationalist power both in politics and society. Never before in the history of Basque nationalism since the foundation of the PNV in 1895, had the followers of Sabino Arana enjoyed such political and social influence as they achieved during the last three decades of the twentieth century. From an historical perspective, the transformation of the PNV, which to begin with was a small, semi-clandestine group of *petits bourgeois* in Bilbao, eventually becoming the dominant, governing, cross-class popular party in the region, was certainly astonishing. If we add the fact that the rise of this major nationalist party had not thwarted the emergence and expansion of other nationalist parties on the left of the PNV, it becomes evident that the institutionalization of post-Francoist democracy in the Basque Country was accompanied by the evolution of a new, historically unprecedented cycle of nationalist power.

There are three basic reasons for this new situation. First of all, after the long and dark experience of dictatorship and repression, Basque nationalism – and especially ETA – was one of the most active political forces in the struggle against Francoism and for freedom, so for public opinion (even within the Spanish state) nationalism had nearly become a synonym for democracy. The claim for self-government and self-determination was no longer the programme of a radical minority. It had become popular and fashionable. In the numerous public demonstrations in the years after 1975, even Basque socialists could be seen side by side with nationalists holding up banners with the slogan 'self-determination' on them. During those years of political and social mobilization, everybody had become a little bit nationalist, or at least 'Basquist'. The Che Guevara image of the ETA activists as fearless freedom fighters was especially attractive for Basque youths. All these circumstances have helped produce a great deal of nationalist votes in the elections since 1977. Summarizing the votes for either the moderate or

45

Table 6.1   Nationalist vote-sharing in the elections to the Spanish (SP) and Basque (BP) parliaments

	SP 77	SP 79	BP 80	SP 82	BP 84	SP 86	BP 86	SP 89	BP 90	SP 93	BP 94	SP 96	BP 98	SP 00	BP 01
PNV	28.8	27.6	38.0	32.0	42.0	28.0	23.7	22.7	28.5	23.9	29.9	25.4	27.9	39.1	42.7
HB	4.3	15.0	16.5	14.8	14.6	17.8	17.5	16.8	18.3	14.5	16.3	12.5	17.9		10.2
EE	6.3	8.0	9.8	7.7	8.0	9.1	10.9	8.8	7.8						
EA								15.8	11.1	11.4	9.8	10.3	8.3	8.7	
Oth.		0.9		1.0											
Total	39.4	50.6	65.2	54.5	65.6	54.9	67.9	59.4	66.0	48.2	56.5	46.2	54.5	39.1	52.9

Note: PNV = Partido Nacionalista Vasco; HB = Herri Batasuna; the figure for 1977 is the sum of the two parties which later would join, together with other parties and groups, in the HB coalition; the result for BP 98 and BP 01 is that obtained by Euskal Herritarrok, which was a new electoral platform of HB, opened also for other groups, initiatives and individuals close to radical nationalism; EH boycotted the elections to the Spanish parliament in 2000; in 2000 and 2001, PNV and EA went in coalition; EE = Euskadiko Ezkerra; EA = Eusko Alkartasuna.

Sources: Llera (1994: 158–9); *El Diario Vasco*, 24 October 1995, 26 October 1998 and 14 May 2001.

radical nationalist blocs, the figures above clearly show evidence of this historically new situation of nationalist power.

Another consequence of this general political climate, and the second reason for the nationalist success was the remarkable particularity of the Basque party system, in which conservative and rightist options were strongly under-represented, at least in the two most nationalist coastal provinces of Bizkaia and Gipuzkoa. In these regions, Spanish parties with links to a Francoist past like the former minister Fraga Iribarne's Alianza Popular party, but also the centre-right reformist party Unión de Centro Democrático of President Adolfo Suárez, the architect of the transition, suffered for their bad reputation as the enemies of the Basque people and the heirs of Spanish fascism. The pressure of ETA violence made it even more difficult for the members and sympathizers of the right to express their political credo in public. This is why many of those social layers which in any other normal West European democracy would probably have voted for conservatives, decided to hide within nationalism and to lend their votes to the PNV, a party that never before had been able to penetrate so deeply into the sectors of Basque big business.

Thirdly, this appeal was linked to the fact that the PNV was the key political party in the new Autonomous Community since the establishment of regional autonomy in accordance with the 1979 Statute. It controlled the administration in each of the three provinces of Alava, Gipuzkoa and Bizkaia. This was of crucial importance, since this control of the three 'Diputaciones' enabled the party to control and manage the whole system of autonomous tax, which is a historical specificity of the Basque provinces not shared by the other Spanish regions. After the abolition of the *Fueros* in 1876, the new conservative government offered a so-called Concierto Económico to the Basque provinces as a means of placating opposition to the abolition of the *Fueros* as well as to integrate the emerging Basque bourgeoisie into the restoration monarchy. This offer consisted of a deal between the Spanish government and the administration of the provinces about the total amount of taxes to be paid by the Diputaciones for a period of five years in exchange for the services rendered by the state in the Basque territories. The system of taxation and the management of the possible surplus, however, would be the exclusive domain of the Basques. As a punishment for the Basque defence of the Republic, after his victory in the Civil War, Franco abolished the *Concierto* in Bizkaia and Gipuzkoa, but not in Alava, where his putsch had succeeded from the very beginning. During the transition, this particular Basque system of tax autonomy was re-established. Now in the hands of the PNV politicians, it became a powerful tool of self-government and the key instrument for raising and distributing financial resources. Any attempt to influence this process had necessarily to pass through the offices of the PNV bureaucrats in the three Diputaciones and the Basque government, where, ever since the establishment of autonomy, the party controlled not only the presidency,[1] but also the Consejería de Hacienda, that is, the Basque Ministry of Finance, which is responsible for the coordination of tax policy put into practice by the three provincial administrations. The political hegemony of moderate nationalism was also reflected by the composition of the Basque Finance Council, which is the supreme body in which the regional government and the three Diputaciones negotiate the annual contribution for each of the three provinces to the government's budget. Until the 1999 local and provincial elections, where the PNV lost its majority in the Diputación of Alava, which would be governed for the first time by the conservative PP, the complete area of taxing and budgeting was exclusively in the hands of the PNV. Conflicting interests which emerged in the Council of Finances among the three provinces, or between one of them and the regional government, would frequently be resolved by a final decision taken by the party's presidency in Bilbao. Even after the party split and Eusko Alkartasuna was founded in 1986, the PNV's loss of hegemony and the onset of a new era of coalitions with the socialists, the party would not give up its control of key positions in the Basque world of finances.

The Basque society of the post-Franco era is a more nationalist society not only in terms of party politics. The increase of power in the parliaments was followed by the growing influence of the two nationalist trade unions: the historically moderately nationalist Eusko Langileen Alkartasuna (ELA), founded in 1911, and Langile Abertzaleen Batzordeak (LAB), a radical nationalist union created during the transition as a part of the so-called

Table 6.2   Delegates of the trade unions elected in Basque companies (percentages, 1998)

	ELA	UGT	CCOO	LAB	Others
Alava	30.77	24.15	16.77	10.94	17.37
Gipuzkoa	44.18	9.80	15.11	24.41	6.51
Bizkaia	40.59	17.42	19.39	10.76	11.83
Euskadi	40.18	15.91	17.46	15.52	10.92
Navarre	21.03	31.35	21.86	11.71	14.05
South Euskal Herria	35.76	19.48	18.48	14.64	11.65

Note: Euskadi refers to the three provinces integrated in the Autonomous Community of the Basque Country, South Euskal Herria to the total of the four provinces on the southern part of the Spanish–French border.

Source: Data provided by the union ELA (Hauteskunde Sindikalak, 31 December 1998).

Basque National Liberation Movement headed by ETA. At the end of the 1990s, ELA was by far the strongest of all unions and the two nationalist unions together outnumbered – at least in the three provinces of autonomous Euskadi, but not in Navarre – the other two state-wide organized unions, the socialist Unión General de Trabajadores (UGT) and the leftist, former communist Comisiones Obreras (CCOO).

If the labour movement was apparently becoming more nationalist, so was Basque culture. Autonomy and its implementation provided considerable resources and instruments for the process of Basque nation-building, which has no comparable example in the history of the Basque Country.[2] One of the areas in which the most dramatic changes were made was that of education. According to the Statute of Gernika, nearly the whole of the education sector was transferred from Spanish to Basque administration, which immediately started to work on one of the central issues not only in the nationalists' programme, but – to a minor extent – also that of the other political forces: namely, the promotion of education in Euskara, the Basque language. With very few exceptions, until the 1960s the whole school system was completely organized in Spanish. Since the end of that decade, some private initiatives have been carried out by Basque parents, generally under the protecting umbrella of the Catholic Church, which created the foundation of the first primary schools in the Basque language, later known as ikastolak. The Basque administration combined the promotion of these schools, which had grown remarkably in number during the years of the transition, with incentives for those public schools willing to introduce or to extend the use of the native language in education. Nowadays, there are three language models in the Basque school system, divided according to

Table 6.3 School education and language models in the Basque Autonomous Community (percentage of pupils in each model). Infant and primary education (2–5 years)

	1990/91	1999/2000
Model A	29	13
Model B	36	32
Model D	34	55

Sources: Etxeberria (1999: 133); *El País*, 22 October 1999.

Table 6.4 School education and language models in the Basque Autonomous Community in 1999/2000 (percentage of pupils in each model according to age levels)

	3–6 years	6–12 years	12–16 years	16–19 years
Model A	13	24	39	76
Model B	32	29	23	–
Model D	55	47	38	24

Source: *El País*, 22 October 1999.

the criterion of a higher or lower level of teaching in *Euskara*. Model A refers to schools teaching completely in Spanish with *Euskara* as just another subject among the others; model B is a mixed system used in schools which teach more or less half the subjects in Spanish, and the other half in Basque; finally, the model D describes those schools, in which education is given entirely in Basque with Spanish as a subject. The following figures for the percentage of students in infant and primary education schools (2–5 years) reflect quite clearly the trend of the last few years, indicating that the parents are asking for monolingual education in Spanish less and less, because they are aware that the only real possibility for their children to learn Basque is offered by models B and D. This demand is especially high during the first few years, since Spanish is still the predominant language in secondary education and the baccalaureate. This trend is, of course, also a consequence of the fact that the knowledge of the Basque language provides Basque speakers with an advantage in the labour market, at least as far as public civil service employment is concerned – but a knowledge of *Euskara* is more and more being considered advantageous in an applicant's CV also in other sectors of the labour market. For the first time in history, the Basque language has not only an emotional and ideological value, but also a material one.[3]

This growing demand for education in the Basque language has produced a strong impact on the public university as well. The Universidad del País

Vasco–Euskal Herriko Unibertsitatea (UPV–EHU) is a fairly new institution created in the years of the transition with the aim of counteracting the notorious historical lack of university education in the Basque region. Until the end of Francoism, Basque students had to go outside to other Spanish universities or pay the high university fees at the Jesuit-run private University of Deusto in Bilbao. The UPV–EHU, where in 2000 about 60,000 students were taught in the different faculties distributed throughout the three campuses, has made an important effort to satisfy the increasing demand for education in Basque, both for the linguistic formation of the academic staff and for the reinforcement of bilingualism in the curricula. Between 1991 and 1998, the number of teachers able to lecture in both languages more than doubled. At the end of the 1990s, in some faculties the students can carry out nearly all their studies in either of the two languages (teacher training; humanities), whereas in others (natural sciences) the bulk of subjects are still offered only in Spanish. The number of new students who choose studies in Basque is increasing by about 2 per cent each year. In 1997, 31 per cent of all the new students were studying the first year of their degrees in *Euskara*. According to the calculations of the university administration, in 2003 this figure will have increased to 40 per cent. According to the same census, about 20 per cent of all students at the UPV–EHU were studying through the medium of Basque.[4]

Thanks to these efforts in education, by the end of the 1990s and for the first time in the history of the Basque language, the historical decrease in the number of those Basques able to understand and speak *Euskara* has been stopped and even turned around. The statistics from 1991 reveal 23 per cent of *Euskaldunak* in the Autonomous Community of the Basque Country, 9.55 per cent in Navarre and 34 per cent in the French part of the Basque Country. In 1998, the fruits of the autonomous education policy have become visible in *Euskadi*, whereas in Navarre and in the Basque territory across the French border the trend remains more or less the same as before. In 1998, the percentage of the Basque-speaking population in the Autonomous Community of the Basque Country has increased to 26. The younger the person, the higher the percentage of *Euskaldunak*. In the three provinces of the Autonomous Community, among young Basques aged between 6 and 20 years, two-thirds are Basque-speaking.[5] This growth in the trend of the Basque-speaking population and the policy of subsidies carried out by the Basque government have produced remarkable effects in book sales. Whereas between 1900 and 1939 less than one thousand publications in *Euskara* have been counted, between 1976 and 1992 there were about 10,500 new books written in Basque.[6] This cultural offer is completed by a daily newspaper written completely in the native language (*Egunkaria*) and by a public TV channel and broadcasting station, both of which work 24 hours a day in Basque.

All these facts indicate that the situation of the Basque language, the most outstanding ingredient of the local traditional culture, has improved thanks to the limited self-government granted by the 1979 Statute of Gernika. The reality has changed considerably. At the beginning of the nineteenth century, Wilhelm von Humboldt had warned of the ruin of Basque nationality and language. One hundred years later, even Sabino Arana, the founder of the nationalist movement, was rather pessimistic when thinking about the future of the language: in his opinion, the language would disappear before the end of the century, unless the necessary funding for its promotion could be raised and its social status could be changed: *Euskara* had to become useful for any Basque, and not just for the peasants.[7] At the end of the twentieth century, money was found and more and more young people learn Basque because it helps in finding a job. We could add other information like the creation of their own Basque police force (Ertzantza) with duties encompassing everything from traffic regulation to the persecution of drug-dealers or terrorists. The nationalist influence in the high management of the most important first-division football clubs like Real Sociedad de San Sebastián or Athletic Club de Bilbao; the nationalist sensitivity of some important sectors of the Catholic church; or, last but not least, the booming new Basque folk and rock music industry. All these facts lead to the same conclusion: the autonomy recovered by the Basques in 1979 has laid an invaluable groundwork for an effective impulse in the process of Basque nation-building. Even nationalist politicians recognized from a very critical manifesto published on the occasion of the twentieth anniversary of the Statute of Gernika, that the Statute had borne 'fruit in terms of the recovery and development of the capacity for self-government'.[8] Furthermore, this devolution of limited home-rule has been guided by moderate nationalism, which – as I have argued – never before in its history had been as powerful and influential as it became after the granting of autonomy in 1979. This power and influence is even visible at a more anecdotal, but not meaningless level, for example when a confessed PNV member became the coach of the Spanish national soccer team, or a PNV supporter became a member of the board of directors of the second largest Spanish bank.

Yet there is always another way to tell the same story. Democracy and autonomy have certainly opened a new page in the history of the Basque Country, leaving behind the sad experiences of dictatorship and civil war. But there were some dark spots that made the new situation less comfortable and positive than many Basques had expected it to be when Franco died. First of all, it should be remembered that democracy was born based on a broad consensus in the Basque region, which, however, had been smaller than in the rest of the state. This became evident in the referendum on the Constitution and even during the debate on the Statute of Autonomy, defended by moderate nationalists and a part of the nationalist left, but rejected by the majority wing of leftist nationalist radicalism close to ETA-militar. HB's electoral results since the coalition's foundation in 1978 (see Table 6.1) show that during the following 20 years the segment of the society which could be described as 'anti-system' could not be reduced noticeably. The granting of a limited self-government and the important steps in the process of nation-building did not work as incentives for those who remained outside the consensus and might reconsider their position. In its 20 years of history, there was no major split within HB and those few leaders who dared to disagree with the mainstream orthodoxy were forced to disappear from the political stage. What was the reason for this situation? Why did autonomy and limited self-government fail to produce a broader consensus among the Basque people?

Any attempt to answer these questions should distinguish between discursive and contextual arguments, that is, between explanations attached to the discourse and ideology of radical nationalism on the one hand, and other facts linked to the context in which that discourse is developed. In the previous chapter, the two main arguments that HB-leaders used to repeat in their public performances against the new status quo have already been mentioned briefly. The most convincing one stressed the lack of legitimacy of the post-Francoist state in the Basque region, whose voters had expressed their disagreement with the Constitution in the referendum. This vote was interpreted as a gesture of the Basque people, who were said to have rejected any political order born out of the ruins of the dictatorship while claiming for a total political and social rupture, which would open the door to the construction of a real democracy in Spain and for self-determination in the Basque Country. Furthermore, and this was a hint to the PNV and the other autonomist parties, if the basis of Spanish democracy had been rejected in *Euskadi*, what then could be the legitimacy of an autonomous regime, which itself was nothing but a part of the new constitutional order?

The second argument against the new system consisted in what later would be known as the problem of territoriality. By collaboration in the establishment of an autonomy which would include only three of the seven historical territories of *Euskal Herria*, abandoning both Navarre and the three territories on French ground (Lapurdi, Zuberoa, Behe Nafarroa, which in Basque are commonly referred to as *Iparralde*, 'the area of the North'), the moderate nationalists were charged with betraying the real interests of the Basque nation. They were accused of abandoning their brothers and sisters in Navarre and on the other side of the border, which only encouraged the perpetuation of the Basque people's separation. Thus, with Navarre and *Iparralde* left out, there was no question of talking about any kind of Basque nation-building by the politics of an autonomous government, whose function was considered similar to that of a fifth column of the Spanish state.

It is obvious that the development of two different Autonomous Communities in the three provinces of *Euskadi* and in Navarre, which is both a province and a single-province Autonomous Community, has created specific political dynamics in both communities, both of which has its own parliament, government, police and political culture. At the beginning of the twenty-first century, the unification or even cooperation of both territories is probably further away than it was in the Second Republic or at the end of the dictatorship. However, even Basque nationalists admit that a primordialist definition of the Basque nation, which would include Navarre for historical and cultural reasons, hardly matches a more subjectivist viewpoint based on Navarrese social and political reality, in which the Basque identity is only expressed by a part of the population, since the political options which back the unification of all Basque territories, including Navarre, have been in a minority in all the democratic elections since the Second Republic.[9] Furthermore, since its shape during the first campaign for Basque autonomy from 1917 to 1919, a conservative Navarrese regionalism has become one of the most influential ideologies in the province. Its basic features are a conservative, populist Navarre-centred regionalism and a virulent anti-Basque Spanish nationalism. The historical origins of this ideology were linked to the tradition of Carlism, and its first outstanding proto-fascist leader Víctor Pradera. Years later, it was in a convent of Navarre where General Mola prepared with the leaders of Navarrese Carlism for the putsch that led to the Civil War. Navarre was one of the first regions to fall under the control of the insurrectionists, and it was from this province that the Carlist paramilitaries (Requetés) started the military conquest of the Basque neighbouring province of Gipuzkoa. Under the new democratic circumstances after Franco's death, this tradition of conservative anti-Basque 'navarrismo político' was adapted to the new context. Its political expression nowadays is the party Unión del Pueblo Navarro (UPN), which in the rest of Spain is allied to the PP. Since the Spanish conservatives decided not to compete with UPN in Navarre, the Navarrese regionalists manage to cover the whole spectrum of political conservativism in the province. Their panic about becoming a victim of Basque 'imperialism' has pushed them frequently towards an attitude of rough rejection of any political or cultural proposal intended to sacrifice the freedom of the Navarrese to Basque expansionism. If this policy was (and is) popular

Table 6.5 Nationalist votes in Navarre (elections to Spanish Parliament; results as percentages of votes)

	1977	1979	1982	1986	1989	1993	1996	2000
HB		8.89	11.73	14.05	12.02	10.52	8.16	
EE			2.84	2.83	2.86			
PNV			5.53	1.82	0.92	1.15	0.97	2.14
EA					4.80	3.73	3.77	4.77
Others	14.61	8.45						
Total	14.61	17.34	20.10	18.07	20.06	15.04	12.90	6.91

Note: In the elections of 2000, HB campaigned for abstention.

Source: Izu Belloso, p. 243.

Table 6.6 School education
and language models in Navarre
(1997/98) (percentages)

Language models[10]	% of pupils
Model A	20
Model D	22
Model G	57.5

Source: Etxeberria (1999: 154).

among important layers of Navarrese society, this is not only due to the long tradition of conservative regionalism, but also to the activity of violent Basque nationalists within the province, who provided the best arguments for UPN leaders and the right-wing press in their campaign for the protection of Navarrese interests against the influence of Basque nationalism.

Yet Basque culture still has an important presence in Navarre. The demand for bilingual education has been growing slowly over the last few years and has reached an important level despite the reluctance of the administration.

Huge areas of the hilly pre-Pyrenean northern part of the province conserve the Basque language and customs. Because of the weakness of modernization, in these predominantly rural areas Basque cultural identity has not been transformed as radically into a political movement as in Bizkaia or Gipuzkoa. Here, speaking Basque is frequently compatible with voting UPN. There is no clash of more or less exclusive identities. In contrast with this complex background, it becomes quite obvious that the so-called problem of territoriality is not rooted in the development of Basque autonomy and the 'betrayal' of moderate nationalism, but in the very heart of the history and the political culture of Navarre. Unless a majority of Navarrese citizens is convinced of the advantages of a hypothetical union with the other three Basque provinces on Spanish territory, there is no possibility of finding a democratic solution to the problem of territoriality.

The situation of *Iparralde*, the Basque region in the French state, is quite similar to that of Navarre. From the time of the French Revolution, the Basque territories lost their self-governing institutions and were henceforth exposed to a radical policy of assimilation into the French nation-state, which, especially under the Third Republic, aimed at turning all the Basque 'peasants into Frenchmen'.[11] The rural character of large parts of the region is only altered by the impact of tourism on the coast. Immigration, instead of industrial workers, brought well-off pensioners from Paris and other French places to Biarritz, Saint Jean de Luz or Hendaye. The Basque culture and language, where it was preserved as in the interior, still cannot count on any institutional support. In contrast with *Euskadi*, where both Spanish and Basque are official languages, and Navarre, where this official status of *Euskara* is at least recognized in the Basque-speaking northern part of the provinces, in *Iparralde*, with 26 per cent of Basque speakers in 1996,[12] the only official language is French. If this situation does not change, the low rates of education in Basque (see Table 6.7) augur the continuity of the trend, that is, the increasing decay of the language in the near future. A minority culture without political and institutional support is not able to survive. French Basques don't have autonomy like that in *Euskadi* or in Navarre, since their region is included, together with neighbouring Bearn, in the Département des Pyrenées Atlantiques with its capital in Pau. Historically, Basque nationalism has been too weak to press for autonomy. Even if in the mid-nineteenth century the Basques were still said 'to have not one sympathy in common with the rest of France', the only expression of the French Basques' 'proto-nationalist ethnic pride' was a 'conservative clericalism' as opposed to the policy of secularization carried out by the governments of the Third Republic. It was not until the 1960s that this traditional attitude and mentality of conservative clericalism and regionalism were challenged by the timid emergence of secular ethnic nationalism.[13] However, nowadays, as in the northern part of Navarre, French Basques – even in the *Euskara*-speaking areas – vote much more for French conservative parties than for Basque nationalists.

At the beginning of the twenty-first century, the only institutional links between *Iparralde* and the southern Basque territories are cultural ones, since intellectuals on both sides of the border cooperate in the Society of Basque Studies (Sociedad de Estudios Vascos – Eusko Ikaskuntza) or in the Basque Academy of Language (Euskaltzaindia), even if the process of European unification and especially the creation of cross-border Euro-regions like that of Aquitaine has permitted more administrative and political contacts and cooperation between politicians of the three Basque areas. This fragmentation of the Basque homeland does not fit into the ideology of any nationalist, and still less into that of a radical nationalist, whose political aim has to be the unification of the nation. Since in the opinion of ETA and HB Basque

Table 6.7 School education and language models in the French Basque Country in 1997/98 (percentage of pupils in each model according to age levels)

	3–6 years	*6–12 years*	*12–16 years*
Model A	7	6.5	11
Model B	10	5	3
Model D	5	3	2
Model X	78	85.5	84

Source: Etxeberria, 1999: 137, 141, 149.

autonomy, even if it brought a higher level of self-government to about two-thirds of the less than 2.5 million Basques living in *Euskal Herria*,[14] did not contribute to the achievement of this aim, it had to be rejected and unmasked as an instrument of Spanish imperialism. The question, however, of how to operationalize Basque unification in terms of realistic and democratic politics in Navarre and *Iparralde*, where the social and political culture was not exactly favourable to this aim, remained on a secondary plane.

While the lack of legitimacy of the constitutional system and the problem of territoriality were the main arguments presented by radical Basque nationalism against the new Spanish democracy and the Basque autonomy, there were other external, contextual reasons that might explain the anti-system attitude adopted by the National Liberation Movement during the transition and the years of post-Francoism parliamentary democracy. First of all, of course, there is the legacy of the dictatorship itself. After the military conquest of the Basque provinces, the abolition of the 1936 autonomy and nearly 40 years of violent repression against any feature of ethnic particularism, the idea of building a new democracy with the help and consent of the reformist elites linked to the authoritarian regime was difficult to sell in Spain, and obviously much more so in the Basque region. If the suggestions are correct that, firstly, in the decades following the Civil War the amount and intensity of both actual and subjectively perceived grievances were higher in the Basque Country than anywhere else in Spain, and that, secondly, the rapid modernization since the 1960s was another important factor accelerating even more the shape of political and social unrest in the region, the rise of extremist political projects like ETA terrorism and its broad active or passive support by large parts of the society becomes understandable.[15] The continuity of torture and police violence against demonstrators during the transition and even the first years of democracy seemed to be solid proof of the arguments of those who stated that nothing had changed since the death of the dictator. The same function fulfilled the cases of anti-ETA terrorism committed by extreme right-wing groups or killer commandos organized and paid by the state. From 1978 to 1991 this counter-violence caused a total of 90 casualties. To take only the period 1983–87, the so-called 'Grupos Antiterroristas de Liberación' (GAL), killed, mostly in the French-Basque territories, 25 Basques with the objective of forcing the French government to reconsider its lax attitude towards ETA refugees and cooperate more directly with the Spanish police forces.[16] During the last few years, Spanish judges have found sufficient pieces of evidence to charge the socialist Minister of the Interior of that period and a number of his direct subordinates with organizing and promoting the GAL. In July 1998, the Supreme Court condemned the socialist ex-minister Barrionuevo and his former State Secretary Vera to ten years' imprisonment because of their participation in the GAL activities. Only a few months after their imprisonment, and despite the protests of all Basque nationalists, both were granted a pardon by the conservative Spanish government.

The legacy of the past and the errors committed by the state agencies were no incentives for the integration of radical nationalism into the new democracy. Another obstacle was the very dynamic of the armed struggle itself. With the split that had led to the foundation and later disappearance of ETA p.-m., any discussion about the relationship or hierarchy between the armed and the political struggle had been aborted. Ever since ETA-militar had been the unquestioned vanguard of the National Liberation Movement, the logic of arms determined the strategy of the politicians. Political violence became consecrated and the celebration of the ETA activists, dead, imprisoned or alive, produced a mystical and emotional aureole around the movement, which penetrated even into the smallest rural area and destroyed familiar and friendship ties between those who joined the movement and those who did not.[17] In this context, political reasoning became extremely complicated, since every proposal for alternative ways towards independence could easily be condemned as a step towards surrender and a betrayal of the nation's real interests. The structure of the movement as a complex network of communitary organizations and initiatives, in which sociability and politics were two sides of the same microcosm, was another wall that sealed off the world of radical nationalism, preventing the penetration of heterodox critical ideas.

Moreover, ETA was no longer a more or less spontaneous underground group. Over the years it had become a well-organized, powerful and internationally related enterprise with its own Ruling Council, bureaucracy and employees. With Irving Louis Horowitz we can refer to a 'routinization of terrorism',[18] not only as far as the public perception of ETA's armed struggle as an everyday event is concerned, but also as to the institutionalization of the underground group itself. Within such long-established underground organizations the social control of its members is usually very strong, the pressure against hypothetical dissidents high, and the means of the struggle tend to become more important than the aims. In these circumstances a shift towards peaceful, democratic and more flexible politics was unlikely to occur.

On the other hand, there were very few incentives to encourage that shift. The proper dynamic of violence and the renouncement or inability of the government and the political parties to think of the conflict in terms other than of security shaped a highly polarized society, in which a very tiny space was left for agreement brokers. Mediation and consensual approaches could not emerge, because they were rejected as betrayal by some, and as backing down in the fight against terrorism by others. ETA, instead of offering gestures of de-escalation, did exactly the opposite by carrying out a more and more indiscriminate strategy of violence against increasingly large numbers of targets. On the other hand, few attempts were made to challenge this strategy by innovative and non-exclusively security-led responses. In 1988, the 'Agreement of Ajuria Enea', to which I shall refer again below, united all Basque parties – nationalists and non-nationalists alike – except HB in the 'democratic bloc' opposed to terrorism and its political supporters. Ever since, efforts to build bridges between 'democrats' and '(philo-)terrorists' have been extremely rare.

The political blindness of paramilitary activism on the one hand, and the limits of security-led approaches on the other, has produced a virtual stalemate in the conflict. In more than 20 years, no progress has been made towards a broadening of the political consensus that sustained democracy. Moreover, factors like the deep socio-economic crisis caused by the industrial recession since the mid-1970s or the accumulation of scandals of corruption and state terrorism in the 1990s during the last period of socialist government until the conservative victory in the 1996 elections, weakened the state, created a climate of unrest and contention, and, provided more arguments for all those like the radical nationalists of the Basque Movement for National Liberation, who contested the very groundwork of the system. During the 1990s, however, slowly but surely, things started to change. New opportunities for a peaceful settlement of the conflict were shaped. After decades of horror and pain, the Basque people became bewitched by the idea that for the first time since the rise of violent nationalism a peace process might be kick-started.

7
'The times, they are a-changin''

One of the most remarkable features of any peace process seems to be the mystery concerning its origins. Why and how, after so many years of violent confrontation, do the actors decide to look for a settlement? What are the factors that break the stalemate and trigger a movement that, if it overcomes the initial obstacles and reaches a certain sustainability, will commonly be referred to as a peace process? What are the reasons that make both contenders, or at least one of them, believe that military defeat of the other is impossible, improbable or politically counterproductive? The mystery that accompanies the initial phases of a peace process is usually also fed by the statements of many involved participants who, frequently for ideological or strategic reasons, argue that there has never been anything similar to a peace process or that this process has definitely ended.

However, during the 1990s some violent ethnic conflicts entered a period of slow transformation leading to a ceasefire and a lessening in the frequency and intensity of violence which most tangibly indicates that indeed, as Bob Dylan would sing, 'The times, they are a-changin'. Probably the most outstanding examples of peace processes, which were started with the aim of smoothing the way towards a peaceful transformation of violent ethnic conflict during the 1990s are the cases of South Africa, the Dayton Agreement for Bosnia, the Oslo Accords following the negotiations between Israel and Palestine, and, finally, the Good Friday Agreement in Northern Ireland. At the beginning of the twenty-first century, some of these attempts to settle violent conflict seem to be successful; others – especially the Israeli–Palestinian example – have already been wiped from our memory by a new period of increasing violence and warfare.

The Basque Country was one of those places where, during the 1990s the situation seemed ripe for a conflict-transformation. When in September 1999 the underground organization ETA called the first unilateral and unlimited ceasefire in its 40-year-old history, a wave of optimistic expectation and even timid euphoria gripped Basque society. Were the actors now involved finally willing to 'start swimmin'' and to adapt themselves to the new circumstances? Never before had Basque politicians, journalists or intellectuals used the phrase 'peace process' so frequently to describe the impression that, finally after so many years of absurd bloodshed, things were coming to an end. In fact, the information available during the months preceding and following the announcement of the ceasefire, seemed to corroborate the analysis that in the Basque Country an embryonic peace process at least had been initiated. According to Darby's and Mac Ginty's definition, we can talk about a peace process if (1) there is a real will to negotiate, (2) the key actors are included in the process, (3) the negotiations address the central issues in dispute, (4) the negotiators do not use force to achieve their objectives, and (5) the negotiators are committed to a sustained process.[1] In the Basque case, the (in other circumstances unthinkable) secret meeting held in Zurich between the leadership of ETA and official representatives of the Spanish conservative government – the 'key actors' – after the mediation of a Basque bishop, could be interpreted as a sign that both contenders were willing to talk with one another. Yet, it was also true that despite the willingness to talk with one another, it was not at all clear what these talks would be about. That meant that the answer to the third condition formulated by Darby and Mac Ginty was not at all evident. While ETA placed the dispute about the distribution of power and the level of self-determination at the top of the agenda as a key issue, the government was only willing to debate the security and prison policy. Concerning the fourth condition mentioned by the two authors, the response in the Basque case was once again neither precise nor categorical. Due to the ceasefire, which lasted for more than one year there was not one single killing by ETA violence. Yet, violence did not disappear, since street violence, arson attacks and threats against non-nationalist politicians did not stop. Moreover, the unwillingness of Herri Batasuna, the political party close to ETA, to condemn these acts cast doubts on the sincerity of the party's commitment to fight for self-determination by exclusively peaceful and democratic means, as had been agreed in the so-called Lizarra Declaration together with the other mostly nationalist democratic parties and organizations of the Basque Country a few days before the announcement of the ceasefire. Finally, both the statements and attitude of the government during the truce, and ETA's eccentric arguments when calling off the ceasefire, were far from proof of the 'key actors'' commitment to a sustained process.

Anyway, despite these doubts concerning the definition of what was happening in the Basque Country in terms of a peace process, at the end of the 1990s many people began to ask why and how ETA had decided to declare its first unilateral and unlimited ceasefire. Since nothing similar had happened before in the history of the Basque paramilitaries, there was apparently enough evidence to suppose that some of the major coordinates of Basque politics had entered a period of alteration. Would this alteration bring peace to the Basque people? After more than a year without killings, the breakdown of the ceasefire and the return, and even increase, of ETA terrorism aborted the hope for a settlement of the conflict in the short run. Frustration, pain, tears and the deepest crisis of the Basque political system since the restoration of democracy made people forget very quickly the hopeful optimism of the months before. Yet, my argument is that despite this fatal outcome of the first real attempt to get a peace process going, the changes which took place in Basque society and politics during the 1990s were not invalidated later. If they made possible the shape of new circumstances within which for the first time a unilateral and indefinite ceasefire could emerge, such circumstances are likely to open up new opportunities in a foreseeable future. The following chapters deal with this new context shaped during the 1990s. Only after this analysis shall we be able to ask why this first embryonic, stillborn Basque peace process collapsed.

7.1 Negotiate with terrorists?

One of the most complex and controversial problems to resolve in every peace process is the question of political convenience and ethical legitimacy of talking and negotiating with those who commonly do not use words but arms to defend their ideas. The arguments are well-known and are repeated everywhere an initiative towards a peaceful settlement of conflict has come up. If a democratic state and its politicians accept negotiations with terrorists, don't they implicitly legitimate the use of violence for political aims? Don't they motivate others to follow the example of the paramilitaries and take up arms? Can democratic negotiations be carried out in a situation of extreme pressure and with the threat that the paramilitaries might break their ceasefire and return to violence, if their demands are not satisfied? Do negotiations with terrorists not mean something like a second killing of their victims committed now by the democrats, who have decided to honour the terrorists, accepting them as equal partners at the negotiating table? And, finally, if negotiating with paramilitaries is acceptable, should constitutional issues be addressed or only those related to problems of security? When at the end of the 1990s the possibility of negotiation arose in the Basque Country, the spectrum of responses was defined by two extreme formulas at either end of the political landscape. Both were inspired by the Palestinian slogan of 'Peace for land'. While the Spanish government defended the option of 'Peace for peace', or 'Peace for prisoners', excluding any political concession to terrorism, ETA and its political wing demanded 'Peace for democracy' or 'Peace for self-determination', considering that constitutional changes were the necessary precondition for the establishment of peace. Majority moderate nationalists moved somewhere in between these opposite poles. However, as we shall see further below, this ambiguous and vague position of the governing Basque nationalists turned out to be closer to the opinion of radical nationalism than to that defended by the Spanish government.

However, the Basque dispute about how to negotiate with terrorists and which issues to address in any negotiation, was no invention of the 1990s. It appears in practically all the contacts between government and paramilitaries since the foundation of ETA. In contradiction to the common official argument that there is nothing to talk about with terrorists except their own dissolution, in reality plenty of such contacts were held in the past. Only in the period of nearly 13 years between the death of the dictator and mid-1988, Robert P. Clark has counted 'between twenty and thirty serious attempts to negotiate an end to insurgent violence in the Basque provinces of Spain'.[2] Clark's list does not include negotiations about the release of hostages or the payment of the 'revolutionary tax'. Among all these attempts, however, only two deserve special attention because the first brought to an end one of the two important paramilitary groups: ETA político-militar, and the second was – until 1999 – the only attempt to establish a direct and lasting dialogue between the ETA leadership and senior politicians as representatives of the Spanish (socialist) government.

The story about the negotiation that led to the auto-dissolution of ETA p-m did not really start in 1981. It actually began in the months following Franco's death. At that time, ETA was divided into two opposing factions. The split of 1974 had been a consequence of the confrontation between those activists convinced of the strategic necessity to push the revolutionary mass mobilization into close coordination with the armed vanguard and those, who placed a higher value on the armed struggle, which had to be carried out by a separate underground organization, organically independent from the legal organizations of mass politics. This concept was put into practice by ETA-militar, whereas the first led to the creation of ETA p-m. Yet, it was only a question of months before the unavoidable contradiction between the military logic and the necessities of mass politics in a democratic system provoked a new conflict within ETA p-m. Eduardo Moreno Bergareche, better known as Pertur, one of the most brilliant intellectual leaders of the organization, dared to go even a step further, theorizing about an anachronism, which in his opinion would mean the armed struggle in the foreseeable new context of a parliamentarian democracy. This theoretical renouncement of political violence proposed by this 'liquidator' brought upon him the anger of the leaders of the organization's armed wing. In an attempt to find an agreement, in July 1976 Pertur met ETA-m's head Miguel Angel Apalategi, Apala, in St-Jean-de-Luz. After that meeting, Pertur was never seen again. Even today, there are doubts concerning his disappearance, even if the most credible version is that of a kidnapping and killing committed by his political enemies within ETA p-m.

In the months and years after Pertur's disappearance, his predictions about the probable democratization of the political system became a reality and the contradictions both within ETA p-m and between the society and the advocates of armed struggle became more acute. Just one year after the

Basques of Bizkaia, Gipuzkoa and Alava had expressed in a referendum by a large majority their support for the Statute of Autonomy, the ETA paramilitaries carried out one of the most intensive offensives in the history of ETA. Between September and November of that year alone 36 people died at the hands of ETA, including for the first time politicians of the governing UCD party. In response to that spectacular increase of violence, in November Basque parties organized in the streets of San Sebastián one of the first massive demonstrations against ETA. In this context, the leaders of EIA, the political wing of ETA p-m, became aware of the necessity to adapt their strategy, rooted in the resistance against dictatorship, to the new situation of parliamentarian democracy. In their analysis of the new situation, violence, instead of being the catalyst for revolutionary mass mobilization towards socialism and self-determination, had become an obstacle to the achievement of this aim. EIA was the heart of the coalition Euskadiko Ezkerra (EE), which during the Transition had played an important role in bringing sectors of the radical-left nationalists back into constitutional politics, backing – from a leftist and critical point of view – the autonomist road to Basque self-government. In the first general elections of 1977, the coalition won two seats in parliament (one deputy and one senator), but losing its senator two years later. Both electoral success and the fascination for the new possibilities of making nationalist politics offered by the Statute of Autonomy were the factors that revalued the function of the party, placing it in a position of certain predominance over the underground organization ETA p-m. From this position of strength, the party leaders embarked upon the debate over the new strategy with the paramilitaries, presenting the idea of a ceasefire as the centrepiece of this new strategy yet to be defined. Statements pronounced by leading EIA members confirm this dominant part played by the politicians who had managed to control the paramilitaries, instead of this relationship being the other way round, as it was in the case of the parties related to ETA-m.:

> I think there has been a total copycat relationship from the armed organization to the party. There has never existed a joint leadership. ETA p-m was the armed wing of the party.[3]

In December 1980, the activists of the underground organization met to discuss the proposal of a truce, which was supported by 44 votes, with only one vote against it and four abstentions. The truce was supposed to be a tactical time out, which would permit the organization's redeployment and preparation for a comeback in the future, when the armed struggle might become necessary once again.[4]

In reality, however, the truce was the first step towards the self-dissolution of ETA p-m. It opened the way for the party leaders, who had been waiting for the green light for their attempt to broker an agreement with the government, which would permit the reintegration of ETA activists into society.

After the resignation of President Suárez and his government in January 1981 and the failed military coup a month later, the EE deputy and leader Juan Mari Bandrés established secret contacts with the new Minister of Interior, Juan José Rosón. Rosón was known as a centralist hard-liner and Bandrés initially had to be convinced by his colleague, the EIA leader, and in March 1982 the General Secretary of EE[5] Mario Onaindia, that even with Rosón negotiation was possible, since Bandrés considered even an informal dinner with Rosón a 'waste of time'.[6] Finally, the contacts started in April 1981, after the formal declaration of the ceasefire issued by ETA p-m on 28 February.

The negotiations between Bandrés and Rosón, accompanied by several more sporadic contacts between ETA p-m leaders and representatives of the Spanish government, were carried out in a climate of growing personal confidence. The EE deputy became aware quite soon that the 'hawk' Rosón was the most appropriate person to deal with, since he was a guarantee for the implementation of any agreement. As Clark puts it, 'Rosón turned out to be an extremely effective spokesman for a negotiated settlement because he was a strong man in an otherwise weak government.'[7] This mutual confidence of the negotiators was the decisive element that protected the talks against the influence of a political atmosphere characterized by increasing tension due not only to the already mentioned military coup, but also to several other factors. The first was the continuing violence not only of ETA-m, but also of the *poli-milis*. Since in their announcement of the ceasefire they had declared that they did not consider it possible to take any measures to make the operational capacity of the group incompatible with the truce, they engaged in several cases of kidnapping, one of them being the father of the Spanish pop star Julio Iglesias. A second element was the activity of the Spanish and French police who were not willing to make any tactical concessions to the negotiations taking place, even increasing the rate of detentions among ETA p-m activists and those close to ETA p-m, whose willingness to lay down their arms was well-known. A third point was the agreement of the Spanish political parties to pass a law on the harmonization of the autonomy process (LOAPA), which the Basque nationalists considered a manoeuvre aimed at a centralist reinterpretation and restriction of the autonomy gained in 1979. The concern about the consequences of the LOAPA was so strong that PNV leader Xabier Arzallus found it necessary to have a secret meeting with the *poli-milis*, in which – according to a later accusation published by Bandrés – he was said to have questioned the convenience of the ceasefire at the very moment a major anti-nationalist offensive had been launched by the Spanish parties.[8] Finally, another element with negative consequences for the political climate was the extremely slow implementation of the partial agreements on individual pardons reached by the negotiators. This cast doubt on the efficacy of the negotiation in the ranks of the paramilitaries, among whom the critical voices of the truce and its political management became louder and louder.

This internal criticism within ETA p-m was transformed into open rebellion when it became evident that Bandrés did not bother too much about the political demands linked to the ceasefire, negotiating instead a settlement guided by the formula of 'peace for amnesty'. Bandrés and Onaindia were realistic enough to realize the impossibility of negotiating any more ambitious political claim with the government only a few months after the achievement of autonomy despite strong pressure from the reactionary and military sectors of Spanish society. The failed military coup was the proof that this pressure was no bluff. At the same time, their political instinct and their knowledge of the internal workings of the underground organization made them feel that the moment was ripe for a reconsideration of the armed struggle by many of the *poli-milis*, who were attracted by the possibilities of autonomy and willing to normalize their personal, familiar and professional situation in the new democratic system. Consequently, the negotiations consisted in the drafting of a list of prisoners and exiles, who agreed with this formula, and to negotiate case-by-case individual pardons for these persons. None of them had to sign any public document with a declaration of remorse. Bandrés did it on their behalf, accepting their willingness to lay down their arms and to fight for their political aims by exclusively democratic means. In his contacts with the government, the Basque deputy had rejected the Italian model of the remorseful terrorist as an obstacle to the success of the operation.

During the following years, about 250 former paramilitaries were reintegrated into civil society by this procedure.[9] Considering the adverse background against which the negotiations were carried out, they can certainly be described as successful negotiations. The success was basically the result of three circumstances. The first refers to the fact that they were, almost from the beginning, inclusive negotiations, which tried to integrate all the relevant actors, including the veto-holders, who were on the side of the hardliner Rosón and had the total confidence of the rest of the government. But Rosón also consulted and kept the military, the police and the Guardia Civil informed, as well as the head of the unified anti-terrorism command and the leader of the socialist opposition, Felipe González. On the other hand, the leaders of EE had frequent contacts with the *poli-milis*, who occasionally met representatives of the government. Nevertheless, in their meetings with the paramilitaries, Bandrés and Onaindia were never in any doubt about the dominant role of the politicians in the negotiations. This attitude permitted fluent contact in an atmosphere of confidence with the government, but also provoked the criticism of those *poli-milis*, who were more sceptical about the negotiations and rejected their philosophy based on the principle of peace for prisoners.

A second positive factor for the favourable outcome of the negotiations was the apparently well-calculated balance between publicity and secrecy. After the secret beginning of the first contacts, the philosophy, the contents and the names of the prisoners and exiles on the list submitted to the government soon became known to the public, even if this happened frequently with a certain time-lag. Years later, Bandrés himself underlined as one of the outstanding positive features of that negotiation the fact that 'nothing was gotten by underhand means' and that there were no 'secrete pacts'.[10] Everybody knew what was at stake and what was not. The negotiators did not need to waste any time with the debate about the definition of the issues to deal with and, on the other hand, no false expectations, which could not be delivered, could arise. Bandrés and Onaindia preferred to push their opponents out of the process at the very beginning and to continue with the compact support of their followers, whom they considered strong enough to resist the pressures and threats of their former colleagues against all collaborators with the enemy. This preference for an early separation of the zealots was not only a consequence of the balance of power between both groups within ETA-pm, which was favourable to the dealers, but was also proof of the EE negotiators' political realism, which was the third factor from which the negotiations would benefit. Since they were aware of the impossibility of introducing any political claim in the agenda of the talks in the very particular, extremely tense atmosphere in which the talks were taking place, they started the contacts by renouncing what the *poli-milis* had demanded when they called the ceasefire, and tried to achieve what still seemed to be enormously complicated, but what could reasonably be expected to be accepted as an issue for negotiation by the government: individual pardons. Furthermore, this decision was backed by a solid argument: the political part of the negotiation had already been achieved previously, the outcome of which was the Statute of Autonomy, passed by referendum only a few months before the contacts with Minister Rosón were taken up. This new instrument of self-government would substitute the armed struggle in the Basques' fight for national sovereignty.

The logical consequence of this discourse was in 1982 the dissolution of the paramilitary group, which was preceded by internal splits. The militants opposed to that decision, the so-called *milikis*, joined ETA-m, which did not accept all of them. That was the definite end of ETA p-m, even if this dissolution has never been formally declared.

During the process of negotiation leading up to the dissolution of ETA p-m, the other wing of the armed organization did not for a single moment abandon its attitude of total rejection of the philosophy, the procedure and aims of the negotiations, which were considered a betrayal of the Basque nation's interests and a cowardly surrender to the Spanish state. Not only were the *milis* unwilling to enter the discussion of a ceasefire, but they even threatened the 'execution' of all those activists who appeared on one of the lists negotiated by Bandrés or later by the PNV lawyer and member of the Spanish Senate Joseba Azkarraga. These threats became a crude reality, when in 1986 a commando shot dead the former head of ETA's political office, Dolores González Catarain, better known by her nickname Yoyes, when she was walking through her home town of Ordizia with her 3-year-old son. Yoyes had broken off the relationship with ETA-m and had returned from her exile in Mexico after having initiated the legal procedure for being pardoned under the shelter of the Azkarraga programme. Two years before, ETA had killed another former activist, Mikel Solaun, who had been charged with being a collaborator with the Spanish police as a means of assuring his release negotiated by Bandrés with Minister Rosón.

Yet only a very few years later, almost at the moment when Yoyes was killed, ETA-m itself would be the centre of a new attempt to find a negotiated settlement of the violent Basque conflict. The negotiations carried out in Algeria between 1986 and 1989 have received much attention by analysts, who have produced a series of – mostly journalistic – accounts of that issue. Beyond the different political approaches and interpretations offered by the authors, there seems to be a broad consensus concerning the importance of that 'Algerian connection' as the 'most serious and the most open attempt to negotiate an end to ETA's insurgency between 1978 and 1989', or as the 'scenario of the most risky attempt of a Spanish government to neutralize ETA'.[11]

During the 1980s, several factors would shape the context in which the negotiations became possible. First of all, thanks to the overall majority the socialist PSOE gained in 1982 and once again four years later, a period of solid one-party rule in the Spanish government became reality. This strength of President Felipe González and his Cabinet broadened the space for political initiatives, which the pressure of a strong opposition might have aborted. Furthermore, the main goal of the socialist administration was the modernization of the country and its complete integration into the political, economic and military framework of the western democracies as a full member of the European Community and of NATO. Failed military coups and the daily problems caused by ETA terrorism were dark spots on the curriculum of a country which was knocking on the door of the select club of western democracies. On the other hand, ETA was passing through a phase of increasing weakness due to the stronger involvement of the French government in the persecution of the commandos and members of the Ruling Council living in French territory, which was considered the organization's 'sanctuary'. In coordination with the Spanish government, Paris had designed a policy of deportation, which consisted in flying ETA prisoners to Third World countries and holding them there under arrest, preventing them from getting in contact with their comrades and reorganizing the structure of the organization. The capture in April 1986 of Domingo Iturbe ('Txomin'), the supreme leader of ETA-m, by the French police was not the beginning of the end of the Basque underground organization, but it forced the radical nationalists both of the military and the political wing into greater flexibility. The word 'negotiation' appeared more and more frequently in the vocabulary used at public meetings, manifestos circulating among the paramilitaries and in secret contacts with senior PNV leaders. Together with these shifts on either side of the barricades, there was another final factor, which favoured the emergence of a political atmosphere in which negotiations became feasible: the existence of a mediator accepted by both the Spanish government and the paramilitaries.

Since the initial years of ETA activity, Algeria had been a positive reference for the Basque activists both as an example of a successful struggle for independence and as an international ally, who permitted the military training of the *etarras* on its territory. On the other hand, the Algerian government was aware of the advantages that an active contribution to the brokering of an agreement between ETA and the Spanish government would offer not only in terms of an economic reward, but also as political backing from Madrid, who would silence the Algerian dissidents living in Spain and help resolve the conflict in the Western Sahara.

After its beginning in September 1986 until the definitive breakdown in April 1989, the negotiation process passed through several phases.[12] Its main protagonists were, on the one hand, several ETA prisoners transferred to Algeria, including the leaders Iturbe and Eugenio Etxebeste ('Antxon'), and, on the other hand, a delegation of the Spanish socialist government made up by Rafael Vera, the director of state security, and two middle-ranking politicians. Other participants were several Basque lawyers close to radical nationalism, and representatives of the Algerian government. The talks were carried out in an atmosphere of tension. Despite the announcement of various short-term ceasefires, violence continued with acts of kidnapping and car bombing. A detailed analysis of the whole process and its different phases is beyond the scope of this book. Yet, we should pay special attention to the outcome of the Algerian talks for two reasons. Firstly, while asking for the reasons for the negotiations' frustration, we might expect some more general indications concerning the problem of how to tackle a negotiation with armed paramilitaries; and second, the breakdown of the ceasefire in 1989 had a remarkable influence on the shape of new opportunities in Basque politics during the 1990s.

As is well known, the final collapse of the Algerian talks came about in spring 1989, when ETA blamed the government for breaking an agreement reached in Algeria, according to which the González administration had accepted the idea of starting 'political conversations' with the underground organization. More than a decade later, not all the doubts concerning the reasons for the final breakdown of the Algerian connection have been resolved. Since the only documents we know about the agreement reached in the last session at the negotiating table are those published by ETA in its press communiqués, it is impossible to know for sure if ETA introduced any change in the text issued by the daily *Egin*, if really all the points were agreed upon and if there was any formal signature, or if the agreement was only verbal and dependent on other unwritten conditions. In any case, what seems to be clear is, firstly, that the government promised something in

Algeria that later in Madrid it was not willing or not able to respect in its totality, and secondly, that ETA was not willing or unable to make a new concession to keep the process alive. Why? What were the insurmountable obstacles that provoked the breakdown of this important and serious attempt to find a settlement of the violent conflict in the Basque Country? I would suggest the following four arguments.

Practically from the very beginning of the last phase of the negotiations in Algeria, the process received broad and detailed media coverage. Real news was mixed up with speculation. The debates held between the two delegations were continued by the media in Spain. Politicians of all colours were asked to give their opinions on the issue, which became media headlines. Thus, the transparency of the process, demanded as a precondition by ETA, was granted, but at the same time media pressure became enormously strong and the necessary space for discretion, not to say secrecy, in which the negotiators could talk without the permanent presence of the media, was lost. When the government's delegates, Vera and Eguigaray, returned from their exhausting last meeting with Etxebeste and his advisers, the Spanish media had already broadcast the message that the socialist government had made political concessions to the terrorists. The confirmation of that news might have meant political suicide for the government.

A second problem was the representativeness of the delegations. The handicap of both Txomin and Antxon was their sidelining by the new ETA leadership in the French underground, which had the effective control over the arms and the active commandos. Txomin did not feel comfortable discussing complicated political issues without any adviser, and requested the transfer of Antxon to Algeria. The latter had already spent several years outside the Basque Country (in Ecuador) and despite his charisma, the Spanish delegates wondered if he had any real decision-taking capacity. In fact, the final breakdown of the talks was decided in France, and though there is very little information about the internal debate during those days of March 1989, there was apparently some kind of disagreement between Antxon, who was willing to maintain the momentum of the process, and the underground leadership, who imposed the suspension of the ceasefire and the talks. Secret documents written by Belén González and Ignacio Aracama, who together with Antxon negotiated on behalf of ETA, confirm the thesis about the disagreement between the negotiators and the organization's Ruling Council in France.[13] 'Once again in the long history of the organization, it becomes clear that the last word belonged to those who handle the arms.'[14] The Spanish socialist party, however, had a similar problem. The political heads of the delegation (Elgorriaga, Eguigaray) were politicians who of course counted on the confidence of the Minister of the Interior, but they neither exercised any remarkable influence on the government, nor were they personalities with much impact in the socialist party. The affair concerning the interference of the Secret Service, who had spied on the meetings in Algeria and used this secret information to put pressure on President González, is significant proof of the relative weakness and vulnerability of the Spanish delegation. Even if we do not know exactly all the inside issues related to the last phase of the negotiations leading finally to the agreement which collapsed, the hypothesis of a draft signed or agreed upon by Vera and Eguigaray in the hurry of the five-to-noon-atmosphere, and rejected later by the Minister or the President, seems quite plausible.

As a third obstacle I would suggest the lack of a real willingness of both sets of contenders to embark upon the search for a negotiated settlement, since neither had yet come to the conclusion that a military victory against the enemy was impossible. The Spanish government sat down at the negotiating table after having achieved – with or without the help of the GAL terror commandos acting on French territory – one of its most important political aims, namely French involvement in the persecution of Basque terrorism. The arrest of several important ETA leaders and members of different commandos helped to increase the hope that the agony of ETA had begun. ETA, although in a situation of growing police pressure, was not willing to rethink its military strategy, reacting with the longest kidnapping and the bloodiest bombing in the organization's history to the rumours about its weakness, which were discussed in the media.[15] ETA could play their joker card (their guns and bombs) whenever they wanted to. So why should there be any compromise in a process of negotiation?

Finally, probably the most complicated obstacle to the Algerian contacts were the serious errors concerning the conception and the timing of the negotiations, underlining what Domínguez Iribarren has called the 'immaturity of the process'.[16] The paramilitaries' desire to negotiate directly with the state modifications to the constitutional framework of the Basque Country and, consequently, of the whole Spanish state, was impossible to accept for any democratic government, rooted in the principles of constitutional parliamentary rule. The historical importance of the Algerian experience consisted in the fact that the ETA leadership apparently, and probably against its will, had an intuitive notion of such an impossibility, realizing that by sticking inflexibly to the demand for a political negotiation between ETA and the state they would hopelessly deadlock the process. What emerged in this context is what Clark rightly has called 'the most significant achievement of these talks, the fashioning of the two-track formula'.[17] Yet this formula only appeared in an embryonic, undefined and confusing manner. No clear definition of the issues to be dealt with by either of the negotiations proposed by ETA was made. In the proposal it was not clear if ETA would or would not take part in the negotiations and decision-making on constitutional themes. The strand set up by the political parties was apparently thought of as a secondary negotiating level with some kind of counselling function for the actors evolved in the first strand of negotiations, that is ETA and the state. Furthermore, the sidelining of the leading nationalist party in the Basque Country, as well as the leading opposition party in the state, was proof of political blindness, since these parties were strong enough to veto any possible outcome of the negotiation. It was easily foreseeable that these parties would not agree to their exclusion from the talks until these entered a second round, nor would they accept any negotiations which apparently depended on the first and decisive ones proposed by the paramilitaries and the central government.

However, the breakdown of the Algerian conversations was more than a dramatic blow to the Basque people's hopes for peace. It was at the same time the beginning of a new era, in which new circumstances for a peaceful settlement of the conflict would be shaped. ETA p-m decided on the group's dissolution because democracy and devolution opened new possibilities in the struggle for Basque home-rule. ETA militar was not willing to accept this analysis of its former comrades, defending the importance of the armed struggle even within the democratic and autonomous system. Yet, in Algeria the formula of the two-strand negotiations emerged, in a confused, timid and contradictory manner. ETA was not yet prepared to delegate its political responsibility to the party Herri Batasuna. On the contrary, after the end of the Algerian experience, the return to violence was followed by political (self-) castration of the civilian arm of the Liberation Movement, which refused to articulate any further discourse or strategy that might go beyond the day-to-day necessities of military logic. During the 1990s it became more and more evident that there was no complementary cooperation between the armed and the political struggle, but a total subordination of the latter to the former. The problem was that Spain was no longer a centralist and repressive dictatorship, nor was the Basque Country a Third World colony, whose frustrated and impoverished inhabitants had nothing to lose and everything to win through armed insurrection. This contradiction between the strategy of revolutionary violent insurrection and the completely different reality of a society that did not fit into the imaginary framework constructed by the paramilitaries turned out to be the seed of a growing separation between violent nationalism and Basque civil society. Out of this increasing distance a new attempt to progress towards a peaceful settlement would emerge.

7.2   The decline of radical nationalism

Contrary to popular opinion, radical Basque nationalism is not exactly a product of Francoism. Since the foundation of the Basque Nationalist Party in the mid-1890s, the history of the nationalist movement has always been that of a complex mixture made up of radical and moderate, by separatist and pro-autonomy patriots. An opportunistic strategy swinging like a pendulum from radicalism to pragmatic flexibility by adapting the party's claims and procedures to the specificity of each political moment facilitated the movement's cohesion over the years.[18] However, before the dictatorship there was neither any leftist, Marxist nationalism in the Basque Country,[19] nor any wing of the movement which would have considered violence a legitimate tool for the conquest of political goals. Therefore, the qualitatively new features introduced by ETA and the organizations of the Basque Movement of National Liberation during the years preceding and following Franco's death, were not the fight for independence, but a leftist anticapitalist rhetoric and the strategy of armed insurrection. After the dissolution of ETA p-m and the frustrating experience of Algeria it had become even clearer than before that ETA was not willing to renounce its self-proclaimed central position as armed vanguard and principal decision-taker, who would guide and supervise the process leading to independence. The enormous bloodshed caused by the bombs in the Barcelona supermarket, the Guardia Civil barracks in Zaragoza and those in the Catalan city of Vic (May 1991; nine casualties), made it evident that from ETA's viewpoint the consolidation of democracy and the implementation of Basque autonomy had not changed the panorama of centralist oppression against the Basque nation. The cases of state terrorism, organized and funded by the Ministry of Interior, and executed by GAL commandos, seemed to corroborate this thesis. Even as late as 1989, two years after GAL's last act of violence, another extreme-right commando burst into a meeting of HB leaders in a central hotel in the Spanish capital, shooting to death Josu Muguruza and seriously hurting Iñaki Esnaola, the HB politician and lawyer. In 1984, a similar act of right-wing assassination had put an end to the life of the HB leader Santi Brouard when exercising his profession as paediatrician. Thus, in the opinion of the paramilitary group, there were no reasons to modify the strategy of violent insurrection or the central position of the underground organization as leader and guardian of the Basque people's fight for freedom.

Consequently, if the state was not willing to meet ETA's demands and those of the Basque Liberation Movement, it had to be pushed to the negotiating table through force of violence. During the 1990s, especially after the conservatives' victory in the 1996 general elections, ETA recommenced its customary activity, which had only been interrupted temporarily during the Algerian talks. The paramilitaries even intensified their violent campaign, not in the quantitative sense of increasing the number of victims, but by broadening the scope of possible targets.[20] The 1980s had been by far the most violent decade of ETA activity, with a total of 417 persons killed by the underground group. During the 1990s, this figure dropped to 163. Yet, in the new context of regional autonomy and anti-terrorist solidarity of all political parties except for HB, the impact of these killings within Basque society was stronger than during the previous decade. Instead of becoming aware of this social and mental transformation of those whom it presumed to defend, ETA added more and more social and professional collectives to its list of potential targets. In the 1990s these included prison officers, members of the Basque autonomous police (Ertzaintza), rank-and-file members of the socialist and the conservative party, especially the latter, quite apart from the traditional targets of ETA's violence – the security forces, including the police and the army, as well as law court judges. Elected conservative or socialist councillors in any Basque (or in some cases even Spanish) town, automatically faced serious death threats as office-holders, who had to be protected by special security measures and personal bodyguards provided by the affected parties or by the Basque government. The escalation of violence did not even stop at the nationalists' doors. ETA killed Basque policemen who were members of the PNV or prison workers, who as members of the ELA union had been involved in the struggle for the transfer of ETA prisoners to Basque prisons. Whereas, to begin with, ETA had been known for the meticulous selection of its victims, at the end of the century, after 30 years of armed struggle, this image had changed substantially: nobody in the Basque Country, except the group's own followers, could exclude the possibility of becoming a target of political violence with complete certainty, and apparently ETA was not especially worried about its new image as a more and more indiscriminate terrorist group, whose political reasoning was no longer comprehensible to the broad majority of Basque society. In February 1996 an ETA gunman shot to death Fernando Múgica Herzog, one of the historic, popular leaders of Basque socialism, this was followed by the assassination of Francisco Tomás y Valiente, the former president of the Spanish Constitutional Court and one of the most brilliant Spanish intellectuals, an internationally known expert in law and history. He was shot when working in his university office. The killing of seven 'easy' targets, that is, PP town-councillors, in most cases without any particular political profile except that of being rank-and-file members of the conservative party, provoked generalized popular stupefaction. Furthermore, the necessity of both raising funds and demonstrating the organization's strength led ETA to intensify the practice of kidnapping. Among the total of 84 kidnappings in the history of the Basque underground group, by far the longest and the most profitable, in terms of the amount of ransom paid by the hostages' relatives, occurred in the 1990s. Between 1993 and 1996, four kidnappings with a total duration of 1,222 days[21] and a ransom sum of 2,130 million pesetas were committed.

Table 7.2.1 Kidnappings committed by ETA during the 1990s

Year	Name	Duration (days)	Ransom
1993	J. Iglesias Zamora (industrialist)	116	500 million pesetas
1995	J. M. Aldaya (industrialist)	342	130 million pesetas
1996	J.A. Ortega Lara (prison worker)	532	Rescued by the Spanish police
1996	C. Delclaux	232	1.500 million pesetas

Source: Asociación de Víctimas del Terrorismo (http://www.avt.org/).

Despite the economic profitability of these kidnappings for ETA, their pro-pagandistic effects were extremely negative for the paramilitaries. During a period of more than three years, Basque society was confronted day after day by the consequences of ETA violence. Every morning, the Basques had break-fast with the daily papers reporting the suffering of the families, the investi-gations of the police, the anti-ETA statements of the political parties and the popular initiatives for the rescue of the hostages. The nightly news on TV and radio stations repeated the now familiar stories, two of which it will suffice to recall here because of their tremendous impact on Basque and Spanish society and for their dramatic reporting by the media.

The two events happened in the summer 1997 and as a result all those who thought that there might still be some kind of humanitarian limits to ETA's strategy had to admit that they were wrong. In July, just a few days after ETA released the young businessman Cosme Delclaux, kidnapped 232 days before, the Spanish police freed the prison worker Ortega Lara. He had been kidnapped and held for 532 days in deplorable conditions in a damp, dark and cold cellar room. His kidnappers had decided to let him die from starvation if the government continued to refuse to transfer prisoners to prisons located in the Basque Country. It was the television images reaching Basque and Spanish homes of a shy and sick Ortega Lara, who was now nothing but skin and bone, which evoked the shocking memories of the lib-erated victims of the Auschwitz and Birkenau concentration camps and awakened public opinion with far greater effect against ETA, even among many of its own followers, than any of the anti-terrorism communiqués of the years before.[22]

But only a week later, ETA took yet another step in its particular spiral of violence by kidnapping a 29-year-old PP town councillor in the little Basque town of Ermua. Miguel Angel Blanco, the son of a Galician working-class family which years ago had settled down in Ermua, was better known in his town as the bass-player of a local pop group than as a politician. ETA declared that the only way of preventing his 'execution' within 48 hours was the immediate transfer of all the ETA prisoners. Since this demand was com-pletely impossible to carry out even if the government had been willing to, the kidnapping became characterized as a televised death penalty. Despite the mobilization of millions of Basques and Spaniards, ETA turned a deaf ear to them and to the petitions of international mediators, some HB politicians and even various ETA prisoners. A few minutes after the expiration of the ultimatum, Blanco was executed with a shot to the back of the head.[23]

The massive mobilizations of several hundred thousand Basques to save the life of Miguel Angel Blanco could not easily be branded as a manipula-tion prepared and staged by the enemies of the Basque people. In reality, the 48-hour ultimatum did not leave enough time to organize anything and, in retrospect, many politicians emphasized the high level of spontaneous mobi-lizations as one of the most outstanding features of the summer of 1997.

These multiple and massive mobilizations, which later would be referred to as the 'spirit of Ermua', were both a popular demand for ETA to stop killing, and to the policy-makers to start working seriously on a solution to the conflict. This spontaneous popular demand, intensified with the multiple effect of media coverage of the mobilizations, delivered one of the most damaging blows ETA had ever received. As we shall see below, during those summer months in the prisons and the political wing of the Liberation Movement the first doubts about the political and military strategy towards independence arose. How should that goal be achieved if those, who were supposed to be liberated, rebelled against their liberators? How should a popular consolidation and broadening of the Movement beyond the limited circles of radical nationalism be reached against the practically total opposition of the mass media? Just as in other parts of the Western world, Basque society on the eve of the twenty-first century was experiencing the impact of the 'Information Age',[24] in which 'the media are an intrinsic part of the political processes of official and public response'.[25] The events of the summer of 1997 jeopardized the survival of ETA and the political party attached to it, casting doubts even on the future of Basque nationalism in general. Indeed, this was so because ETA had been the result of a split within moderate PNV nationalism and because the reluctance of this party during the transition and the years after to break radically and definitively with their 'lost sons' became an easy argument for the state-wide parties. It served to transfer part of the responsibility for terrorism to the moderate nationalists and could be extremely useful in the struggle for votes within, and (especially) outside the Basque Country. In the summer of 1997, even for some radical nationalists who used to think more in military than political terms, it became evident that something had to change if, after losing the important battle of Ermua, the whole war for self-determination was not to be lost.

In fact, the crushing supremacy of military activism over any kind of more political reasoning was jeopardizing support for ETA even within the constituency of HB. The only occasions in which the paramilitaries appeared in the media – except, of course, those linked to the Liberation Movement – was related to bombs, guns, kidnapping or blackmailing, and the number of people who were still able to see a political purpose in these acts of violence was becoming smaller with each new act of violence. Despite the inevitable problem of perceiving the surrounding beyond the microcosm of underground life, this dangerous tendency of losing popular support was apparently noticed at ETA's headquarters too. One of the measures taken in order to stop this tendency was the drafting of a new political programme issued by the paramilitary organization, the so-called 'Democratic Alternative' in 1995.[26] Once again, the publication of this programme was preceded by a spectacular act of violence, a car bomb against the leader of the conservative party and – one year later – new Spanish President José María Aznar. Miraculously, Aznar survived unhurt. The 'Democratic Alternative' was officially announced as an updated version of the 'KAS Alternative'. The new text was more nationalist than the previous programme. As a late tribute to the breakdown of the Soviet Bloc, no more reference to socialism could be found in the paragraphs referring to the aims of ETA. Furthermore, it was a return to the period of the Algeria negotiations, during which the concept of the two-track strategy had emerged. Now it was officially recognized as a core idea in the new ETA programme. But the 'Democratic Alternative' was a return to Algeria also in another sense, since the same confusion as to the functional definition of each of the two strands appeared in the 1995 document too. In other words, ETA continued demanding an active participation of the organization in the negotiations on political issues with the state. It was not willing to delegate the constitutional part of the negotiations to the political parties with electoral mandate. It was ETA who would negotiate with the state on behalf of the Basques about the three fundamental questions, which – according to the paramilitaries – shaped and sustained the conflict: the recognition of the Basque Country as a political and cultural entity, the Basque people's right to self-determination and the unification of the politically and territorially separated parts of the country. This negotiation carried out by ETA with the state was considered 'a tool at the disposal of Basque society', but nothing was said about the hypothetical possibility that Basque society might not be willing to make use of this tool, preferring the use of others of greater democratic legitimacy. A ceasefire would be called only after the state's public agreement to the 'proposed plan to initiate a democratic process in the Basque Country'. With ETA as the protagonist of this peculiar 'democratic process', the political parties were supposed to enter the political stage only after the crucial political questions had already been decided. The proposal was the dizzy result of a tactical attempt to recover the offensive in an adverse situation, marked by an increasing social and political decline of ETA and the Liberation Movement.

In fact, ETA was not able to produce any kind of fragmentation between the political parties with its proposal formulated in the text of the 'Democratic Alternative', which was a step away from and not in the direction of the negotiating table. The only political party not willing to recognize this fact was Herri Batasuna. Its leadership reacted with unbounded enthusiasm, converting the 'Democratic Alternative' into the new totem of the party's political activity. In fact, just at the moment when ETA issued its new programme, HB was involved in the internal debate on the party's future political and strategic activity. The draft of what was going to be the party's new programme, known as the 'Oldartzen Report' and defended by the coalition's collective leadership against two alternative and more moderate documents, was endorsed by HB's rank-and-file-members in 1996. 'Oldartzen' closed the door on any attempt to broaden the space for autonomous radical nationalist policy-making and confirmed the subordination of policy to the dynamics of the armed struggle.

The document reveals a severe criticism of the Spanish and French states, which pursue 'the disappearance' (article 81) of the Basques as nation, and against all parties, organizations and institutions which collaborate in one form or another in this aim (political parties, mass media, Basque policy, peace movement). Even if the authors recognize the 'false dependence on the activity of ETA' as an error committed by HB (197), no attempt is made to break this dependence and articulate a deeper autonomy of HB by adopting a more critical attitude towards violence. On the contrary, there is no doubt about the legitimacy of ETA violence as a heroic act of self-defence. Furthermore, the enormously destructive street violence committed by gangs of young radicals received the *placet* of the Oldartzen Report, which referred to it as 'expressions of the political struggle of our people' (212). Far from establishing a possible link between the uncritical support of violence on the one hand and the increasing loss of political representativeness in the Basque society on the other, Oldartzen insinuates the opposite conclusion: it is necessary to leave the strategy of resistance and pass to a new offensive phase (287), 'theorizing and practising everything that allows us to accelerate the political process right now' (283).[27]

The meaning of these ambiguous and nebulous formulations becomes evident with a look at the statistics concerning street violence. During the last years of the 1990s, and as compensation for both the loss of ETA/HB influence and the more and more successful mobilisation of the Peace Movement, the figures register increasing and extremely destructive violence of well-organized gangs made up mostly of teenagers, which by night burned and destroyed hundreds of telephone boxes, bank offices, public buses and trains, politicians' private cars or offices and bars of the political parties, all of which is done without any consideration for the health and life of the persons affected by this vandalism. During 1996, the material damage provoked by these acts of sabotage was calculated at more than 3,500 million pesetas. That means an increase of 125 per cent on the year before. The year 1996 brought the highest economic losses since 1988. This was due to the spectacular increase in the number of acts of violence with major destructive consequences, namely incendiary destruction. While the growth rate of the general number of acts of street violence from 1995 to 1996 was 20.4 per cent, incendiary destruction increased by 60 per cent.[28]

From 1992, when this type of violence appeared in the streets of the Basque Country, up to 1997 the police have arrested more than 500 youths. About 100 were sent to prison.[29]

According to media information, this street violence was designed by 'Txelis', one of ETA's leaders in prison, who is now critical of the organization's strategy, which was a consequence of ETA's weakening following the capture of its Central Committee in 1992.[30] Ever since, ETA, KAS and HB have backed these always well-prepared and organized destructive activities.[31] The political aims of the street violence, if there are any, and its functionality, were not at all understood by the vast majority of the Basque society. A public-opinion poll published in May 1997 showed that about 83 per cent of the population in the Basque Autonomous Community denied that the street violence might help to achieve the political aims of those who commit it. Only 9 per cent thought it did. Even among the voters of HB a majority of 47 per cent gave a negative answer to this question, 32 per cent a positive one and 21 per cent didn't answer.[32] If there has been any effect of the street violence within Basque society, it is probably this: an increasing ghettoization of the Basque Movement of National Liberation and the growing identification of radical nationalism and violence in the eyes of the broad majority of the Basque people, for whom it became more and more difficult to recognize politics beyond the burning of buses, banks, cars or even historic town halls. This growing identification of violent nationalism with criminality generated a counter-productive boomerang effect against all those demanding a negotiated solution of the conflict.

This latter affirmation is also true in another sense. Kepa Aulestia, a former ETA activist and then leader of Euskadiko Ezkerra, the political heir of ETA p-m, makes the point that while the high intensity of political violence has damaged the social reputation of those linked to it, at the same time it also acted as an integrating and cohering symbol of all ETA activists and sympathizers:

> Violence in Euskadi has managed to build around it a separate society, a world of uncertain boundaries, of varied human profile; a 'society within the society', and even a sort of 'a state within the state'. This is its great success, and because of this it is so difficult to deactivate violence: because it protects itself with social armour, which has proved to be hermetic faced with the call made by the rest of the Basques in favour of concord.[33]

From this point of view, street violence took on the function of an 'initiation rite', which permitted the transfer of this central symbolic role of violence in the social behaviour of a minority of society from one generation to the next. Within this violent microcosm, this is the conclusion drawn by Aulestia, 'a very small part of the reality is projected as a collective delirium, as organized paranoia'.[34] Within this extremely pessimistic panorama – 'Pessimism is also a requisite for optimism' is the last sentence in Aulestia's essay – a hint concerning a possible way out of the confrontation can hardly be found. Yet the publication and presentation of his book coincided nearly on the same day with the announcement of ETA's unilateral and unlimited ceasefire of September 1998. Had Aulestia, like so many others, underestimated the influence of civil society on the compact microcosm of the Liberation Movement? Or – and this would be another interpretation of the ceasefire more in accord with the thesis concerning the 'hermetic society within the society' – was the ceasefire a tactical reaction to a shift within the Liberation Movement, instead of a concession to pressure articulated from outside? In reality, I would suggest that both questions and their corresponding answers should not be treated as strict alternative explanations, but as a double-sided response to the same problem. In other words, the external pressure had weakened the Movement, which was no longer hermetic. In this situation, only shifts carried out first on the fringes, then adopted by the very core of the Liberation Movement, were likely to be a valid strategy aiming at the recovery of the lost political and social influence of radical nationalism.

One of the most reliable barometers for measurng HB's influence within Basque society are the elections. The year 1987 stands for both the peak of the coalition's electoral influence and the beginning of a long process of political decline, which would not be stopped until the new post-ceasefire scenario. Significantly, 1987 was also the year in which ETA planted its bloodiest bomb: that of the Barcelona supermarket, with 21 fatalities.

These figures in Table 7.2.2 are very significant, especially if we contrast them with the ascendant voting trend characteristic for HB from 1979 to 1987. If we include in the results those for Navarre, the difference between the 1987 result and that of 1996 would be about 70,000 votes, more than a quarter of the total votes gained in 1987. This phenomenon has also attracted the attention of sociologists, who have tried to explain it with data proceeding from biographical case-by-case studies.[35] The leaders of HB, however, had enormous problems with the interpretation of these figures, which in any democratic party should have provoked an internal discussion about the party's political strategy. Instead, they continued business as usual. To mention just one example, after the kidnapping and assassination of the young town councillor Miguel Angel Blanco and in response to the massive popular mobilizations of protest, the first reaction by HB consisted in criticizing the rest of the political parties for having 'put into practice a state of emergency' in the Basque Country. Some days later, several leaders blamed the Spanish government for the death of Blanco because of its refusal to transfer the prisoners. This was a clear legitimization of the assassination, which had so upset Basque society, and even sectors close to the Liberation

Table 7.2.2   HB votes in the Basque Autonomous Community

Elections	Votes
Europ. parliament 1987	210,000
Span. parliament 1989	187,000
Basque parliament 1990	186,000
Span. parliament 1993	175,000
Basque parliament 1994	166,000
Span. parliament 1996	155,000

Sources: Mata (1993, 33); El País 20.7.1997.

Movement, more than any earlier act of violence committed by ETA. At least from this moment on, the public image of HB was exactly identical to that of ETA, and this, of course, made the party and its leaders much more vulnerable in the area of the juridical confrontation. The result came soon. In January 1997, the Spanish Supreme Court summoned all the 23 members of the Directing Council of the coalition to appear in court to answer charges of hypothetical 'collaboration with an armed gang'. The reasons for the trial were for two communiqués justifying the killing of a Basque socialist politician and of the ex-president of the Supreme Court, as well as the fact that during the 1996 electoral campaign HB had tried to use the space for party broadcasts granted by the public television channels to all political parties represented in parliament for the showing of a video produced by ETA, in which armed and hooded members of the group explain the contents of the 'Democratic Alternative'. After the temporary imprisonment of the HB leaders, who were released on bail, and after having concluded the hearings in a climate of strong pressure and even threats, in December 1994 – a few months after the mobilizations of Ermua had taken place – the judges of the Supreme Court sentenced them to seven years' imprisonment plus a fine of 500,000 pesetas for each of the leaders. The judges rejected the imputation of 'apology of terrorism' and 'membership of an armed gang', considering only the crime of 'collaboration with an armed gang' by granting a terrorist group the coalition's political broadcast on TV. The judges stressed that it would have been absolutely legal if the party itself had explained in the broadcast the content of the ETA video, and that it was not the so-called 'Democratic Alternative' which had to be punished by the law, but the facilities they had provided to an illegal terrorist group to perform on public TV.[36]

But the work of the judges had not yet finished. In July 1998, *Egin*, the daily paper close to HB, its radio station and a number of near-HB enterprises were closed down because the instructing judge found important evidence to prove his theory that all these organizations formed part of ETA's financial network.

Contrary to what many political observers had expected, this juridical offensive against the Liberation Movement did not provoke any particular reaction of protest and solidarity within Basque society, excluding some critical comments on the juridical basis of the sentences by the moderate nationalists, who did not consider it very solid and thought it overly influenced by the political background of a widespread anti-ETA/HB atmosphere. Apparently, these criticisms were correct, since in July 1999 the Constitutional Court revoked the sentence against HB's Ruling Council, and the National High Court permitted the reopening of the daily *Egin* and its radio station. The Court released the members of the HB leadership considering 'the sentence disproportionate' with respect to the extent of the crime, in this case the intended diffusion of ETA's video on public TV.

Table 7.2.3   Detentions in France for relationship
with ETA

Year	Arrests	Imprisonments
1988	85	33
1989	64	28
1990	57	23
1991	76	19
1992	149	36
1993	99	23
1994	84	21
1995	47	23
1996	98	28
1997	64	19
Total	823	253

Source: Domínguez Iribarren, Negociación, p. 293.

During the 1990s, the political decline of HB was accompanied by a loss of ETA's military effectiveness. To a great extent, this was the consequence of the more active role played by the French government and its police in the persecution of the underground organization.[37] It should be remembered that one of the reasons justifying the activities of the anti-ETA commandos organized by Spanish government agencies was the reluctance of the French police to fight against terrorism. Whatever the influence of this state terrorism on French politics might have been, the fact is that during the last decade of the century the number of spectacular blows against the Basque organization on French territory increased remarkably. In 1992, the French police arrested the complete collective leadership of ETA, known under the pseudonym of Artapalo. During the following years, some of the successors of Artapalo and other high-ranking members of the organization were sent to jail. Plenty of other persons were arrested and imprisoned for their relationship with ETA. Many prisoners were delivered to the Spanish police after serving their sentence in a French prison.

These figures provide evidence that what traditionally had been called the 'French sanctuary' of ETA had ceased to exist. Under growing police pressure on both sides of the frontier, isolated by the rest of the political parties and suffering from permanent electoral decay, the Basque Movement of National Liberation faced a complicated situation, which in reality transformed what the Oldartzen programme called a political offensive into a forced withdrawal with no realistic prospect of recovering the lost initiative, which had not only been jeopardized by the police and the parties, but also by the Basque business community and the peace movement.

7.3   Violence and the economy

Until the 1970s, the Basque provinces have historically occupied the leading positions in nearly all socio-economic statistics, which compared growth rates, per capita income, and levels of salaries or rates of professional occupation registered in the different provinces or regions of the Spanish state. Bizkaia and Gipuzkoa were, together with parts of Catalonia, the first regions to industrialize at the end of the nineteenth century. The second 'industrial revolution' of the 1960s and first half of the 1970s pushed Alava and Navarre, the Basque 'late-comers', into a similar position to their neighbours on the coast, transforming the Basque region into one of the most modern and dynamic centres of the Spanish economy.

This privileged situation has changed dramatically since the end of the 1970s. The growing liberalization of the Spanish economy, strong international competition, the technological backwardness of Basque factories, which had rested on their laurels instead of adapting production to the new necessities of the international market, and the oil crisis, are the most important factors which explain the sudden and dramatic change in the fate of the Basque economy, which sank into deep recession. Many of the traditional industrial plants in the historically leading sectors of iron and steel and shipbuilding had to be closed down or at least restructured. About 180,000 jobs disappeared in the three provinces of the Basque Autonomous Community. In 1994, unemployment reached a peak of 25 per cent of the working population. All the indicators of wealth and income registered a drastic decline of the Basque territories in comparison with Spanish ones. Terrorist violence was both a by-product and an active promoter of this acute crisis.[38]

Nevertheless, it is probably impossible to measure the degree of responsibility that can be attributed to violence in the process of socio-economic decline in the Basque Country. On the one hand, there is no doubt that the kidnapping and killing of businessmen, as well as the collection of 'revolutionary taxes' among threatened employers have obviously had – and still have – a negative impact on economic activities. Even without taking into account the incalculable cases of lost investment opportunities, which were not implemented in the Basque Country or were transferred to other regions, the damage produced by the violence to Basque and Spanish society has been enormous. According to the data offered by Domínguez Iribarren, the financial costs of ETA's violence and its consequences would come to more than one billion pesetas for the period between 1978 and 1992, more than half of this amount corresponding to the direct and indirect costs incurred by the dismantling of the nuclear plant of Lemoniz, a small town near Bilbao. ETA had targeted the nuclear plant, its owner Iberduero and its workers between 1977 and 1982, killing two of the engineers responsible in 1981 and 1982. In that same year, the government decided to cancel the construction of the plant. In 1983, when the decision became definitive, the government created a public fund in order to meet the considerable expenses originated by the closing down of the (unfinished) Basque nuclear plant. A part of the financial resources in this fund is generated by a percentage of the electric tariffs fixed yearly by the government and paid by all the electricity consumers. Analysing these facts, Domínguez Iribarren concludes that 'probably only very few terrorist campaigns throughout the world have been so expensive for the economy of a country like that carried out by ETA against the nuclear plant' of Lemoniz.[39]

However, despite the high financial and human negative impact of terrorism, the development of the last decade of the twentieth century proves that the persistence and even increased violence has not impeded a vigorous renaissance of the Basque economy after its exit from the long tunnel of recession and industrial restructuring. Since the 1990s, except for the years of 1992 and 1993, which included a short, but deep recession, the economic figures have turned out to be quite optimistic once again. Between 1985 and 1995, the per capita income in the three provinces of Alava, Gipuzkoa and Bizkaia has grown by 39 per cent that is, about five points more than the Spanish average.

Compared with the EU average, up to the beginning of the crisis in the mid-1970s, the Basques were even wealthier than other Europeans. After the end of the 'golden years', Basque per capita income dropped beneath the European average, remaining there until the end of the century. Yet, during the 1990s, the Basques were more successful in their efforts to make up the difference in income with their European neighbours than the Spaniards were. In 1998, the Basque income-rate was only seven points beneath the European level, whereas the difference between the European and the Spanish average was still about 20 points.

Alava is the Basque province which has most benefited from the economic recovery during the 1990s. It has climbed to third position in the ranking of all Spanish provinces based upon the per capita income rates. All the other Basques provinces are situated in positions above the Spanish average.

Table 7.3.1 Per capita income:
Basque Autonomous Community
(Spanish average: 100)

Year	PCI
1955	170.89
1985	107.54
1987	107.06
1989	107.13
1991	110.1
1993	109.09

Source: Cambio 16, 27.10.1997, p. 12.

Table 7.3.2   Per capita income in the Basque Autonomous Community (BAC) and in Spain (EU average: 100)

Year	BAC	Spain
1959	95.04	58.29
1965	108.71	68.75
1969	109.72	75.37
1975	108.07	85.29
1979	84.03	73.04
1985	80.03	70.60
1991	87.69	79.07
1993	85.82	78.20
1998	93.38	81.45

Source: Fundación BBV, Renta Nacional de España (1999); Diario Vasco, 8 December 1999.

Table 7.3.3   Per capita income in 1998 (Spanish average: 100)

Ranking	Province	Rate
1	Balearic Islands	147.86
2	Girona	133.58
3	Alava	132.96
4	Madrid	128.29
5	Barcelona	123.58
7	Navarre	117.70
8	Bizkaia	115.66
15	Gipuzkoa	105.91
52	Granada	64.62
53	Badajoz	64.49

Source: Fundación BBV, Renta Nacional de España (1999); Diario Vasco, 8 December 1999.

During this process of socio-economic rally, *Euskadi* has also recovered its attraction for foreign investment. In the 1990s, the Basque provinces, which – not counting Navarre – made up about 1.43 per cent of the total territory of the Spanish state, have climbed from attracting only 1.01 per cent of all foreign investment in Spain (1991) to the figure of 7.12 per cent (first semester of 1997). Moreover, according to research done by the Basque University, since 1996 foreign investment shows an increasing tendency to flow into high-tech sectors with important perspectives of economic growth, and not – as had been the case up to then – into the traditional heavy and the service industries.[40]

This optimistic impression was confirmed by the development of the Gross Domestic Product (GDP). Still in 1996, the Basque GDP growth rate was similar to the Spanish average. Yet during the following years the Basque economy performed remarkably better than the Spanish one. In 1998, the year the ceasefire was declared, it reached its peak, growing nearly two points more than the Spanish economy, which was one of the most dynamic economies in the EU. This ranking did not change in the last two years of the century: the Basque GDP growth rate continued surpassing the Spanish rate and the EU average by an even greater difference (2.63 in 1999; 3.33 in 2000).[41] The 1980s, with several years of negative growth, seemed far away. The year 2000 was, after the last negative growth rate in 1993 (−0.8 per cent) the seventh year of continuous growth for the Basque economy, which at the end of the twentieth century had become one of the most prosperous regions of the EU.

Table 7.3.4 Evolution of the Gross Domestic Product (%) in Spain and *Euskadi*

	1996	1997	1998	1999	2000
Spain	2.4	4.0	4.3	4.1	4.1
Euskadi	2.5	4.4	6.0	5.2	5.3

Sources: www.eustat.es; www.ine.es/daco.

Table 7.3.5 Rates of unemployment in the Basque Autonomous Community

Year	Euskadi	Alava	Bizkaia	Gipuzkoa
1985	21.1	16.4	22.3	21.0
1986	21.0	16.7	22.1	21.0
1987	21.7	18.8	24.2	18.8
1988	21.6	16.8	24.3	19.0
1989	18.8	15.8	20.2	17.7
1990	16.2	13.2	18.2	13.2
1991	17.3	15.7	19.8	13.8
1992	19.9	18.7	21.9	17.2
1993	24.3	21.3	26.6	21.8
1994	25.0	22.0	26.5	23.8
1995	23.8	21.3	25.4	22.4
1996	22.4	19.7	24.6	20.1
1997	21.1	17.1	24.3	17.7
1998	17.8	13.9	20.5	15.1
1999	15.5	13.2	18.0	12.6
2000	13.7	11.6	16.8	9.5
2001	11.1	9.2	13.5	8.3

Source: Basque Institute of Statistics (http://www.eustat.es).[43]

As in the Spanish economy and in most of the other European economies, economic growth in the Basque Country did not automatically lead to a similar level of decrease in the rates of unemployment. Basque unemployment reached its peak in 1994 with 25 per cent of the working population looking for a job. At the end of 1997, the statistics still registered a percentage of 21.1 per cent in the Basque average with remarkable inter-provincial differences and a regional peak of 27 per cent in the traditional industrial areas on the left bank of the river Nervión. Only in the following years did the number of unemployed decrease remarkably.[42]

The sector of Basque society which most suffers from unemployment is young people. According to a report of the major Basque trade union, the nationalist ELA, at the beginning of 1998, that is, within the quite favourable context of decreasing general unemployment rates, 43.4 per cent of the Basque working population aged less than 25 years was jobless. The European average rate was 12.5 per cent.[44]

There is no reliable sociological data on the relationship between youth unemployment and violence, especially street violence. It seems that in any case there is no direct cause–effect relationship, since probably most of the youngsters engaged in the radical nationalist street gangs are teenagers that have not yet entered the labour market. There is no evidence either of a relationship between the rates of unemployment and the numbers of acts of sabotage in the different Basque areas, since Gipuzkoa, the most nationalist area is where street violence has reached a peak, rather then Bizkaia, the most populous area, which has the highest number of unemployed people.[45]

Analysing these figures in the introductory chapter to a plan elaborated by the Basque government with the aim of contributing to the 'expansion of the democratic values and the promotion of attitudes of solidarity, tolerance and responsibility among the Basque youth', the authors deny any interpretation of street violence in terms of a more or less logical product of social deprivation. Instead, violence is interpreted as politically 'induced' behaviour.[46] The conclusion from this analysis is that an active employment policy is necessary to improve the situation of young people and to promote

Table 7.3.6 Local distribution of acts of street violence, 1992–94 (percentages)

	Population	*1992*	*1993*	*1994*
Gipuzkoa	25.8	43	55	54
Bizkaia	44.5	36	23	27
Alava	9.9	11	8	6
Navarre	19.8	10	14	13
Total	100	100	100	100

Source: Plan de Actuación (1997).

their integration into society, but it will not provide the key for a solution to (street) violence. More jobs, as well as other measures (education, policing), might contribute to reducing the level of receptiveness towards violence, but the final decisions for this kind of 'induced' violence is taken in the headquarters of ETA, KAS and HB. Only in the moment when the leading strategists of the Liberation Movement recognize that street violence is no longer profitable will it decline in importance, if not disappear altogether. The situation during the first months following the ceasefire in September 1998 seems to provide evidence for this thesis concerning the strategic character of street violence. During that first period, marked by the consolidation of the pan-nationalist entente and the still more or less optimistic expectation that a positive outcome of the recently initiated process of apparent détente would be possible, arson attacks and threats vanished almost completely from Basque streets. Only later, when these initial hopes of a political settlement of the conflict had already been dashed, did street violence return, with two consequences: first, it provided the non-nationalist parties and the Spanish government with arguments for their political strategy of not discussing political issues until all expressions of violence disappeared. And secondly, street violence jeopardized the survival of the pan-nationalist entente. Through virulent media pressure, the moderate nationalist parties of PNV and EA had to pay a high political price for their alliance with a political party like EH,[47] which was blamed for being the political instigator of the street violence.

It is obvious that a hypothetical disappearance of street violence, and politically motivated violence in general, would immediately produce a peace dividend for the whole of Basque society, which is currently financing through taxation the millions in damage caused by youth-gang vandalism and the yearly increase in public spending in law and order needed to protect the victims. The figures concerning the costs of terrorism mentioned above are quite significant in this sense. Tourism, which despite terrorism has grown slightly over the last few years, is still suffering from the image of violence that characterizes the Basque Country, especially abroad. An anecdote by the British Foreign Office advising tourists against visiting the Basque Country for safety reasons is quite eloquent, even if this report has been withdrawn after protests from the Basque government.[48] In the above report on foreign investment, terrorism is blamed as the 'principal culprit' for the traditional reluctance of foreign investors to take their capital to a region historically known for its good infrastructure network and the skilfulness of its human capital.[49] In the same sense a major Basque banker warned that a continuance of terrorism would probably block the positive effects the introduction of the euro is supposed to generate in the Basque economy, since it would divert investments linked to the common European currency to other European regions.[50]

Nevertheless, returning to the original theme of this chapter, it is interesting to observe that the spokesmen for Basque businessmen, certainly one of the sectors of Basque society most affected by violence, despite all the pressures and suffering, maintain a fairly realistic attitude of coolness and pragmatism. Nearly a year before the ceasefire was announced, in an interview with the president and the general secretary of the employer's Association of Gipuzkoa ('Adegi'), the latter answered as follows to a question about the relationship between violence and industrial investment in the Basque Country:

> Talking about investment in the Basque Country and elsewhere in Europe, and I am thinking especially about foreign investment and in general about enterprises of a certain dimension, before deciding about the placement of their capital, they check all the conditions like infrastructure, the skilfulness of the people, the industrial culture, the market and its foreseeable perspectives of growth, public subsidies, tax system. (...) I don't think that much investment is being diverted only because of terrorism. What is happening is that when all the other factors are weak, inevitably terrorism will be more important. On the other hand, if those factors are strong and favourable, in the end investment will be forthcoming despite terrorism, and there are some examples to prove that.[51]

Mr Ruiz Urchegui, who said this, had already been targeted by ETA. The terrorists placed a bomb in his car. The General Secretary of Adegi saved his life, because the bomb exploded when a relative was driving the car. The driver survived, but lost his both legs. Mr Korta, Adegi's president, was killed after the ceasefire was called off, as one of the victims caught up in the new wave of ETA terrorism. On the background to this crude reality, it is in fact not easy to understand how the spokesmen of the Basque business community are still able to issue statements like the one quoted above, in which there is no place for a fatalistic interpretation of the Basque economy. Furthermore, the facts and figures concerning the development of the economy seem to corroborate the impression that despite political unrest, daily threats and lethal terror, the Basque economy is still doing quite well. This is without doubt a consequence of the favourable social and economic conditions mentioned by Ruiz Urchegi, but also of the daily restless struggle against fear and desperation carried on by Basque employers, whose attachment to their country is still too strong to provoke a massive flight of capital. On the contrary, the Basque provinces are still surprisingly attractive places for investment from outside. One of the most effective instruments, which is producing a remarkable pull-effect for Spanish and foreign capital is the Basque tax autonomy, which after the agreement on 'special taxes' signed in May 1997 by the Spanish and Basque governments has nearly reached a level of complete financial sovereignty. This capacity for financial self-management, legitimized for historical reasons and granted by the Constitution of 1978, is an absolute exception in the Spanish fiscal system and provides the Basque administration with an important tool for the public regulation of the regional economy. According to information published by the economy supplement of the major Spanish daily paper, *El País*, in September 1996, at least seven multinational companies had expressed their interest in investing in the Basque Autonomous Community.[52] The lower taxes offered in the Basque Country and the important public subsidies have attracted capital from the surrounding regions, provoking an angry response from the affected regional governments. Between July and August of 1996 only, there were 23 cases of capital-transfer to one of the Basque provinces.[53] These subsidies provoked a formal complaint presented by the Spanish government to the EU administration, which was accepted by the European Commission. Several regional governments that border the Basque region backed this complaint. Brussels has opened legal proceedings to check if the Basque subsidies can be considered as illegal financial help offered to certain enterprises by public agencies. If this is the case, the courts would have to act against an infringement of the law of free competence. Finally in January 2000, an agreement was reached between the Basque and the central governments. It consisted in the withdrawal of the juridical complaints against the total of 87 different Basque tax norms and dispositions by Madrid. In return, the Basque government dropped the most controversial of those tax incentives with the hope that an agreement with Madrid would consolidate the Basque tax system and, incidentally, make the European administration refrain from acting against the *Conciertos*.[54]

To summarize, without doubt it can be stated that an end of violence would bring important dividends to the whole of Basque society, especially to its economy. Even the short experience of the 14-month period of cease-fire provides enough evidence to prove that this peace dividend will not only become visible in the long run, but also in the short run. According to José Guillermo Zubia, the secretary-general of Confebask (Basque Business Confederation), the ceasefire especially affected the services sector, since the industrial sector is not likely to alter its development over the influence of short-term circumstances. Even so, Zubia attributed the decision of Mercedes-Benz to invest about 100,000 million pesetas into a new Basque factory over the next ten years with the prospect of 'political and social stability' in the Basque Country created by the ceasefire.[55] During the summer of 1999 and even of 1998, the Basque Country registered a massive influx of tourists both from other Spanish regions and from abroad. Among the different factors mentioned by the experts on the sector, the spectacular new Guggenheim Museum in Bilbao and what the head of the Department for Economy and Tourism at the Provincial Government of Gipuzkoa called the new 'socio-political climate'[56] are the two most important reasons for the increasing tourist attractiveness of the Basque Country. The figures for 1999 confirm the positive tourist pull-effect of the truce. During that year, the three provinces of the Autonomous Community of *Euskadi* were visited by a total of one-and-a-half million tourists, which meant an increase of 7 per cent on the year before. This was an absolute record in the history of Basque tourism.[57] After the return of violence, the Basque region lost once again part of its appeal and the figures for visitors dropped.

Nevertheless, as I have tried to show, it seems that in the Basque Country a peaceful 'socio-political climate' is not a *conditio sine qua non* for economic growth and social welfare. The figures for the socio-economic Basque apogee during the 1990s, a decade of permanent violent conflict, are quite eloquent. The Basques have learned to live with violence and to recover little by little their traditional economic strength despite continuing violence. As a consequence, certainly a controversial, paradoxical conclusion concerning the relationship between peace and economy might be put forward: the peace dividend is important, but not important enough to generate inside the Basque business community stronger pressure on policy-makers to request a stronger commitment in the search for a settlement of the conflict. As a matter of fact, there is no single opportunity of checking out how (economic) life would be without violence since ETA arose in the 1960s. For businessmen, and for society in general, violence had become a fatal, but nearly natural feature of the Basque everyday reality. Everybody criticized the violence, but nobody really knew how to stop it. And furthermore, if it was possible to get the economy moving and expanding despite ETA, why waste energy, racking one's brains, inventing possible scenarios for a peaceful settlement and an even more prosperous economy? The day-to-day resistance against terrorism and the temptation to abandon the Basque Country already requires a lot of personal energy and in such circumstances a stronger, more active concern for more 'political' issues like that of peace can hardly be expected from the Basque business community. Yet, this reluctance was criticized by speakers of the Basque peace movement Elkarri, who – referring to a report about 'Peace and the Economy in Northern Ireland' – compared the situation in Northern Ireland and in the Basque Country, urging Basque businessmen to take a more active part in the promotion of a negotiated solution to the Basque conflict.[58]

This happened to a certain extent after September 1998. The hitherto unknown 14-month experience of life without ETA's shooting and bombing also produced an impact on the Basque business community. For the first time since ETA started to act, tangible prospects for an end to violence had arisen. Even if it was only for a few months, it became evident that the unilateral and indefinite ceasefire had apparently blown away for a moment the crude reality of so many years of violence. There is no statistical data available, but analysis of the public manifestos, reports and media briefings delivered by the spokesmen of the Basque business community would probably reveal both for the 14 months of the ceasefire and for the period following its breakdown at the end of November 1999, a more frequent presence of statements concerning violence and the search for it than was the case before 18 September 1998. This had become evident already in April 1999, when the ceasefire was still in force, but the sense of a certain paralysis of the peace process as a consequence, among other factors, of the government's passivity, was increasing day by day. In fact, it was during a visit of President Aznar to Bilbao that the most spectacular and controversial gesture of this stronger commitment to the peace process was performed by the most outstanding representatives of Basque big business. In a meeting between Aznar and the business community in the hall of the new Congress Centre of Bilbao, the Euskalduna Palace, the addresses of the three spokesmen[59] were full of references to the peace process and appeals for dialogue as a tool for peace.[60] This could only be interpreted as a badly disguised criticism of the government's lack of initiative during the period of the ceasefire. In fact, responding to a question concerning this surprisingly critical reception of President Aznar in Bilbao, Mr Zubia, the secretary-general of Confebask, refused to make any comment on political issues, but confirmed the fear of Basque businessmen concerning a possible 'paralysis' of the peace process, which was the basis for the statements made during Aznar's visit to Bilbao, where the 'desire for dialogue was general'.[61] However, before the opportunity of consolidating peace arose and before the stronger commitment of the Basque business community to the solution of the problem of violence was shaped, it was civil society that would generate an important stimulus to the efforts to find a way out of the conflict.

7.4   The end of the silence

One of the common features of all violent ethnic conflicts is that in certain circumstances the suffering of the affected population multiplies the people's war-weariness and stimulates a popular desire for peace. This general assertion, however, raises important questions, which do not only deal with the characteristics of peace processes all over the world, but with some of the most relevant problems concerning the very nature of politics and democracy. The first question addresses the linkage between grievances and popular protest. Since the debate about the thesis presented by the promoters of the theory of relative privation we know that the intensity of popular responses provoked by grievances and frustration does not always correlate with the intensity of these grievances. Applied to peace processes I would say that there is no automatic relationship between the level of violence and the extent of popular protest. The history of mankind is full of examples that demonstrate human beings' surprising capacity to tolerate any kind of atrocity. On the other hand, popular protest may be mobilized in situations where the intensity of conflict and violence is lower. Popular protest relies more on opportunities than on frustration, or, as John Darby puts it, 'courage in condemning atrocities is not enough. What converts outrage to action is condemnation within the context, or at least realistic hope, that agreement is possible, and that further violence could threaten it.'[62]

A second question has to do with the relationship between mass mobilization and the behaviour of the political elite. It deals with the influence of popular unrest in the development of politics, and in this case more particularly in the genesis and the development of peace processes. If the popular desire for peace is mobilized, how strong will its influence on the peace process be? In other words, can grassroots protest be a motor for a peace process, or is it the political elite which fuels and manages this process?

Turning from theory to our specific case study, in the Basque Country we can find evidence for both the important role of the contextual structure in the development of the peace process and for the key function performed by civil society in the preliminaries of the process. The 1980s was the decade with the highest intensity of violence. During those years ETA killed 417 persons and perpetrated devasting outrages. The 1987 car bombs in Barcelona and Zaragoza caused a total of 32 casualties. However, the popular mobilization for peace in the Basque Country did not really start until the 1990s, despite the decrease in the number of fatal victims caused by ETA's activities (163). Several factors might help to explain this phenomenon. First of all, the consequences of the devolution policy and the subsequent (partial) recovery of home rule have to be mentioned. As already indicated above, the granting of regional autonomy in 1979 meant the construction of a new institutional, political, cultural and economic framework, which provided a remarkable push-effect in the Basque process of nation-building. It was true that Basque autonomy only worked in part of the territory considered the historic homeland by the nationalists, and that, as a consequence, this autonomy deepened the separation of the Basques living in *Euskadi*, in Navarre and in *Iparralde*, the French Basque Country. But it was no less true that the possibilities of broad self-government enjoyed by the wide majority of the Basque citizens, that is, those living in *Euskadi*, undermined the radical nationalist discourse, according to which nothing had changed since Franco's death. Basque society was aware of the limitations of this form of autonomous self-government and of the obstacles the central government or the Spanish courts created from time to time. But why kill and harm, if now other instruments and channels for the articulation of discontent and the formulation of new demands were available, contrary to what had happened during the dictatorship and even before? Moreover, political normalization since the establishment of democracy and the increasing implementation of the Statute of Autonomy revealed an image of a Basque society which was much more heterogeneous and pluralistic than a political observer during the 1970s and the early 1980s might have thought. As a matter of fact, both the electoral results and public surveys made it clear that the image of a more or less completely nationalist society fighting for self-government or even independence, had been a mirage created by Francoist repression. Given the possibility of expressing their will freely and democratically, the Basques demonstrated in every election and opinion poll that only a little more than half of them defined themselves as nationalists. Within Basque society multiple types of Spanish–Basque–European identities existed along with those who identified themselves as purely Basque or Spanish. Thus, the obstacles to a broadening of Basque self-government could not only be attributed to Spanish 'repression': They were consubstantial to the pluralistic Basque society itself. Thus, it is obvious that, if more and more nationalists, who might agree with the political aims of ETA, refused the armed struggle in the new context of democracy and regional autonomy, those Basques who did not consider themselves nationalists would oppose with even more emphasis the use of terror for the achievement of political goals. Public surveys confirm this slow, but finally visible change of mind produced in the Basque society of the 1980s. In 1979 17 per cent of the Basque population described the ETA activists as 'patriots'; ten years later this figure had dropped to 5 per cent. In the same period, the percentage of Basques, who regarded the *etarras* as 'idealists' decreased from 33 to 18 per cent, while those who considered ETA members 'lunatics' or 'common criminals' increased from 13 to 32 per cent.[63]

This change of mind was also a consequence of the greater proximity of ETA activity since the end of the 1980s and during the 1990s. As indicated above, the three bombs with the greatest number of fatal victims, had all been exploded outside the Basque Country. Madrid was another place with a high number of victims. If ETA acted in the Basque territory, most of the victims were members of the different police forces or the military, nearly all of them being from other Spanish regions. This is what the journalist L. Rincón has called the 'social and physical remoteness'[64] of terrorism, which in the conscience of many Basques acted as a barrier, transforming terrorism into a phenomenon without direct personal relevance. This situation changed when, from the end of the 1980s, ETA started broadening the groups of possible targets. In 1988, in the Basque towns of Eibar and Elgoibar two locally very popular persons were killed after having been charged by

Table 7.4.1 The public image of ETA activists

	1978	1979	1989
Patriots	13	17	5
Idealists	35	33	18
Manipulated	33	29	11
Lunatics	11	8	16
Criminals	7	5	16
Don't know	1	8	34

Source: Llera, *Los vascos*, p. 103.

ETA with drug-dealing. Very few people believed this accusation, and even those who thought that ETA might have been right, rejected the 'death penalty' as absolutely disproportionate. The shock and stupor caused by the assassinations ended as a popular revulsion of ETA. During the 1990s, the paramilitaries continued acting against Basques, even against members of the PNV or the nationalist union ELA. The long periods, during which three Basque businessmen were kidnapped by ETA (1993: Iglesias Zamora; 1995: Aldaya; 1996: Delclaux), as well as the capture for 532 days of the prison-worker Ortega Lara or the assassination of the young PP town councillor Blanco (both in 1996), were further important milestones in the process of increasing Basque abhorrence and rejection of ETA violence. In the 1990s, it was no longer possible to be neutral towards ETA. If the suffering of the relatives of a killed Spanish Guardia Civil had only been indirectly present in the Basque living rooms via their TV screens, the personal experience of seeing or hearing about the tears of a neighbour or a friend of that neighbour caused a much more direct and impacting experience in a small area like the Basque Country, where the network of social relations has not yet been totally disrupted by the anonymity of postmodern mass society. This was the background, which made important sectors of Basque society abandon their traditional attitude of more or less complaisant silence[65] and show in public their disagreement, rejection or loathing for ETA violence.

Within this changing context since the end of the 1980s, Basque civil society would play an active part in the shaping of a political process, which would lead to the first unilateral, indefinite ceasefire ever called by ETA. The first popular demonstration against violence, however, had already been held in 1978, organized by the PNV. About 35,000 Basques demonstrated in Bilbao for a 'Basque Country in Peace and Freedom'. The ambiguous wording of the slogan that without any concrete reference to violence could be endorsed even by ETA supporters indicated that the time was not yet ripe for more explicit criticism of the armed group. After so many years of critical solidarity and the traumatic experience of Francoism, in 1978 and during the following years the attitude of the PNV leaders towards ETA was not as clear as the demonstration implied. Basically for two reasons it was difficult to break completely with the paramilitaries. First, many democratic nationalists considered the *etarras* as the 'lost sons' of the huge nationalist family, who in reality had the same, correct political aims, but the wrong strategy. Secondly, terrorism was quite helpful as an additional pressure in the negotiations with the central government for the implementation of autonomy. It is unrealistic to blame only the PNV for its ambivalence towards the persistence of ETA violence, but the fact remained that, while unease and discontent with terrorism was growing in civil society, the PNV and the rest of the political parties were unable to find a solution to the problem. This is the context in which the Basque peace movement would emerge.

The first attempt to coordinate the different groups and initiatives created before was realized in 1989 with the foundation of the Coordinadora Gesto por la Paz de *Euskal Herria* (Coordination for a Gesture for Peace in the Basque Country). Since then, Gesto has developed and can be considered one of the most dynamic and representative organizations in the peace movement. It has been very successful among Basque youth. In 1997, from about 160 local groups integrated in the Coordinadora, 40 were linked to schools or universities. There are only a few statistics available for the number and the social profile of the members, but it has been calculated that the average age is not much higher than 25 years.[66] According to a survey from the end of 1992, neither the political parties, nor the labour unions played any outstanding role in the shaping of the Basque peace movement.[67]

The name 'Gesto por la Paz' is a reference to the group's decision to hold silent protests after every act of political violence involving the death of victims. During the long kidnapping of the industrialist Aldaya in May of 1995, Gesto added a silent act of protest every Monday evening to petition for the release of the hostage. Since then until February of 1998, the members of Gesto have organized a total of about 15,760 silent protest meetings in 150 places of the Basque Country.[68] A key aim is to carry the rejection of violence from the streets to everyday life of Basque society. The group invented the symbol of a blue ribbon, which since one of the last acts of kidnapping (of the industrialist Julio Iglesias Zamora) became more and more visible on people's clothing, on TV screens, in newspapers, placards and even on the Internet. The increasing success of the popular mobilizations promoted by Gesto provoked the reaction of the Basque Liberation Movement, which, afraid of losing the control of the streets, started to organize simultaneous counter-demonstrations everywhere a Gesto group appeared. The tension raised on these occasions led to the intervention of the Basque police, who would form a kind of *cordon sanitaire* between the opponents in order to defend the Gesto pacifists against possible aggressions from the other side.[69]

The core element in the ideology and the discourse of Gesto por la Paz is the total rejection of the idea that in certain circumstances the use of violence might be legitimate for the achievement of political aims. It is a discourse based on ethics, in which any kind of violence is condemned. Significantly, one of the major acts this peace group used to organize is the demonstration on the day Gandhi was assassinated. The task of Gesto focuses on the promotion of a conscience-raising process to undermine the mental basis of political violence in Basque society. This does not mean that the political implications of violence are denied, but, according to one of the veterans of Gesto, 'our task does not consist in presenting concrete political solutions to the problem'.[70]

Despite this auto-restriction of the work done by Gesto, the group's ideas and proposals do not elude the political debate. In general terms, these pacifists are backing the idea that the way out of the conflict must be that of a 'solución dialogada', that is a solution agreed upon by dialogue. In the above-quoted interview, X. Azkazibar, one of the senior members of the organization, distinguishes between three levels of dialogue. The first is political, carried out between parties and institutions with an accredited democratic legitimacy. The key issues on the agenda of this first stage of dialogue would be the problem of self-determination and the transfer or pardon of the prisoners. On a second, social, level of the dialogue, all interested citizens and especially the social movements would be involved. Finally, on a third level ('nivel fáctico') the dialogue/negotiations would be between the state and ETA, its principal aim being the achievement of 'the end of armed violence' and the establishment of conditions that would facilitate the fulfilment of this objective. The only basic, indispensable precondition for these talks between the state and ETA would be the exclusion of political issues, which have to be discussed and agreed upon by the Basque citizens.

Gesto por la Paz is politically a very heterogeneous organization, drawing support from voters from nearly all political parties in the Basque Country except HB and PP. The group has undergone some splits during the last few years (Bakea Orain = Peace Now; Denon Artean = Among All of Us), but none of these groups has matched Gesto's capacity for mobilization.[71]

The origins of the other mass-mobilizing peace group called Elkarri ('One to the Other', or 'Mutually') can be found in the Basque National Liberation Movement. Elkarri, was founded in 1992, the same year that the ETA leadership structure was dismantled. It came about as the result of the transformation of a single-issue ecologist organization close to radical nationalism (Lurraldea). At first, Elkarri's public performance was stigmatized as the result of a new strategy of ETA and HB's aimed at breaking the cohesion of the democratic parties in their attitude towards ETA. In recent years however, this image has changed, basically for two reasons. Firstly, Elkarri has demonstrated in public and after each of ETA's acts its profound opposition to the violent nature of political struggles. Consequently, it has become a target of severe HB and ETA disapproval. Secondly, the leaders of the group have proved the coherence between their discourse and their day-to-day activities on plenty of occasions. They try to avoid all reasoning and activity that might contribute to increasing the polarization between the different sectors of society. Their discourse evolves in the spheres between the opposite poles of black and white, good and bad, criminals and heroes. Elkarri's leadership has endeavoured to establish links with the different contenders in the conflict. As a result, the group has gained a positive reputation. It is accepted – despite all criticism – by all political parties from HB to PP as a serious partner, worthy at least of being heard and taken on board. This capacity for building bridges between the extremes of the political spectrum is not really very usual in the highly polarized Basque society. Since the process of political realignment leading to the Lizarra Agreement and the ceasefire, however, this generally positive image of the group has been jeopardized as a consequence of the reproach formulated by the non-nationalist parties, according to which Elkarri was accused of giving up its independence after joining the Nationalist Front. Ever since, the conservative PP has boycotted any initiative organized by Elkarri.

In comparison to Gesto, Elkarri – working with a staff of 13 full-time employees and coordinating about 2,500 members and collaborators – considers politics the principal arena for its activity, not ethics:

> Its main purpose is to promote a process of democratic dialogue in *Euskal Herria* for the transformation of conflict through social mediation.[72]

This implies a critical attitude towards all those pacifists like Gesto that stress the ethical dimension of the conflict. For Elkarri it is impossible to separate ethics from politics in the analysis of the Basque conflict. According to this argument, violence is rooted in a contention between a significant part of Basque society and the Spanish state, in which the distribution of political power and, finally, the right of the Basque people to achieve self-determination are the issues at stake. Elkarri, like all Basque nationalists, backs this right.[73] According to the group's analysis, the already century-old confrontation between those who claim self-determination and the power-holders who deny this right has provoked the intensification of the struggle and – since the 1960s – the rise of political violence not exclusively carried out by ETA.

Over the last few years, Elkarri has performed a very broad repertoire of mobilization that has included the collection of signatures, debates between and workshops with policy-makers, publications, creation of educational material for the school and public demonstrations, the main objective of all these activities being the breaking-down of intransigence as the main obstacle to peace. One of the highlights of the group's work previous to the cease-fire was the peace proposal called Izan ('To be') presented in November 1997. It anticipated some of the basic ideas of President Ardanza's March 1998 peace proposal, which – after being harshly rejected by the non-nationalist parties, kick-started the political realignment and the subsequent process, which led to the Lizarra Agreement and the truce.

The openly political character of Elkarri carries an evident double risk: first, the efficacy of the work will depend, much more than in the case of Gesto, on the support of the political parties. From the moment, in which a concrete political proposal is adopted and defended, the peace group will be looked upon as one more political contender in the conflict and its proposal will immediately raise support or criticism. Consequently, the group's image of neutrality and its capacity of brokering agreements are likely to decrease. The post-Lizarra situation seems to confirm this thesis. A second point is, that – due to its political implications – the peace group becomes vulnerable to the criticism of those reluctant to accept the intervention of organizations without electoral mandate and parliamentary representation in the solution of political problems. This criticism has been formulated against the organizations which tried to set up a 'third space', one of them being Elkarri, as we shall see further below.

Besides Gesto, Bakea Orain, Denon Artean and Elkarri, the spectrum of the Basque peace and human rights movement is made up of other minor groups, some of which form part of the National Liberation Movement like Senideak (relatives of the ETA-prisoners and refugees) or Gestoras Pro Amnistia (organization demanding a total amnesty for all ETA-prisoners).[74] On the non- or anti-nationalist side, organizations like 'Asociación de Víctimas del Terrorismo' represent the relatives of the victims. The 'Foro de Ermua' and the initiative 'Basta Ya' are groups of anti-nationalist hardline intellectuals and politicians, who oppose any concession to terrorism, while considering nationalism the real root of terrorism. Except for these three latter organizations – the Ermua Forum and 'Basta Ya' had not yet been founded at that time – Elkarri promoted a round-table debate between all these groups, which in the 'Maroño Agreement' (January 1994) called to 'substitute all expressions of violence by mechanisms of dialogue as the best route to peace'.[75] The subsequent attempts to introduce a more political dimension into the agreement by discussing the roots of the conflict and possible solutions (self-determination) broke the fragile union of the peace groups. After the kidnapping and assassination of the young town councillor Blanco in the summer of 1997 and the refusal of Senideak and Gestoras to condemn this act, the cooperation and discussion between the different groups was definitively brought to an end.[76]

What is the balance of the peace movement's activities in the Basque Country? Or, returning to our introductory remarks in this chapter, can any evidence be found to prove that the Basque process leading to the ceasefire was, at least partially, a bottom-up exercise, instead of a phenomenon managed by the political elites? Neither in the text of the Lizarra Agreement, nor in the wording of the ETA communiqués was there any direct hint of the importance (or insignificance) of the peace groups. This influence, and its positive results, however, are visible in the area of consciousness. At the end of the 1990s, Basque society made important efforts to leave behind the long period of lethargy in which violence was, if not openly backed, at least accepted as something normal with a frequent and inevitable presence in everyday life. A new sensitivity towards all expressions of violence arose and the level of legitimacy of the armed struggle decreased even among many Basques close to the Liberation Movement. As already indicated above, there is a wealth of data confirming this impression. Asked for the personal 'opinion or attitude towards ETA in this moment', between 1981 and 1996 the percentage of Basque citizens who expressed their 'total support' for ETA came down from 8 to 1 per cent. During the same period, the percentage of those manifesting their 'total rejection' rose by 28 points.

Table 7.4.2 Attitude of the Basque citizens towards ETA (in percentages)

	1981	1987	1996
Total support	8	1	1
Critical support	4	6	5
Aims yes, means no	3	12	11
Before yes, now no	12	19	18
Indifferent	1	2	2
Fear	1	4	7
Total rejection	23	34	51
No response	48	22	5

Source: Funes, *Salida*, p. 197.

According to another public opinion survey done in 1997, 84.1 per cent of the youth in the most nationalist Basque province, Gipuzkoa, declares itself 'opposed to the violence of armed groups'.[77] Basque youth, traditionally more given to radical nationalism than other sectors of society, seem to have developed a special attachment to this new sensitivity. The surveys register an involution in the attitudes shown by the young people aged from 18 to 29 towards ETA violence. The sociologist J. Elzo has summed up this impression: 'the young people have been ETA's source of supply, in the future they are going to be the organization's gravediggers'. The new critical sensitivity concerning ETA violence has also been present in the streets. The massive demonstrations during the summer of 1997 as an answer to the kidnapping of Ortega Lara and the assassination of the PP town councillor from the little town of Ermua mobilized a total of about six million Basques and Spaniards. In November of that year, according to the survey quoted above, nearly five out of every 10 Basques (47 per cent) said that they had participated in one or more of the demonstrations organized to protest against ETA. After the summer mobilizations, politicians and the media started talking about the so-called 'spirit of Ermua' that has been interpreted as a grassroots call to stop violence and to endorse unity against terrorism. Nevertheless, the increasing rejection of violence – and this was not only the case of the youth but of society in general – did not close the door to a negotiated way out of the conflict. The sum of those backing contacts with ETA with or without ceasefire was 65 per cent (43 per cent with ceasefire; 22 per cent even without). Only 22 per cent of the Basque population rejected any contact with ETA.[78]

In short, the peace movement played an important role in the process of consciousness-raising. It helped Basque society to leave behind the period of silence and to enter a new phase of active mobilization against violence and in favour of peace. It shaped a new dualism, in which a tougher rejection of ETA and all forms of violence went hand in hand with growing support for a negotiated way out of the conflict. Like all social movements, the peace movement in the Basque Country has been (and still is) both a product of this process of (ideological and mental) transformation of society, as well as an actor intervening and promoting it. Even if the work of Elkarri, Gesto and the other groups has not yet been very fertile in the political arena, it has contributed to creating a new context in which – unlike only a very few years ago – proposals endorsing dialogue based upon solutions of the conflict can no longer be considered the fruits of wishful thinking born of the minds of some dreaming pacifist Utopians. Without the day-to-day work of the different peace groups, both the September 1998 ceasefire and the previous political process, which, despite all the errors which were committed, smoothed the path to the truce, would have hardly been imaginable. The peace groups did their job, but it was, and still is, up to the political parties to transform the popular call for a settlement into tangible political proposals. At the end of the 1990s, within this context of grassroots mobilization for peace, a new attempt to find a peaceful settlement of the conflict was put into practice.

8
Give Peace a Chance: on the Way to the Ceasefire

During the 1990s, the decline of radical nationalism, the military and political weakness of ETA, and the pressure articulated by the peace movement were some of the factors which helped shape favourable circumstances for new efforts towards peace in the Basque Country. Yet, other elements were still necessary in order to mobilize the structure of Basque politics and to operationalize the new opportunities. Scholars like Sydney Tarrow or Charles Tilly[1] have emphasized different kinds of alteration within the ruling elite as some of the most decisive triggers of mobilization. Conflicts between elite groups, the shift of traditional political alignments and, consequently, the availability of new allies are some of the theoretical ingredients usually mentioned by authors close to the political opportunity structure theory. My point is that in the explanation of the 1990s political process in the Basque Country, besides the factors indicated above, this triple alteration of the Basque political system was the most important catalyst which definitively mobilized Basque politics and kick-started the process leading to the truce of the summer of 1998. Translated into the Basque context, the triple alteration produced the crisis and final breakdown of the relationship between nationalists and non-nationalists, the rapprochement between moderate and radical nationalism, and, finally, the open alliance between both sectors of Basque nationalism. Since in the eyes of Basque nationalists the Irish example seemed to corroborate the political efficiency of this new strategy not only in terms of new parliamentary majorities, but also as a means of de-escalating violence, a further important argument was available to continue exploring the possibilities of the new pan-nationalist strategy. The question of how to tackle the problem of ETA prisoners offered a first opportunity to bring together both branches of Basque nationalism.

8.1 The problem of the prisoners

From the time the police scored its first successes against ETA, the group's prisoner collective has always played an important role within the Basque

National Liberation Movement. In 1970, during the famous Burgos trial, the 16 ETA prisoners used the publicity to campaign against the regime and in favour of their ideas. In the opinion of Basque and Spanish democrats, they became heroes of the anti-fascist resistance. Their popularity helped them to mobilize a wave of popular protest even in the Basque region, Spain and other European countries. When even the Vatican intervened with a petition for clemency, Franco no longer dared to carry out the six death penalties, commuting them to long prison sentences. But in the history of ETA the Burgos trial is also significant for another reason, because neither in Burgos, nor in any other later circumstance were the important political and strategic decisions taken in the prisons and by the prisoners, however popular they might have been. During its history, ETA has demonstrated a surprising capacity for reorganizing its own leadership after police successes, maintaining its headquarters and centres of decision-taking in the underground outside the prisons. Thus, it was those militants who controlled the arms who decided the organization's future. This had also become clear during the talks in Algeria, where a more flexible and political-minded Antxon was unable to convince the underground leadership of the advantages that continuing the negotiations with the Spanish government might bring. The consequence of this problem was that during the 40 years of ETA history, the balance between military and political reasoning was generally favourable to the former. Those activists who tried to correct this uneven relationship were likely to end up losing influence on the group.

Owing to the strong link between the control of the arms and the internal political empowerment of those who possessed the arms, the role of the prisoners within the Liberation Movement was not a political, but a symbolic one. The fact that on several occasions the ETA underground leadership designated different prisoners as the organization's spokesmen for hypothetical contacts with the government or political parties did not really change this circumstance. According to the philosophy of the Liberation Movement, the political prisoners symbolize the existence of a political conflict with the Spanish (or French) state and their unwillingness to give up their militancy or to abdicate from the armed struggle is interpreted as an heroic sacrifice of their personal interest for the Basque nation's benefit and its fight for freedom. On the contrary, those prisoners who might consider a return to civil life automatically become the anti-heroes, the collaborator with the enemy, charged with betrayal and, in an extreme case, sentenced to death by the organization. When during the 1980s the policy of reinsertion put into operation by the first socialist government of Felipe González became one of the core elements in the government's anti-terrorism strategy, ETA decided to act in order to prevent their prisoners from accepting the offer made by Madrid. Prisoners who had not been convicted of blood-crimes were offered release from prison, if they signed a legal document declaring that they were willing to renounce violence, to break all links with

ETA, to respect the law and to acknowledge the suffering they had caused. María Dolores González Catarain, Yoyes, was the first former member of the ETA-m leadership to take up this opportunity. In 1984, after apparently having received the permission of their former comrades, or at least part of them, Yoyes returned from exile in Mexico to her hometown in the Basque Country. While the social reinsertion of this high-ranking ETA member became an important political triumph for the authorities, it also became more and more dangerous for the paramilitaries, who saw their control over the prisoner collective jeopardized. In September 1986 – as already mentioned – Yoyes was shot dead in the marketplace of her hometown Ordizia in the presence of her young son.

This assassination provoked incredulity and protest even within sectors of the Liberation Movement, but it also cut off the way to social reinsertion as a means of conflict de-escalation, since the paramilitary leadership recovered total control of the prisoners. When after the breakdown of the conversations in Algeria all hopes for a negotiated settlement were aborted, the González administration introduced a major shift in its penal policy by distributing about 500 ETA prisoners in small groups throughout all Spanish jails, including those of the Canary Islands, which were about 4000 km away from the Basque Country. As Von Tangen Page puts it, this policy of dispersion was put forward with the intention of 'destroy(ing) group cohesiveness and thus encourage the prisoners to defect and accept social reinsertion'.[2]

When in 1996 the conservatives came to power, the new administration of President José María Aznar, who during the electoral campaign had strongly ciritizised the socialists for what Aznar considered an indulgent attitude towards ETA terrorism and its prisoners, continued with his predecessor's policy of dispersion. Lacking an overall majority, Aznar depended on the votes of the Catalan and Basque moderate nationalists and, as a consequence, his pre-electoral ideas and proposals concerning a tougher policy of anti-terrorism had to be postponed. At the end of the 1990s, when the political process leading to the ceasefire was started, the dispersion of the prisoners had already proved unable to achieve its aims. Neither had a significant number of prisoners chosen the way to social reinsertion, nor had the iron control exercised by the paramilitary leadership on the prisoners been seriously questioned. On the contrary, now even the relatives of the ETA militants in jail became more directly linked to the Liberation Movement and its organizations such as Gestoras Pro Amnistia or Senideak, which organized and sponsored the long and very costly travel expenses to the prisons, where the prisoners were usually allowed to receive only two twenty-minute visits a week (or in some prisons one of 40 minutes). According to a spokesman of Senideak, the organization representing the interests of the prisoners' relatives, the families spend yearly about 3,000 million pesetas on these trips, that is about 18.3 million euro.[3] Instead of breaking the cohesiveness of the compact microcosm of the prisoners, these grievances produced the opposite result.[4] Furthermore, the prison policy encouraged ETA to open a new front targeting all prison workers, who were blamed for being willing lackeys of the Spanish repression against the Basque people. The above-mentioned cruel kidnapping of Ortega Lara is only one of the most spectacular examples – followed by many others with fatal outcomes on several occasions – of this new escalation of paramilitary violence.

As a consequence of the Spanish governments' unwillingness to reconsider its penal policy, during the 1990s one of the first steps on the way to the pan-nationalist *entente* was taken precisely in this area. Despite their alliance with Aznar's administration, the moderate nationalists got increasingly upset because they felt that the Spanish government was only interested in administering the problem of violence for its own political benefit, instead of trying to find a solution to it. In fact, when the PNV signed the pact of parliamentary cooperation with Aznar, the problem of peacemaking was excluded from the agreement. Backed by opinion polls which revealed that a broad majority of Basque citizens were opposed to the penal policy of dispersion as being contrary to human rights, the Basque nationalists started mobilizing against this policy not only out of humanitarian concern, but also for political reasons: a shift in penal policy could be regarded by ETA as a confidence-building measure and was thus likely to bring about some response in terms of conflict de-escalation by the paramilitaries. From this point of view, the demand for a transfer of the prisoners to Basque jails, which was one of the already traditional demands of the Liberation Movement, might become a worthy tool if a peace process was to be kick-started.

Yet the first step in this campaign against dispersion was already negotiated a few months before Aznar came into office. In December 1995, the Basque parliament passed a resolution urging the Spanish government to transfer all the prisoners of Basque origin to prisons in the Basque Country. This resolution had neither been backed by the Socialist nor the Conservative parties, but by the nationalist and leftist majority. A consequence of this initiative was the drawing up of a concise plan to approach all the Basque prisoners to the four prisons in the Basque Country, as well as to another ten prisons near the Basque borders. A total of 826 Basque prisoners were located elsewhere.[5] Taking into account only those prisoners with a political background, that is ETA members or supporters, the number was reduced to 554 in April 97.[6] Graph 8.1.1 shows the geographic distribution of these prisoners throughout the different Spanish and French prisons, indicating as well the distance between these centres and the Basque Country.

Besides the already mentioned humanitarian and political considerations, the principal argument of the promoters of the plan was a juridical one, since in their opinion the plan's implementation would be nothing else but

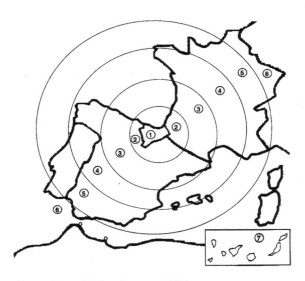

Graph 8.1.1 Dispersion of ETA prisoners (1997)

1. Basque Country	30 prisoners
2. Less than 300 km	41 prisoners
3. 300–600 km	205 prisoners
4. 600–900 km	124 prisoners
5. 900–1,200 km	122 prisoners
6. 1,200–1,500 km	17 prisoners
7. 2,600 km	15 prisoners
Total:	**554 prisoners**

Source: *Egin*, 25 April 1997.

an implementation of the existing law. In fact, the General Penitentiary Law (1979) indicates that the administration in charge of the penal system should 'endeavour' (*procurar*) to accommodate the prisoners in centres near their homes, in order to 'prevent a social uprooting of the convicts' (Art. 12.1). In September 1996, the European parliament adopted a resolution with a similar content.[7] Yet it was obvious that the initiative of the Basque parliament in the field of penal policy was not only carried out in order to grant the implementation of a certain law, but aimed, in the short run, at the freeing of the hostage Ortega Lara, and in the long run, at the brokering of a peace process.

However, once again the crude political reality buried all optimistic expectations. Lacking the support of the two strongest political parties in the Spanish parliament, the Basque initiative was born pretty lame. Moreover, not even ETA's political partner Herri Batasuna felt comfortable with it, since it was an initiative which had escaped the control of the Liberation Movement, and HB could not accept that the democratic nationalists transformed one of the very few really popular claims in the discourse of radical nationalism into their own political benefit. Furthermore, an open support of the plan would also have contributed to legitimizing the Basque system of regional autonomy and its institutions, which had traditionally been rejected by ETA and HB. Finally, HB adopted some kind of in-between attitude, which was closer to a rejection of the initiative than to its support, arguing that not all the prisons included in the plan were located in the Basque Country and that therefore the plan was not a real tool for the ending of the dispersion policy. When a delegation of the Basque parliament's Commission on Human Rights visited Txikierdi, the speaker of the ETA prisoners, he rejected the plan and refused to discuss any petition related to the fate of the hostage Ortega Lara. The reaction of the Spanish Minister of the Interior was not very different, since he even refused to meet the delegates of the Basque parliament, considering that they had put him on the same level as an ETA criminal. The minister Mayor Oreja needed about two months to reconsider his decision and finally meet the president of the Commission. A month later, in June 1997, his response was delivered to the media; in his opinion, there was not one single reason to change the penal policy. Besides raising a series of virtually insurmountable technical problems, a general transfer of the prisoners would be a total political mistake, since it would be looked upon as a victory for ETA. Consequently, any transfer of a certain prisoner could only be the result of an individual case-by-case study.[8]

So far, nothing new under the sun: once again a timid initiative of conflict de-escalation had failed in the Basque Country. The hardliners both of ETA and the conservative Spanish government were unwilling to move, not one single step towards confidence-building was taken and the Basque stalemate continued blocking any attempt to settle the conflict. Yet, there was one novelty. For the first time, democratic nationalists and radical nationalists of the Liberation Movement had shared in public a claim with a humanitarian, but also with a political background, even if HB was keen to display its disagreement with the technical details of the plan drawn up by the Basque parliament. However, in 1997 this coincidence could not yet be transformed into open cooperation, since the political system in the Basque Country and its major cleavage between the nationalist and non-nationalist democratic bloc on the one side, and the radical supporters of violence on the other, had not yet been directly challenged. When in the summer of 1997 the initiative on penal policy came to a (temporary) end, very few Basque politicians and journalists could imagine that only a year later, thanks to the break-up of the political alignments, this challenge of the Basque political system would become a reality. Yet this alteration should not have been that surprising, since the principal advocates of a political reorientation within democratic nationalism had been thinking about the outline of a new strategy for years.

8.2 The break-up of traditional political alignments

During the second half of the 1990s, Basque politics changed completely. The party system went from a long period of consolidation into a new phase of confusion, conflict and strategic realignment. Political parties, which had been allies for years, became antagonistic enemies. The main cleavage separating (nationalist and non-nationalist) democrats from the (radical nationalist) supporters of violence disappeared. It was substituted by the cleavage between two political blocs: the pan-nationalists, and the non-nationalist (or Spanish nationalist) bloc. In September 1998, ETA demonstrated its agreement to this process of political realignment by announcing the ceasefire.

This chapter deals with the reasons for this transformation of the Basque political landscape. If this mutation is to be explained, it is not enough to look for the good guy and the bad guy to blame for what many observers call the destruction of the unity of democrats or, later, the new offensive of terrorism. My point is that the political alteration was not the result of a unilateral strategic decision taken by a certain actor, but of the confluence of different circumstances and decisions taken by different actors. Neither was the PNV's political shift the consequence of an evil plan of ethnic cleansing and nationalist authoritarianism, nor was the increasingly virulent antinationalism of the socialists and conservatives the product of Spanish nationalists' desire to destroy Basque nationalism and its very roots in society. Yet this attempt to avoid simplistic black-and-white approaches and to look for multi-causal models of explanation does not mean that the attention paid to the complexity of the structural context while asking for the reasons of certain patterns of political behaviour should be carried out without asking for the consequences of this behaviour. On the contrary, the fatal outcome of that experience after the ceasefire was cancelled places the question of the errors committed during the process in the agenda of historians or social scientists who oppose postmodern nihilism and have not yet completely lost the conviction of the enlightening and emancipating effect that a better knowledge of the past might provide for a better future. In other words, the breakdown of the ceasefire, the following return of political terror with a much higher intensity than ever before and the subsequent deepest crisis of the Basque political system since the restoration of democracy are reasons enough to analyse the alteration of Basque politics during the 1990s, taking into account both structural circumstances and the decisions of the political parties, understood as human agencies with responsibility for their activity and per definition guided by their goal of conquering larger spaces of power. As we shall see, both the shape of consensus politics cutting across the nationalist/non-nationalist cleavage during the 1980s, and the shift towards politics of confrontation and polarization along the line of that cleavage during the second half of the 1990s are as much the results of a particular political context as of the parties' struggle for power and the decisions taken according to calculated strategies, which were supposed to be beneficial for that struggle.

The Basque parties' search for consensus after the dictator's death in 1975 was a direct consequence of the traumatic and to some extent unexpected experience: the experience that a policy of devolution was unable to bring an end to ETA terrorism, considered by observers of nearly all political colours as the most dangerous challenge to the young democracy. After 1975 there was a broad agreement among most of the political actors that the end of terrorism required some kind of satisfaction of the historical Basque wish to establish self-government. This basic agreement did not exclude controversial discussions about the extent and the level this self-government should reach. The increasing ETA violence as well as the growing nervousness and conspiratorial activities among right-wing militaries during the years of the transition put permanent pressure on the politicians. When the Spanish president Suárez and the Basque nationalist leader Garaikoetxea negotiated the details of the Basque Statute of Autonomy during a dramatic night-session, they were both aware that in case of a breakdown in the negotiations the country would run the risk of a violent confrontation between Basques and Spaniards, and in more than one political commentary the danger of a new civil war was mentioned.[9] Finally, as I have pointed out above, autonomy was passed and ratified in a referendum, after which the negotiations for its specific implementation started.

Yet it was not long before it became evident that it was an infantile illusion to hope that this first important step towards Basque self-government would produce an immediate impact on the paramilitaries. After 1979, ETA violence indeed diminished, but it did not disappear completely. Moreover, contrary to what occurred for example in Germany with the Baader-Meinhof Group or in Italy with the Red Brigades, ETA terrorism was not the result of the political desperation of some petit-bourgeois individuals who lacked any significant roots in society. ETA's political violence in the Basque Country continued receiving the support of a minority, but not a negligible part of Basque society. Owing to its emotional and symbolic power ETA had become the centrepiece of the political, social and cultural microcosm made up by the organizational network of the Basque National Liberation Movement.

One of the reasons that might explain the continuity of ETA violence despite the devolution policy was the lack of a common strategy by the democratic (nationalist and non-nationalist) parties when tackling the problem of terrorism. The major clash was between those, usually nationalists, who emphasized the political nature of the problem, and the rest of the parties. As a consequence, in the nationalists' opinion the resolution of the problem required political measures, not police pressure alone. For parties like the leading PNV, EE or later EA, the major obstacle on the way to peace was the Spanish government's unwillingness to fully implement the Statute of Gernika. This same argument was interpreted by the state-located socialist and conservative parties into a crude, polemical attack against the nationalists, who were blamed for the persistence of terrorism, because they were said to have no interest in an end to violence since they got political benefit from it. If violence itself was already a serious and painful problem for society, its polarizing effect on the political parties gave it an even more central and traumatic transcendence within post-Francoist Spain.

It took some years for the political parties to realize that the only one who really benefited from their polemics was ETA. Policy-makers became aware of the growing gap between a society that desired peace, and a political system immersed in never-ending polemics, incapable of designing any kind of basic consensus concerning violence. Hence, it was society and the brutality of terrorism, which pushed the politicians towards an agreement. After the bloodiest period of ETA terrorism during the last trimester of 1987, when ETA killed a total of 32 people with two bombs, the first agreement between all political parties in the Basque parliament – except for HB – was signed. The promoter of the agreement and the chairman of the previous negotiations was the Basque president Ardanza and it was in the president's official residence 'Ajuria Enea' where the Agreement for the Pacification and Normalization of *Euskadi* was signed on 12 January 1988. That is why the agreement is known as the 'Pact of Ajuria Enea'.

The Agreement contained three fundamental statements. Its basic starting point was the common rejection of all attempts to reach political aims by means of violence. The violent paramilitaries would not have any right either to represent the will of the people, or to take part in any political negotiations, which could only take place among the 'legitimate representatives of the popular will'.[10]

The second statement consisted in the reaffirmation of the nexus between the full development of the autonomy and the subsequent 'progressive resolution of the conflicts of the Basque society' as a contribution to the 'reinforcement of democracy and peaceful coexistence'. All the signatories confirmed their willingness to contribute to the complete implementation of autonomy, while leaving the door open to a future revision of the Statute of Autonomy by the means established in the Constitution and the Statute itself, since it was Basque society that had to decide on the 'validity or invalidity of the Statute as an instrument of self-government'.

The third important assessment expressed in the 'Pact of Ajuria Enea' referred to a solution of the conflict based on dialogue. After stating that 'all political ideas democratically expressed can be defended within the parliamentary framework' and offering the possibility of 'social rehabilitation' to all those who had decided to 'abandon violence', in point 10 of the agreement the parties formulated the possibility of a 'dialogue between the competent powers of the state and those willing to abandon violence', if certain conditions were given.

During its ten years of existence, president Ardanza chaired a total of 32 formal meetings of the Pact's members. The Agreement's main achievement was its contribution to the strengthening of anti-violence feeling in Basque society. It created a new cleavage separating those backing the use of violence for political purposes from those who rejected this idea. This rift overlaps and cuts across the historical one dividing Basque and Spanish identities. Despite the political controversies between the parties, once the text was signed, there was no longer any real basis for criticizing any of the parties for their ambiguous attitude towards violence. This was, of course, also a consequence of the fact that during the 1990s members of all the parties – including occasionally the nationalists – became targets of ETA.

The common rejection of violence as a tool for political bargaining created an atmosphere of mutual confidence between the Basque parties, which enabled them to discuss their disagreements with each other and to find at the end basic points of consensus. The most evident indicator of this ability to bridge the gap separating nationalists from non-nationalists is the coalition between the nationalist PNV and the Basque branch of the Spanish socialist party after the loss of the PNV majority due to the party's split and the foundation of Eusko Alkartasuna. Between 1987 and 1998, this coalition in the different governments headed by the *Lehendakari* José Antonio Ardanza became the axis of Basque politics. It was the best proof that in the Basque Country the clash between competing identities, cultures and policies did not suppose any insurmountable barrier between two clearly defined, closed communities. The political party that most benefited from this situation was the PNV. As a moderate party of the democratic centre and with a long historical experience of combining the defence of long-run claims with an opportunistic and pragmatic day-to-day policy, the PNV took advantage of its appeal as a partner for any of the other parties. Its coalition with the Basque socialists was helpful for the negotiations with the central government during the era of President Felipe González. Yet, when the Spanish socialists left power and the elections of 1996 brought the conservative leader José María Aznar into office, the PNV president Xabier Arzallus negotiated the party's vote of confidence for Aznar in return for remarkable gains especially in economic terms, while at the same time maintaining the coalition with the socialists in the Basque government and exploring new contacts with HB.

At the end of the 1990s, this political climate of negotiated contention reigning among the parties of the so-called 'Democratic Bloc' in the Basque Country came to an end. Just as ten years ago the Ajuria Enea Agreement had been the centre-piece upon which this policy of consensus had been built, now it became the origin of a major conflict and, as a consequence, of a political realignment. The first fundamental disagreements became evident as early as 1993, when the National Assembly of the conservative Popular Party voted for a programmatic document on terrorism, which included two demands opposed to the text and the spirit of the Ajuria Enea

Agreement: first, that the prisoners convicted for terrorism should in no case be released before having served their complete sentence in prison, excluding all possibilities of reducing the duration of their sentences offered to all prisoners by the penal law, and second, that no negotiations should be carried out with any terrorist group, even if its members were willing to lay down their arms. This resolution was part of a broader radical strategy against the ruling socialist government, which was blamed for being too indulgent to terrorism and therefore, according to Aznar's conservatives, should be voted out of power. Hence, the PP started moving away from the common anti-terrorism consensus, because its tougher attitude concerning Basque terrorism was supposed to produce an electoral dividend, as in fact occurred in 1996.

On the other hand, the leadership of moderate nationalism, including the Basque President Ardanza, was gradually reaching towards a more critical interpretation of the Ajuria Enea Agreement. The PNV leaders criticized the fact that the Agreement had been handled as a defensive instrument in the struggle against terrorism, and not as a useful strategy for the achievement of peace. The argument was that if ten years after the Agreement had been signed violence was still continuing, something must have failed. Something was wrong, if nothing had changed concerning the percentage of 12 to 15 per cent of the voters who continued supporting an openly anti-system and pro-ETA party like HB, a party which had always rejected the Agreement as a badly disguised instrument 'in the strategy against the separatist movement'.[11] Hence, the Agreement had not been a tool for 'the pacification and normalization' of *Euskadi* as in the very title of the text it announced. In the opinion of the moderate nationalists the pact had been devalued as a mere anti-terrorism pact. This, on the other hand, was not that surprising, since the more and more indiscriminate military activity of ETA and the increasing 'militarization' of HB's political discourse could not at all be interpreted as an invitation to the lowering of tension and dialogue.[12]

Based on this criticism of the multi-party Agreement and its deficit, President Ardanza, who had announced that he would retire from politics after the regional elections to be held in October 1998, adopted a more active attitude towards the problem of political violence and peace. In January 1998, the *Lehendakari* called the 'fathers' of the Ajuria Enea Agreement to the tenth anniversary commemoration of the pact, manifesting his wish to start the still unexplored 'second phase' of the Agreement. Two months later, after many secret and public contacts with the political parties represented in the Basque and in the Spanish parliaments, as well as with the conservative central government of President Aznar, an unknown informer leaked Ardanza's peace proposal to the press.[13] Quite apart from the positive or negative assessment of its contents, the document can already be considered a text of historical significance in the history of Basque nationalism, because it is the first serious and specific peace proposal presented practically since the beginning of political violence in the Basque Country.[14] Moreover, on this occasion it was not a political party that designed and supported the proposal, but the supreme institution representing all Basque citizens, namely, the Basque presidency. Ardanza defined the document not as a new proposal born exclusively of his own (nationalist) mind, but as a reflection inserted in the history of the Ajuria Enea Agreement signed by all nationalist and non-nationalist parties, which ten years ago had agreed on the possibility of offering a 'solution based on dialogue' to ETA and HB if some basic conditions were given.

Excluding the general introduction, the document consists of three main parts: I The Premises; II The Proposal; and III The Conclusion.[15] The basic goal of the proposal is to check out possible answers to two questions: What can be done, firstly, to stop ETA from intervening in politics by 'armed struggle (terrorism)', and, secondly, how can political dissidents backing HB start 'integrating themselves definitely into the political activity characteristic of the democratic system?' How can a broader political consensus within Basque society be achieved? One of the main premises formulated in the text is that the achievement of this double aim will not be possible by policing only. Instead, some kind of 'political incentive', that is, the possibility to 'influence the current juridical and political system' was considered necessary, as well as a complete and unconditional ceasefire. Thus, the talks about the 'negotiated end' of violence would be the result of the ceasefire, and not vice versa. The participants in the negotiations had to be 'politically legitimate agencies', who should move within the framework of the established democratic system, but nevertheless be aware of the legal possibilities of modifying this framework fixed in the Constitution or the Statute of Autonomy. Table 8.2.1 mentions some of these constitutional doors to consensus quoted in President Ardanza's peace proposal in order to show

Table 8.2.1 Ardanza's peace proposal (I): constitutional doors to consensus

Spanish Constitution	Recognition of the historical rights of the 'foral territories' (Basque provinces)
	Possibility of updating the foral system within the framework of the Constitution and the Statute of Autonomy (First Additional Disposition)
	Possible integration of Navarre into the Basque Community
Statute of Autonomy ('Statute of Gernika')	'The acceptance of the regime of autonomy does not imply the renunciation of the rights which might correspond to the Basque people by virtue of history.'
	These rights can be updated according to what is prescribed in the legislation.

that a modification in the structure of Basque self-government is perfectly feasible in accordance with the laws.

There was still another point in the proposal, which made it different from mainstream nationalist discourse. The conflict was interpreted not as a clash between *Euskadi* and Spain, but as a contention between divergent opinions among the Basques themselves. These differences were about 'what we are and what we want to be (of course, also as far as our relationship with Spain is concerned)'. As a consequence, it should also be the Basques themselves who should take the decisions and find ways out of the conflict. Obviously, both the problem itself and its solution affect the Spanish state, which has to participate in the negotiations. According to Ardanza's document, this participation would be guaranteed by the involvement of those Basque parties linked to Spanish state-wide parties like the socialist PSE–EE, the conservative PP or the leftist IU. According to this methodology, the Spanish governing party PP and the government's interests would be represented at the Basque negotiating table by the PP's local branch. Once granted the presence of the state, the Spanish government and the competent institutions would make a previous formal declaration manifesting their commitment 1) to leave the negotiated resolution of the conflict in the hands of the Basque parties, 2) to assume whatever agreements might be reached, and 3) to negotiate with the representatives of the Basque parties the incorporation of the agreement into the juridical framework in order to make it operative. The final step would be a referendum in the Basque Country about the contents of the agreement. Table 8.2.2 summarizes these main features of the peace proposal.

Table 8.2.2   Ardanza's peace proposal (II)

Conditions	Indefinite ceasefire
	Dialogue as consequence of the ceasefire, and not vice versa
Interlocutors	No direct participation of ETA
	ETA must delegate HB as its legitimate representative of a sector of the Basque people
	Rest of the Basque parties
	Spanish state (via Basque parties with state-wide representation)
	Competent agencies of the state: disposition to accept and to implement the agreements reached by the parties
Contents	Issue: 'national question'
	Fixed time-table
	No previous (political) conditions and limitations
	After a period of testing: referendum
Procedure	'Talks before talks' between the Basque democratic parties, central government, opposition parties in the Spanish parliament, ETA (secret contacts) and HB
	Information on public opinion
	Continuous advice concerning the possibilities of consensus embedded in the Constitution and the Statute of Autonomy

There is not a single allusion to the peace process in Northern Ireland in the 16 pages of Ardanza's text. Yet, both the coincidence in time and the contents reveal the similarities of both cases. In fact, the PNV has followed the Northern Ireland peace process very closely, sending high-ranking party delegations to Ulster on several occasions. In private, Ardanza himself admitted that he and his advisers have had contacts with practically all the important actors involved in the Northern Ireland peace process.[16] Apparently, the president was very well informed of the progress of the peace process in Northern Ireland, because he incorporated several of the core ideas raised since that process started after the Joint Declaration of the British and Irish Governments in 1993. Ardanza and his advisers picked up some of those ideas and shaped them to the Basque situation: no direct participation of armed groups in the negotiations; the previous establishment of a peaceful atmosphere (ceasefire) as an indispensable precondition for the participation of parties linked to armed groups; the commitment of all participants in the negotiations to abide by any agreement reached; the fixed time frame; the referendum.[17] On the other hand, the idea of exploring the juridical possibilities of political reform granted by the proper Constitution, especially by its 'First Additional Disposition', was not new either: A few months before Ardanza's proposal was published, the peace group Elkarri presented another document (*Izan* = 'To be') with a similar suggestion.

It was foreseeable that, due to the fundamental differences between the parties as to the character, causes and the resolution of the conflict, the reactions given to the president's proposal would also be very heterogeneous. In fact, even before Ardanza's initiative forced the parties to define their positions, there was a serious clash provoked by extremely divergent interpretations concerning what each of the parties considered the 'Basque problem'. The nationalist parties, and partly also the leftist IU, stated the existence of a political conflict of historical dimension. This core idea, shared by all nationalist parties including HB and *mutatis mutandis* by IU, asserts the existence of a deep-rooted political conflict between the Basque Country and the Spanish (French) state, violence being one of its elements. What happens is, according to Joseba Egibar, the spokesman for the PNV directing council, that the use of violence not only against the state, but also against the state's (Basque and even nationalist) 'lackeys', has converted the conflict also into a conflict among Basques. But the main problem still remains:

> We have a conflict with the state (...) (after 100 years) the conflict is still alive. I think that our political *Transition* has not yet ended, because a large group of people does not see itself within the system.[18]

In complete contrast to this interpretation we find the position of the conservative PP. For Jaime Mayor Oreja, at that time Spanish Minister of the Interior, of Basque origin, and the government's and PP's principal peace and security strategy ideologist, there is no real conflict between *Euskadi* and the central state. Terrorism is not the consequence, but the origin of the existing problem, which incidentally is considered a problem among the Basques:

> The terrorist problem is essentially that of a minority, which wants to take unfair advantage of the lack of articulation of the majority, and which wants to do it with the gun. The Basque problem is the lack of articulation of a majority, of a political project shared by nationalists and non-nationalists. The order of priority of these conflicts is usually wrongly enunciated. It says: In order to resolve the terrorist problem it is necessary to resolve the Basque problem. And this is an error. In order to resolve the Basque problem, we have to resolve the terrorist problem, because unless there is full freedom we can't resolve a problem of the Basques and their failure to engage.[19]

Within this discourse there was no place for any kind of political dialogue or negotiation, and if there were, the dialogue would in any case take place after the disappearance of terrorism, since in Mayor's logic, dialogue is not considered a valid means of resolving the problem. This discourse seems to match very well the mood of a party and its Basque and Spanish followers, who all are targets of ETA terrorism. Moreover, this toughness was politically very profitable. During his years in office as Minister of the Interior, Mayor Oreja used to get the best popularity scores among all the ministers in President Aznar's government in all Spanish opinion polls.[20] This attitude of combining a strategy of toughness against terrorism and Basque nationalism with a popular Spanish neo-nationalism produced the votes that made possible the first conservative government in 1996 and four years later permitted another triumph, now with an overall majority, in the elections to the Spanish parliament. At the same time, the PP was also growing in the Basque Country both in the elections and the party's affiliation. According to information facilitated by the PP about the most nationalist province of Gipuzkoa, in 1997 alone the party's affiliation in that region increased by 20 per cent.[21]

After a first round of contacts with President Aznar and the Spanish socialist leader Joaquín Almunia, who both had not dared to reject the proposal completely, the Basque *Lehendakari* manifested in public his hope to find an agreement. This optimism, however, was not realistic. The moderate responses given by the non-nationalist leaders were nothing but a political tactic, since no one wanted to assume the risk of being considered the bad boy, whose dogmatic obstinacy was responsible for the abortion of the first real peace proposal in the whole history of the violent Basque conflict. While some of the leaders were still making moderate statements, other politicians of the PSOE and the PP, with the help of some of the most influential media, started to create an atmosphere in which it soon became very clear that Ardanza's proposal, which had been received by HB with surprisingly moderate criticism, would not have any future, at least for the time being. The main arguments of the socialists and conservatives, who in their common opposition to the document seemed to overlook the political confrontation that divided them on other issues, can be summed up in the following points.

- The philosophy that inspires the proposal can be described by the formula of *peace for more nationalism*. This philosophy suggests the existence of a 'democratic deficit' (lack of self-determination) as the real cause that feeds terrorism. The reality, however, is that there is no such deficit, because the Basque people have self-determined themselves in every single election since democracy was reestablished, about 50 per cent of them voting for non-nationalist and Spanish-wide political parties.
- The offer of 'political incentives' to ETA in order to insure the end of violence is nothing but a buckling of the democrats in face of the supreme power of terrorism.
- The hypothetical modification of the Spanish Constitution and the Basque Statute of Autonomy might satisfy the radical sectors of nationalism, but this 'solution' would create new grievances among all those Basques who do not consider themselves nationalists and feel comfortable inside the current constitutional framework.
- The rest of the Spanish state and society cannot be expected to accept passively anything decided by the Basques if this decision has consequences for the state, which would be as if Tony Blair had been asked to accept any political decision taken in Ulster by the local political parties.
- The pre-electoral period is not the appropriate moment for the discussion of the proposal.

Consequently, in a decisive new meeting of the Pact of Ajuria Enea, the proposal was radically rejected by the PP conservatives and also, even if in more moderate terms, by the socialists. For Jaime Mayor Oreja, the Basque PP leader, the rejection of Ardanza's initiative was a question of personal righteousness. 'In life', he commented in an interview to one of the biggest local papers, 'you let yourself be blackmailed or you don't.'[22] The same attitude was defended by President Aznar who in private talks to his political friends and advisers made use of historical parallels to argue his position of vigour against terrorism: 'I am not going to be Chamberlain, and my policy won't be that of appeasement', was one of his comments picked up by the press.[23] The polls seemed to back this toughness, and so did the police forces: a few days after the Ajuria Enea meeting, two of the most active ETA commandos (Araba and Andalucía) were put out of action. Wasn't Mayor Oreja right in affirming over and over again that only military weakness would convince ETA of the necessity to lay down their arms? And wasn't it also true when he, his conservative followers and many socialists considered the Ardanza proposal a badly disguised strategy of the nationalists to push the Basque Country towards independence, even against the will of the non-nationalist Basques? Just at the moment when the parties were preparing their Ajuria Enea summit, the Spanish right-wing daily paper *ABC* had published a document with a record of a secret encounter between Xabier Arzallus, the leader of the moderate nationalist PNV, and Rafa Díez, the General Secretary of the radical, pro-ETA union LAB. In the record of this meeting held in 1992, Arzallus is quoted with such literal affirmations as 'in the question of self-determination, our party will go until the end', or 'we don't think that for *Euskal Herria* it would be good that ETA is defeated'.[24]

In this adverse atmosphere, with the two major Spanish parties and their Basque branches rejecting the plan, and some of the most important media against it as well as the 300 Basque intellectuals and artists of the 'Forum of Ermua' campaigning against any political concessions to the 'fascist movement (...) directed by ETA, HB and other organizations of their ilk',[25] and finally without any real gesture of conflict de-escalation from ETA, nothing could be done. Consequently, despite the favourable votes of the nationalist parties and the left-wing IU, the first Basque peace proposal had disappeared from the political stage.

This political stage, however, was no longer the same after the debate about the *Lehendakari*'s proposal. It was the first time in the ten-year history of the Ajuria Enea Agreement that the parties of the 'Democratic Bloc' met without reaching any kind of minimal consensus. Behind the cleavage between democrats and supporters of violence, there lay the old historical cleavage of nationalists versus (conservative and socialist) non-nationalists that vigorously emerged once again. The frustrated experience of the abortion of Ardanza's peace proposal had an important impact on many moderate nationalists, who became more and more convinced of two facts. The first was related to their impression that it was very unlikely that there would be any kind of support from the socialists or conservatives for a peace initiative that encompassed the idea of an 'end of violence based on dialogue' expressed in the Ajuria Enea Agreement. While the conservatives and socialists blamed the moderate nationalists for betraying the common front of all democrats against terrorism, the democratic nationalists, and President Ardanza himself, accused the PP and PSOE of 'not taking on board the core ideas of the Ajuria Enea Agreement'.[26] It was evident that the rejection of the proposal was only a consequence of a much deeper general political disagreement concerning the issues of peace and self-government. This disagreement buried not only Ardanza's proposal, but also the Ajuria Enea Agreement itself. After ten years of existence, the 'Democratic Bloc' was dissolved.

The second conclusion drawn by moderate nationalists from the collapse of the 'Democratic Bloc' following the rejection of the *Lehendakari*'s peace proposal was the conviction that, if any peace process was to be started, the initiators had to be the nationalists themselves, including the radical nationalists of HB. According to the electoral results in the Basque Autonomous Community, a new pan-nationalist entente backed by the left-wing IU would produce a political majority in parliament, which could trigger and consolidate such an initiative. The core idea which this entente could be built upon was the thesis of the link between peace and self-determination, because the claim for self-determination had never disappeared from the PNV programme as the goal to be achieved in the long run. Years before the 'Democratic Bloc' broke down, the PNV had initiated an internal process of strategic rethinking, in which some senior leaders anticipated some of the main ideas, which would become dominant in the party at the end of the 1990s. In 1994, the PNV ideologist Juan María Ollora published an important book, *A Future for Euskadi*. Ollora made a critical interpretation of the political operativity of the Ajuria Enea Pact, which in his opinion had not brought peace, nor had it permitted any remarkable progress towards Basque self-determination. In the prologue of the book, the former Basque President Garaikoetxea shared this point of view, arguing that the way to 'normalization' in the Basque Country would be impossible without a previous 'basic agreement among the nationalist forces'. Both authors, however, were aware that such a 'basic agreement' would also be impossible if violence continued.[27]

At the end of the 1990s, when these thoughts received a new impulse within moderate nationalism, for the PNV and EA leaders the problem of terrorism was no longer only a problem of Basque society in general. It had become a problem that seriously jeopardized the political future of both parties. Since the massive popular mobilization following the brutal assassination of the young PP councilor Blanco in the summer of 1997, the spontaneous rebellion of the people against terrorism had taken the PNV by surprise. The so-called 'Spirit of Ermua', which was a mixture of popular protest against terrorism and a claim for the unity of all democrats in the struggle against ETA, strongly supported the non-nationalist parties and their points of view, according to which ETA continued killing because the governing nationalists were not really interested in bringing terrorism to an end. As a consequence, pushed by the 'Spirit of Ermua' and politically directed by the conservative PP and most of the Spanish media, a political campaign was started against the PNV, which was blamed for being the secret protector of ETA and the cause of the continuing bloodshed. For the PNV leadership, this was not only a fierce and dirty controversy. It was a concrete political threat, because a growing number of Basque voters were rewarding the party, which had made toughness on terrorism and Basque nationalism the centrepiece of its discourse. Indeed, during the 1990s the conservative PP had realized a really spectacular apogee in the ballot boxes. Starting with 98,000 votes and 9.64 per cent vote-sharing in the regional elections to the Basque parliament in 1990, in the elections to the Spanish parliament held in 1996, the PP got 230,000 votes and 18.63 per cent. It had even become strong in the big cities normally controlled by the PNV, such as Bilbao, where it was competing with the moderate nationalists for the vote of the upper middle classes.[28] Hence, in the PNV headquarters it became more and more evident that due to the rise of the conservatives, for the first time since the establishment of the autonomic institutions the political hegemony of moderate nationalism was at stake, and that this situation was also a consequence of the persistence of ETA violence. At the end of the 1990s, from the PNV's point of view, the – at least temporary – cessation of violence had become an indispensable goal not only in terms of ethics, but also as a tool for the consolidation and enlargement of the party's political power.

Yet the problem was how to reach this goal. Apparently, for ETA nothing had changed. In May and June 98, the organization killed another two Basque PP councilors[29] and a retired Civil Guard policeman. Contrary to this crude reality, the PNV was receiving inside information about internal debates taking place within the Movement. Spokesmen for the party had initiated secret informal contacts with the HB leadership a few weeks before HB's Ruling Council were imprisoned in December 1997. These contacts continued later with the new leadership. The information provided during these meetings was interpreted by the PNV as a clear signal that there was for the first time for many years a growing willingness to reinforce the political dimension of radical nationalism and to bring it out of the social and political ghetto. According to the PNV analysis, it was unrealistic to think that the Liberation Movement could remain insensitive towards the changing reality of Basque society and its desire for peace. The growing rebellion of the Basques against the culture of violence was indeed a corrosive challenge to the military orthodoxy of radical nationalism, and that was so for one particular reason. It was no longer, as it had been years before, a rebellion articulated and directed exclusively by anti-nationalist and anti-HB policy-makers. It had become a popular, grassroots rebellion, which cut across political and national identities, including for the first time even people with open sympathies for the philosophy and the aims of radical nationalism, who could not so easily be described as 'enemies of the Basque nation'. From this background, the PNV's political strategists became increasingly convinced that, if the military and political problems of ETA and HB were evident, political cooperation offered by institutional nationalism might smooth the way to a ceasefire and, at the same time, open the door to a new majority favourable to Basque self-determination. Yet, before this new party alignment was put into practice, there were still some barriers to break down. The initiative of the so-called 'third space' helped to do this.

8.3 The appeal of the 'third space'

Contemporary Basque history is the history of polarization between nationalist and non-nationalist identities. Contrary to the experience of other ethnic movements on the Spanish periphery (for example, that of Catalonia), in the Basque Country none of the political projects created to mediate between the opposing poles (Nationalist Republicanism 1910–13; Acción Nacionalista Vasca during the Second Republic; Euskadiko Ezkerra during Post-Francoism) was successful. As explained above, once democracy was re-established and Basque regional autonomy granted, the continuity of ETA violence introduced a new cleavage, which covered traditional nationalism versus non-nationalism, namely, the cleavage separating democrats, united in the Ajuria Enea Pact, from the supporters of violence. After the successes of the summer of 1997 (the release of ETA hostage Ortega Lara; the kidnapping and killing of the young PP town councillor Miguel Angel Blanco; the massive and spontaneous anti-ETA mobilizations), the wall that separated both political blocs had become higher than ever before, but the problems were far from being resolved: ETA kept on killing and street violence had become a common feature at least every weekend. Everybody talked about peace, but a paramilitary underground organization continued its particular warfare against the 'Spaniards', considering the physical elimination of the 'enemy' as a logical and legitimate means of warfare. The long history of the armed struggle had demonstrated that it was completely unrealistic to expect a military victory of ETA against the state. But it was also evident that the different police strikes against the group had not achieved ETA's defeat. In the Ajuria Enea Agreement, the political parties had drawn their conclusion from this experience, including in the text the possibility of an end to violence 'based on dialogue', if certain conditions were met. Those conditions, however, were unlikely to be met, if the total lack of communication between the 'democrats' and the Liberation Movement continued. The only possibility of breaking the stalemate seemed to consist in making the frontier between the two blocs less insurmountable and in promoting an exchange of ideas that might contribute to the de-escalation of the conflict.

This was the idea behind the conversations between the PNV and HB, and it was this same reasoning that inspired the project of the so-called 'third space'. It is practically impossible to find any real attempt to define this concept, but it is probably more than mere coincidence that the references to the 'third space' appeared in the political discussion of the Basque Country more or less at the same time as Tony Blair, Anthony Giddens and others began their search for a way out of the crisis of international social democracy introducing their ideas of the 'new centre' or the 'third way'. In the Basque Country, the project of the 'third space' was neither a product of the social democratic crisis, nor was it conceived of as an instrument to bridge the gap between the nationalist and the non-nationalist communities. It was imagined as a political and social area of encounter between all those in favour of Basque self-determination by peaceful and democratic means. It was thought of as a meeting point for all citizens dissatisfied with the bipolarization of society into two opposite blocs.

Behind these basic ideas there was no concrete and tangible programme attached to the concept of the 'third space', and it was precisely this (calculated?) ambiguity, which made it so attractive to many Basques inside or close to the Liberation Movement. This special attraction was due also to a second important fact. The promoters of the 'third space' were nearly all linked to civil society and to social movements, and not to the political system. This reinforces the argument that in the Basque case grassroots pressure was an important factor, which – while impacting on the political system – helped to trigger the process which led to the ceasefire. The principal agencies engaged in the project of the 'third space' were the majority Basque, nationalist and left-wing trade union Eusko Langileen Alkartasuna (ELA); the HB-allied union Langile Abertzaleen Batzordeak (LAB); the union of the Basque peasants, Euskal Herriko Nekazarien Elkartea (EHNE); the peace movement ELKARRI and a number of politicians and intellectuals, some of whom were related to an extreme left-wing group, Zutik, which was close to the Liberation Movement, but critical of its military bias.

The origin of the 'third space' project and its centrepiece was the *entente* between the two Basque nationalist unions ELA and LAB.[30] The following table indicating the percentages of worker-representatives elected in the Basque enterprises in 1994/95, shortly after the *entente* was initiated, provides evidence for the importance of both unions, especially that of the moderate ELA, in the Basque labour sector.

Previous to this *entente* was a growing disagreement between ELA and its traditional partners, the socialist UGT and the left-wing Comisiones Obreras, due to what ELA considered an extreme subordination of these unions to the directives and interests of their mother-organizations in Madrid. Since neither UGT nor CCOO were willing to defend what ELA

Table 8.3.1 Delegates of trade unions elected in 1994/95 (percentages)

	ELA	UGT	CCOO	LAB	Others
Alava	30.65	22.70	16.10	11.86	15.0
Bizkaia	39.76	17.88	17.66	12.12	9.73
Gipuzkoa	45.30	9.86	15.21	22.32	3.80
Navarre	20.64	32.23	20.24	11.52	11.54
Total CAPV	40.21	15.86	16.55	15.64	8.51
Total EH	35.96	19.41	17.35	14.74	9.17

Note: ELA = Eusko Langileen Alkartasuna, moderate nationalist union; LAB: Langile Abertzaleen Batzordeak, radical nationalist union; UGT = socialist Unión General de Trabajadores; CCOO = Comisiones Obreras, leftist union; Total CAPV = total results in the Comunidad Autónoma del País Vasco; Total EH: results in *Euskal Herria* (= CAPV + Navarre).

Source: Internal document from ELA, Bilbao 30 October 1995.

leader José Elorrieta called a 'Basque framework of industrial relations', for the moderate unionists the only way of working in favour of this aim was by breaking the traditional alliance with those 'Spanish' unions and constructing a new one, together with the only nationalist union remaining, even if that organization (LAB) was a part of the Liberation Movement commanded by ETA. This process of emphasizing the more political and nationalist dimension of the union's discourse led in 1993 to the breaking up of the ELA–UGT–CCOO alliance and ELA's rapprochement with LAB, which became public in the first common manifestos issued by both organizations on the 'Day of the Basque Fatherland' (Aberri Eguna, Easter Sunday) and then on 1 May 1995.

This new alliance was a risky gamble for José Elorrieta, ELA's general secretary and the principal promoter of this new strategy, since for many of the more than 80,000 members[31] of the union the reasons for this strategic turn were not really comprehensible. Why should a democratic and moderate union like ELA form an alliance with a worker organization, which for years had been blamed for being one of the strongest supporters of ETA terror? This unrest became open rebellion when ETA started its campaign against the Ertzaintza, the Basque police. This campaign caused fatalities among policemen and other workers who were members of ELA (Gómez Elósegui, Olaciregui, Doral, Goikoetxea, Zabalza, Agirre). Yet LAB was not willing to change its traditional attitude and criticize in public any of the activities committed by ETA, not even the killing of unionist members of its new nationalist partner. As a consequence, Elorrieta received strong internal[32] (and external) pressure inviting him to put an end to the alliance with LAB. After the killing in March 1997 of another active ELA member, the prison psychologist Gómez Elósegui, the general secretary admitted that 'the relationship between ELA and LAB has been seriously affected'.[33] In an attempt to calm the internal unrest, ELA opted for slowing down the dynamics of the *entente* with LAB. In 1997, neither on the Aberri Eguna, nor 1 May was a common Manifesto of both unions published. In the summer of that year, the massive popular mobilization against ETA after the kidnapping and killing of Miguel Angel Blanco and the release of the hostage Ortega Lara asphyxiated any initiative related to the idea of the 'third space'. The 'Spirit of Ermua' re-established the frontier between (nationalist and non-nationalist) democrats and the supporters of violence. Now, even the leaders of the moderate nationalist parties PNV and EA close to the project of the 'third space' stated that 'the conditions for defending the idea of a third way' had not been met'.[34]

Yet, the 'spirit of Ermua' and the growing popular rebellion against ETA violence froze the idea of the 'third space', but did not bury it. In October, the political conflict between the Basque and the Spanish governments concerning the implementation of the social part of the Statute of Autonomy, especially the transfer of the national employment agency, demanded by the Basque government and rejected by the Spanish government, was the background against which the revival of the project took place. While the Basque conservatives and socialists were preparing for the festivities to celebrate the 18th anniversary of the Statute of Autonomy, Elorrieta announced the holding of a public meeting in the symbolic town of Gernika as ELA's particular contribution. In previous declarations to the media, he declared the 'death' of the Basque Statute of Autonomy and the necessity of exploring 'a new framework of self-government'.[35]

LAB understood the message. A week after Elorrieta's spectacular press conference, the leaders of the radical nationalist union sent a public proposal to ELA, which was invited to use both organizations' majority 'with the aim of going beyond the Statute of Autonomy'.[36] This proposal brought the idea of the 'third space' back on to the political agenda. Socialists and conservatives immediately criticized the 'betrayal' of the spirit of Ermua by this new flirtation with violent nationalism, defending at the same time the validity of the autonomy as a place of encounter for all Basques, nationalists and non-nationalists.

Finally, despite the criticisms and a new lethal interference by ETA (killing a Basque policeman and a member of the ELA union), Elorrieta confirmed the meeting at Gernika, which had received the support of LAB, the farmers' union EHNE, the social democrat nationalist party EA, the philo-nationalist wing of the leftist IU called Ekaitza, HB, the peace group ELKARRI and other minor organizations. Several PNV leaders were also present. This meeting was the public baptism of the 'third space' and Elorrieta's speech its Magna Carta. It was, in the words of a left-wing commentator, the 'presentation ceremony of Basque sovereignty, its first public act'.[37] In Gernika, the ELA leader's message was threefold. The first was his already mentioned diagnosis of the death of Basque autonomy:

> The Statute of Autonomy is dead; it has been killed by the centralists. What once upon a time could have been an opportunity has now been converted into a snare. Don't misinterpret our words. We don't say, we have never said, that we don't want any Statute at all; what we are underlining is that what we have is insufficient, completely insufficient and moreover unrecognizable. Please, understand us well, we don't have any particular interest in self-government with no kind of social dimension.

The second message was about the means of the struggle for Basque sovereignty:

> 'ELA is completely conscious that the way towards a new self-government won't lead us anywhere unless it is democratic; unless it is peaceful, we shall never ever get the majorities and the social support we need. Consequently, ETA must know that there is no place for it, that we don't

need it, that it is an obstacle to the future. The power of our reason, the support for our project, the dreams of our people – all these are sufficient weapons to help us win. Other weapons are not necessary, they only obstruct.

After explaining the *why* (the death of autonomy) and the *how* (democratic and peaceful means), Elorrieta defined the *who* or the social agency of his project. It was the 'majority' of all Basque citizens '(...) who accept that sovereignty, the right to decide our future as a people, concerns the Basque citizens'.[38]

Elorrieta's proposal to create a new nationalist, democratic and peaceful majority in favour of Basque sovereignty had an important impact on the media and the political parties. The presence of high-ranking PNV and EA members seemed to symbolize the fact that the idea of a new political and social majority beyond the traditional lines of conflict was not just a dream of a nationalist union leader who, after all, had never passed the test of elections. Consequently, the reaction of the Basque conservatives and socialists was much more directed against the democratic nationalist parties and their collaboration with HB than against the thesis and proposals formulated by Elorrieta. This was understandable for two reasons. Since the dramatic experience of summer, ETA had not changed its violent strategy and for conservatives and socialists, the principal victims of terror, the speculations and hypothesis about gradual changes taking place inside HB and the Liberation Movement were nothing but wishful thinking and attempts to break the solidarity of the democrats. Even so, the political instinct of conservative and socialist leaders made them aware of the possibility of a future realignment in the Basque political system, which would be motivated by discontent within moderate nationalism over traditional policies towards terrorism, the growing desire of peace within Basque society, and the step-by-step integration of HB – as well as its 15 per cent vote share – in the political system.

The 'third space' was becoming a remarkably attractive political idea for various important sectors of Basque society. This attraction and success were consequences of the calculated ambiguity of the idea. Elorrieta had explained the why, how and who of the project, but, apart from the general references to self-government, sovereignty and self-determination, he did not say anything about the question of purpose. If autonomy was dead, what was the concrete alternative? Elorrieta himself had no special problem in admitting this lack of definition. When he was asked about the alternative to the framework of autonomy, he answered as follows:

> There are different alternatives, and it is not a question of us offering formulas. We just define a principle: sovereignty rests with the Basque people. How we give political or practical shape to this principle can be discussed by taking into account factors like time or gradualism.[39]

One of the very few participants in the debate about the 'third space' was a leading PNV politician, the former head of the Department of Culture in the Basque government, Joseba Arregi. In a very critical comment on the 'third space', Arregi expressed his opinion that 'we do have the name, but we do not know what it corresponds to'. At the same time Arregi criticized a certain totalitarian bias of some of the ideas related to the 'third space' (for instance the tendency to speak in the name of the whole of Basque society). He interpreted the project of the 'third space' as an attempt to defend the same concept of society defended by ETA, with the only difference that it renounced the use of violence.[40]

The PNV politician was right, and at the same time he was wrong. He was right in criticizing the project's lack of definition, but he was not in denouncing the 'totalitarian' concept of society behind the project, because there simply was no real concept of society attached to the idea of the 'third space'. This idea was no political programme aiming at the construction of a new, alternative society. It was just an idea based on a number of fundamental principles (the solution of the conflict through dialogue; self-determination; no violence) with three immediate political objectives: firstly, the creation of 'spaces of de-escalating tension' – an expression used frequently by Elorrieta and ELKARRI leader Jonan Fernández[41] – in order to contribute to the de-escalation of the violent confrontation; secondly, the breaking of the stalemate between the 'democrats' and the 'people of violence' that was blocking any step towards peace; and thirdly, the design of a hypothetical new majority for the promotion of Basque sovereignty as a realistic alternative to armed struggle. Only a sufficiently fuzzy and ambiguous concept like the 'third space' was capable of generating this future new majority, since it did not exclude by definition any of the different (nationalist) sensibilities. Just as in other moments in the history of Basque nationalism,[42] at the end of the 1990s there was once again a magic formula with integrating capacity and popular impact on different sectors of nationalism, the vagueness of this formula being its principle guarantee for success. It was a formula for the internal use of Basque nationalism and not Basque society. Even if the philosophy of groups like ELKARRI was rooted in the idea of mediation, the 'third space' was never really conceived as a concept of mediation between nationalists and non-nationalists, as the philosopher and hard-line anti-nationalist A. Arteta seems to understand it.[43] Mediation was supposed to take place first of all between different sectors of nationalism, and the expected outcome was a de-militarization of the struggle for self-determination. Only if this objective were achieved, in the long run the conditions for a reconciliation of both communities in a process of what some analysts have called the 'second transition'[44] would be given. In other words: It was understandable that neither Elorrieta nor any other of the different architects of the 'third space' could admit it in public, but for many of the political observers it was no secret that the real addressee of the message transmitted by the 'third space' was ETA. Even critical commentators recognized the potential of this message: 'It has to be admitted that Elorrieta's third space is becoming configured as the only political factor that can really move ETA.'[45]

The ETA paramilitaries understood the message and its potential corrosive consequences. The answer came in December 1997. By injuring a PP councillor's bodyguard and, a few days later, assassinating a PP councillor (J. J. Caso Cortines) in Renteria, the underground organization tried to torpedo the growing cooperation of the third space organizations and thereby recover its control over organizations attached to the Liberation Movement, especially the union LAB. The reaction of the radical nationalist union in the days after the killing was extremely confusing. It reflected the nervousness of an organization struggling for greater autonomy from the military direction of the Liberation Movement without upsetting the 'armed vanguard'. In a series of successive, partly contradictory communiqués, the leaders of the union achieved this goal of performing their loyalty to the Liberation Movement and not criticizing directly the armed struggle, while maintaining their commitment to the idea of the third space. Thanks to this, LAB had saved the 'third space'. In fact, Elorrieta declared in public that the relationship between ELA and LAB had been consolidated and Jonan Fernández, the ELKARRI leader, stated that violence 'conditioned' the evolution of the project, which in his opinion would nonetheless 'continue with more power'.[46] Was that a realistic forecast? Some pieces of evidence might be found when analysing the behavior of the Liberation Movement and its organizations in the days before and after the killing. Against a background characterized by a long history of complete subordination of political reasoning to the military imperative, the very deed of signing a communiqué together with other organizations just the day after a fatal intervention of ETA had a special symbolic significance. This is also true as regards the publishing of some articles with critical opinions of ETA's strategy in the Movement's daily paper *Egin*. Of course, these were only a few details, but they were unusual in the Basque political context. Their confluence seemed indeed to indicate that something had started to change within the Liberation Movement.

The meaning and the extent of these timid and for other observers nearly invisible movements in the symbolic microcosm of the radical nationalist universe was best understood by ETA. The paramilitaries had become aware that within the Liberation Movement for the first time ETA's function as armed and political vanguard in the struggle for Basque independence was being questioned. The latest lethal interventions had the objective of reinforcing this leading role, emphasizing that in the struggle for Basque emancipation no limitation of this traditional dominance would be accepted. An ETA communiqué issued a week after the killing of Caso, was further proof of the organization's self-appointed position as the supreme judge or referee in the national liberation struggle. Apart from the habitual railing against the PP politicians and their 'war for the destruction of *Euskal Herria* as a nation', the text contained a severe criticism of the organizations of the 'third space', including LAB. Others (ELA, LAB, EHNE and ELKARRI) were blamed for 'their equivocal and biased humanitarian ethic'. They were said to have committed a 'political error', which was a result of their 'lack of maturity'.[47]

This was a new serious blow for LAB. Never in the history of ETA had an organization that defended the legitimacy of the armed struggle and considered itself part of the Liberation Movement received such a direct and open warning from the paramilitaries. The consternation of Rafa Díez, its general secretary, was total. The only answer he was capable of giving to the communiqué was that his organization would take 'into account' the considerations expressed by ETA and that he regarded this 'political criticism' towards the attitude of the unions as 'legitimate', because ETA was a 'political organization'. This behaviour of submission and docility had nothing to do with the answers given by the other organizations mentioned by ETA. ELA emphasized 'the enormous distance between the perception of reality shown by ETA and that shared by the majority of the Basque people'. ELKARRI added the impression that 'ETA ignores the social reality of the Basque Country'.[48]

Did the re-establishment of the old frontiers signal the end of the 'third space'? It was a linguistic trick that permitted HB and LAB to find a double answer to this question: 'yes' was the answer sent to ETA, and 'no' the answer to the other nationalist groups outside the Liberation Movement. HB's new spokesman Arnaldo Otegi declared that 'here in the Basque Country there are no third ways'. 'Here, there are only two projects: the Spanish one and that of *Euskal Herria*'. Two days later, LAB picked up the same idea of the confrontation between two ways, 'the autonomist Spanish way that ignores the sovereignty of *Euskal Herria*' as opposed to the way towards a 'scenario of real democracy rooted in the recognition of Basque sovereignty'. Joseba Permach, the other new spokesman of HB, was more explicit. He stated that 'there is no third *way*, but there is a third *space*'. But what was this 'third space' for HB and LAB? For LAB leader Rafa Díez the 'third space' was a space of 'social, trade-unionist and cultural sectors that are betting on a Basque national project and moving away from autonomous statutism which has become an important pillar of the "shared project" defended by Mayor Oreja (the Spanish Minister of Interior, L.M.)'.[49]

Behind this semantic exercise of contrasting two ambiguous and confusing concepts, lay the equally confusing reality of the Liberation Movement. While on the one hand the idea of exploring new ways into the future was emerging with growing support, on the other hand, links with the past were strong enough to prevent an open challenge to ETA's leadership role. In fact, after the shooting of Caso, anonymous ELA commentators were said to interpret that violent interference of ETA as an attempt to 'short-circuit the increasing prominence of the third space, because ETA does not control a socio-political movement that, in the end, (...) can politically harm violence a lot more than the antiterrorist discourse of the PP does.'[50] In order to recover complete control, it was necessary to establish the antagonism of the two ways, taking for granted that the way towards 'Basque freedom' would be directed by ETA. Once this premise was accepted, there was no problem for the recognition of the third space, composed by all the people 'convinced of the necessity to go beyond the current status quo by the means of a democratic solution that recognizes the sovereignty of the Basque people'.[51]

Two conclusions might be drawn from this confusing reaction of the Liberation Movement to the 'third space' idea. Firstly, ETA seemed to have difficulty supporting initiatives towards a Basque peace process, if pushed by organizations not under paramilitary control. Secondly, the contradiction between armed struggle and mass movement had become so evident that it could no longer be silenced inside the Liberation Movement. Despite its nebulous ambiguity, partial failures and scarce political dividend, the idea of the 'third space' had become a rolling stone, which ETA was unable to stop before it affected the Basque National Liberation Movement. It anticipated the notion of a pan-nationalist *entente* as a first step to peace and self-determination. Its promoters were the nationalist unions and some peace groups, while the parties played a secondary role. At the end of the 1990s, after the break-up of the political alignments and these first movements towards a pan-nationalist rapprochement, the Northern Irish example supplied an important argument to all those Basques who were convinced of the idea's political efficacy. The result came in 1998, when the initiative passed from the unions to the parties and the hope that politics would finally overcome violence was raised.

8.4   The Irish mirror

In the Basque Country, and in Spain in general, it is practically impossible to mention in any political or academic debate the example of the Northern Irish peace process without immediately polarizing the discussion around two types of opinions: firstly, the reaction of 'nothing to do' by those, who put emphasis on the completely different backgrounds in which politics in Northern Ireland and in the Basque Country have developed; and secondly, the response of others, who use the Irish example as proof that a settlement of violent ethnic conflicts is possible if certain conditions are met. Usually, the first group is politically close to Spanish and non-nationalist points of view and one of its main arguments is that the political autonomy demanded by Irish republicans and granted in the Good Friday Agreement is remarkably less than that granted and implemented in the Basque

Country since the establishment of regional autonomy in 1979. The mainly nationalist supporters of the second position, however, tend to put emphasis on what they consider common features of both situations and argue that the recognition of the right to self-determination as expressed in the Downing Street Declaration of December 1993 issued by the British and the Irish governments, was the key to progress towards a peaceful accommodation of the conflict. Frequently, instead of being the product of intellectual reflection, these statements of one or another group were motivated by predetermined political interests. They can easily be changed, if this alteration is supposed to bring political benefit. This happened, for example, when ETA cancelled the ceasefire and started its new violent offensive. Then, suddenly all the references to the parallels between the Basque and Northern Irish cases were dropped in the public discourse of radical nationalism. Several months later, non-nationalist politicians and commentators had no problem in becoming enthusiastic supporters of the Northern Irish peace process when in 2001 and after pressure from Unionists the IRA announced its commitment to begin decommissioning its arms. Anyway, whatever the motivation of these statements might be, there is no doubt that during the 1990s the Northern Irish peace process accompanied the evolution of Basque politics very closely. This link is also reflected by the fact that some of the best (and bestselling) books on politics in Ulster published in Spain and in Spanish have been written by Basque authors.[52]

This presence of Irish politics in the Basque Country was not new. On the contrary, since the very beginnings of the movement, Basque nationalists have not stopped glancing at themselves in the Irish mirror.[53] Sabino Arana, the conservative and Catholic founder of the PNV, could not understand how such a Catholic nation as the Irish was able to entrust the struggle for independence from the British Empire first to a leader 'attached to Protestantism' (O'Connell) and then to a Protestant and 'libertine' like Parnell.[54] Some years later, the different interpretation of the 1916 Easter Rising given by Basque nationalist radicals and moderates was one of the first signs to reveal the party's split in 1921. According to Juaristi, this insurrection became the 'myth of the third nationalist generation' among Arana's followers. Consequently, for the re-founded PNV, in the years before Primo de Rivera's dictatorship (1923–30) Sinn Féin became a model to emulate: after one of the visits paid by the Irish party's propagandists to the Basque Country, in 1922 the nationalist women's organization Emakume Abertzale Batza was created as a direct imitation of the Irish model Cumann na mBan.[55] These contacts continued throughout the 1930s, with Irish politicians turning up on several of the most important and spectacular public festivals and meetings like that of the Fatherland's Day (*Aberri Eguna*). After the Spanish Civil War and two decades of Francoist repression, ETA was founded as an armed anticolonialist, underground guerrilla movement, and it was this conception of the Basque Country as a colony oppressed by one, or rather two, foreign power(s) that refreshed the traditional attractiveness of Ulster in Basque politics. Ever since, there have been plenty of contacts between the IRA and ETA, including mutual logistic support,[56] as well as between Sinn Féin and Herri Batasuna or, to a less extent, the rest of the nationalist parties in the Basque Country. Despite the multiple, evident differences in the constellation of both conflicts, their location in the European Union, their far-reaching historical roots and, above all, their violent dimension, there were important common elements that not only impressed the nationalist politicians looking for similarities, but also different scholars interested in comparative approaches to ethnic conflicts.[57]

At the end of the 1990s, this Irish connection maintained by Basque nationalism reached a new peak. After looking into the Irish mirror, radical nationalists from the Liberation Movement started transferring the experiences of Ulster to the Basque conflict. Indeed, comparing both cases, there were some apparent similarities between militant Irish Republicanism and radical Basque nationalism. In Ulster, the 'long war' strategy, the police repression and the Unionist paramilitary violence had contributed to weakening the political position of the Republican Movement. Its leadership began to rethink the conflict, since it became more and more evident that – as Darby and Mac Ginty put it – 'rather than an asset, the use of violence was an increasing liability'. Gerry Adams and his followers had become aware that 'the continued use of violence was increasingly counter-productive for Republicans and resulted in their exclusion and demonisation'.[58] As the armed struggle was unlikely to bring about a united Ireland, new ways of achieving this aim had to be found. The result of this rethinking was the idea of a pro-nationalist coalition with John Hume's Social Democratic and Labour Party (SDLP). In the strategy of militant Republicanism, Constitutional politics based on new majorities substituted the armed struggle as the valid tool for the realization of the political programme.

In the Basque Country, as we have seen above, the situation of radical nationalism was no better than in Ulster. During the 1990s, HB and ETA lost political influence due to the growing popular protest against ETA and the street violence, the increasing pressure against terrorism articulated by the police and the judges, the devolution policy, and the common front of all democratic parties against terrorism. But only when the traditional political alignments entered crisis as a consequence of the Ajuria Enea Agreement's breakdown, a new 'contextual structure'[59] was shaped, in which the door was opened to alternative ways of making politics according to the Irish model. If the Ulster republicans looked to South Africa or Israel–Palestine, Basque nationalists looked into the Irish mirror and became a new example of what Sydney Tarrow has called the 'transnationalization' of social movements and their 'cumulative power', consisting in their capacity to learn from each other and to 'build on the practices and institutions of the past'.[60]

Hence, if in Northern Ireland Sinn Féin and the IRA had managed to overcome a situation of political and military weakness, why should this same prescription not be possible for militant Basque nationalism? During 1998, the Northern Irish model performed a powerful demonstrator effect on the Basque National Liberation Movement.

In an interview given to *The Irish Times*, HB's new leader Arnaldo Otegi confessed that 'Ireland was a mirror for us, and so was the republican movement. Negotiation was always regarded here in the Basque Country as something suspect. But Sinn Féin and the Republican movement showed us that negotiation did not have to lead to political treachery. If it could happen in Ireland, why not in the Basque Country?'[61] This new emphasis on politics and negotiation was the answer given by militant nationalists to the challenges of an adverse contextual structure, in which violence and political projects attached to it became increasingly contested by a broad majority of the Basque people.

ETA and the Liberation Movement were unable to protect themselves against the impact of this new context. The Ermua mobilizations during the summer of 1997 were a catalyst for a timid process of internal debate on the relationship between armed struggle and politics and on violence in general. This debate took place in the local HB assemblies, the pages of the daily paper *Egin* and within the ranks of the prisoner collective. The very existence of this discussion between different sectors of the Liberation Movement, which normally tried to project a public image of monolithic loyalty towards the military leadership, was a significant indicator of some major movements apparently going on within the Movement. Some pieces of evidence seemed to confirm this impression.

The first is related to the union LAB and dated even before the successes of the summer of 1997. In an internal document drafted in April 1997 and leaked to the press three months later, the authors show a very critical attitude towards the political strategy of KAS and HB, blaming them for the total subordination of any kind of political or unionist activity under the dynamics and internal logic of the armed struggle and its complement, the street violence. According to LAB, this radical, violent strategy based on the Oldartzen Report was 'drowning' the possibilities of the union's activity, producing at the same time a strong 'wearing down' and isolation of the Liberation Movement and its organizations. The authors criticize the leading hardliners who were said to 'feed on the ideas of exclusivism' and to be inspired by the slogan of 'the more alone, the better'.[62]

The popular mobilizations protesting against the kidnapping and killing of the young PP councillor of Ermua gave a new strong impulse to the critical voices within radical nationalism. Patxi Zabaleta, the most popular representative of HB in Navarre and deputy in the regional parliament in that province, demanded in public the liberation of Blanco; a group of former ETA and HB members asked ETA to declare an indefinite ceasefire;

Eugenio Etxebeste, Antxon, one of the leading historical members of ETA and considered one of the group's representatives in future negotiations, tried from his residence in Santo Domingo to prevent the execution of Miguel Angel Blanco; several ETA prisoners broke the collective's discipline and manifested in the press their disapproval of the murder.[63]

Yet, probably the most effective criticism was written by the former head of ETA's political branch and one of the principal 'inventors' of the street-guerrilla: José Luis Alvarez Santa Cristina, better known by his pseudonym Txelis. He was captured in 1992 by the French police together with the rest of the former ETA leadership known as the 'collective Artapalo' in the famous Operation Bidart, which was one of the strongest blows struck by the police against the underground organization. Still under the impression of the Ermua-mobilizations, affected by a personal evolution towards religious (Catholic) spiritualism and motivated by a debate on future politics and strategies of radical nationalism taking place in the columns of *Egin*, in August 1997 Txelis delivered a seven-page manuscript written in a very elaborate *Euskara*, from his French prison, where he was serving a 10-year-sentence. The draft was titled 'Abertzaleon estrategiaz' ('About the strategy of the patriots') and started immediately circulating within the different sectors of militant nationalism. It was signed by two other famous ETA prisoners (Kepa Pikabea and Roxario Pikabea). The importance of this document concerns the fact that its author had been considered as ETA's political head and principal ideologist. Furthermore, his new critical attitude was not the result of a previous break with ETA and militant nationalism as had been the case with other former leading ETA prisoners like Soares Gamboa. The philosophy of the analysis was guided by the willingness to overcome the problems of the Basque struggle for self-determination by defining new ways of achieving the Liberation Movement's aims. Txelis himself summed up the three main statements of his analysis as follows:

1. Recently, the Spanish powers are profiting remarkably from the armed conflict to the detriment of the present and the future of our people.
2. The balance of the human and political costs generated by the armed struggle are very high and the absence of a climate for lowering the tension implies an insurmountable obstacle to a negotiated political settlement.
3. The armed struggle led by ETA is being politically and socially discredited as never before. Recently, we have seen and heard the increasingly manifest rejection and disapproval of violence expressed by an absolutely broad majority of our people.[64]

A new ETA killing in December 1997 led to greater internal and public criticism. Again it was an important and recently captured (in France) ETA prisoner who expressed similar arguments in an article published in *Egin* collaborating in a readers' discussion about the question 'Is the example of Ireland valid for *Euskal Herria*?' Joseba Urrosolo Sistiaga stated that the last assassination had provoked a 'high level of commotion' 'especially among the patriotic left', whose members 'cannot understand the decision to commit such kinds of activity in the current context'. He asked ETA to take into account the behaviour of the IRA and to push for negotiations instead of blocking them.[65]

A month later, ETA's intervention and the debate on violence raised another critical comment issued by an important personality within the orbit of the Liberation Movement. Iulen Madariaga, one of the founders of ETA in 1959, manifested in the pages of *Egin* his astonishment and disapproval of the underground organization, which in his opinion was showing a strange tendency to destroy one by one all of the 'favourable moments for us' and backing adverse tendencies. The astonishment of Madariaga was such that the only explanation he found for the counter-productive behaviour of ETA was the hypothesis that 'the enemy has infiltrated our ranks'.[66]

HB could no longer silence increasing unrest within the Liberation Movement. Pressure for a strategic reorientation had become too strong and the party was urged to respond to the cumulative effects of popular discredit, police successes and judicial vigour. The first step towards a gradual abandonment of the Oldartzen strategy and a re-evaluation of the efficacy of military opposition was announced by Rufi Etxeberria, a leading member of HB's (later imprisoned) Ruling Council and at the same time member of KAS. In October 1997, Etxeberria announced in a radio interview the 'beginning of a new phase', in which HB would push forward politics of 'national construction' and cooperation with the rest of the nationalist forces. After the imprisonment of Etxeberria and the HB leadership, a new and more heterogeneous and moderate 'Mahai Nazionala' was elected. Arnaldo Otegi, a former ETA prisoner and since December 1997 spokesman for the new Ruling Council, became the public face of the new wind blowing through HB and the Basque National Liberation Movement.

This shift of the political wing of radical nationalism would not have been possible without the consent of the paramilitaries. Although inside information on the situation within ETA in late 1997 is scarce, there seemed to be a nervousness and anxiety about increasingly successful police action against the organization, which in the past was well known for its safety and inner protection. This nervousness was especially due to the growing pressure of the French police.[67] Because of this increasing irritation and annoyance, the ETA leadership no longer felt safe in the French underground. It was forced to move to Belgium in order to establish its 'new centre of operations' there.[68] This military weakness was an important factor to bear in mind when explaining the reasons for the gradual shape of a new contextual structure in the Basque Country of the 1990s in which major political shifts and, as a result, the preliminary steps towards what many observers considered a peace process, became possible. The first to move was HB and its new Ruling Council, completed after an internal electoral process in February 1998. Although there was no official abandonment of the Oldartzen programme, the sum of the everyday declarations and timid political gestures committed in public by Arnaldo Otegi and Joseba Permach, the two spokesmen of the new 'Mahai Nazionala', indicated that the discourse of radical nationalism was passing through a phase of gradual transformation. In this new situation – despite all the previous criticism – the core ideas of the 'third space' project became visible as the principal guidelines for HB's politics. After the negative experience of Oldartzen, for the new HB leadership it had become quite clear that the way out of political weakness and towards independence could not be through blind militarism and political exclusiveness. The new strategy had to focus on the achievement of a new political majority, which would be more heterogeneous than the Liberation Movement, and the configuration of this new majority was impossible without some, perhaps symbolic, gestures by HB. An internal document discussed in the local groups of the party during the electoral process previous to the constitution of the new Ruling Council put it like this: 'We alone won't construct *Euskal Herria*', although HB is still the 'fundamental piece' in the process of national construction.[69] In other words, the political aims remained the same as always, but the strategy to achieve them had to be adapted to a new reality. Political observers referred to a more flexible 'political waist' in the new HB leadership when analyzing this relationship between the objectives and the strategy. Words and deeds evidenced this 'political waist'. In public appearances, Otegi and Permach distinguished again between the political project represented by HB and ETA's armed struggle. In contradiction to the traditional concept of ETA as the vanguard of the struggle, Otegi admitted that he knew 'very clearly that the majority of the Basques do not share ETA's armed struggle'. Both Otegi and Permach stated that HB did not give 'political coverage' to the 'street struggle' of the urban guerrilla.[70]

Alongside HB's efforts to stress its political autonomy from ETA's militarism – a strategic turn that had to be carried out very carefully and eluding the impression of an open break with the underground organization – HB leaders also reassessed their attitudes towards the other nationalist parties. Perceptions of these parties changed from lackeys of the Spanish oppressors to potential allies in a new project leading towards Basque sovereignty. The accidental coincidence in time with the favourable evolution of another historical ethnic conflict, the Northern Irish one, provided radical Basque nationalism with an idea, which was likely to facilitate a process towards sovereignty and, as a consequence, towards peace: the idea of a pannationalist agreement as a first step that was supposed to trigger this process. In other words, since the beginning of 1998, HB endeavoured – also through personal contacts – to create the conditions in which a Basque John Hume and a Basque Gerry Adams could emerge. If this were the case, somebody would necessarily have to play the part of a Spanish Tony Blair.

In 1997 and early 1998, however, the lack of synchronization between events in Northern Ireland and *Euskadi* seemed total. On 20 July, a week after PP councillor Blanco was kidnapped and assassinated by ETA, the IRA restored its ceasefire in response to changes brought about by the Blair administration. Exactly a week after the beginning of multi-party negotiations in Northern Ireland, which included Sinn Féin (7 October 1997), ETA killed a Basque policeman in front of the new Guggenheim Museum, thus aborting the planned 'third space' demonstration. Only two days after Gerry Adams's historical first visit to Downing Street (10 December, 1997), ETA shot dead another PP councillor. As Adams was being received by the first British Prime Minister since the creation of Northern Ireland, his 23 political allies in the HB leadership had only passed three nights of their seven-year sentence for collaboration with terrorism. In the three months following to the Good Friday Agreement (10 April 1998), ETA killed another three people.

Yet, even during the most intensive and dramatic moments of terrorist activity, the message from Northern Ireland reached the Basque Country. From late 1997, it affected the general political debate as well as nationalism. The nationalists defended more than any other political force the 'Northern Irish Way' to a solution based on dialogue and the first concrete result of this discourse was the *Lehendakari*'s first peace proposal of March 1998. Xabier Arzallus, the president of the moderate nationalist PNV insisted frequently on the validity of the Northern Irish model, considering that 'the world around ETA is not monolithic' and that therefore it was probable that also in the Liberation Movement the idea of dialogue and negotiations hand in hand with the silencing of arms would find followers.[71] In April 1998, the strange coincidence of events taking place in both countries at the same time manifested again the parallels between the Irish and Basque cases. Two days after the Stormont Agreement was reached, Basque nationalists of all colours celebrated their supreme national festival, *Aberri Eguna*, with the Northern Irish peace process at centre-stage.[72] The reaction of the non-nationalist parties contributed to this spectacular effervescence of the Northern Irish example in the Basque region, although the purpose of Spanish and Basque socialists and conservatives was exactly the opposite. They braced themselves to reject any parallelism between the Basque and the Northern Irish cases. Carlos Iturgaiz, the leader of the Basque PP, put it this way:

> The situation is not comparable. In the counties of Ulster an agreement has been produced between two communities confronting one another, whereas here there is a fanatic minority, ETA and HB, that is trying to impose by force and coercion its authority on a democratic and peaceful majority. HB and ETA have always tried to Ulsterize the Basque Country

and to show a conflict between two parts which simply does not exist here.[73]

The socialists agreed basically with this argument and pointed to the high level of self-government already attained by Basques in contrast with the lack of autonomy in Northern Ireland. HB leader Otegi called conservatives and socialists the 'Spanish Orangist Alternative'.[74] This political debate was accompanied by a debate in the media. In the weeks following the Stormont Agreement very few of the opinion-makers in the leading Spanish and Basque daily papers could resist the temptation to discuss the hypothetical lessons to be learnt (or not to be learnt) from the Northern Irish case.[75]

These are only a very few examples to show that in 1998 a real 'Ulsterization' of the main conflicting discourses was taking place in the Basque political process. The influence, however, was not only symbolic and theoretical. It was also translated into concrete political praxis by those who were keen to draw conclusions and learn the lessons from abroad, pushed towards this attitude both by rational calculation of opportunities and by the HB/ETA radical nationalists' basic instinct for political survival. The bitter experience of winter 1997, when the Spanish Supreme Court jailed 23 HB leaders for seven years, with no significant reaction from those sectors of Basque society not directly involved in the Liberation Movement, accelerated the strategic reconversion of HB from intransigent militarism to compromise-oriented policy-making. Thus, in the Basque case, the initiative on the construction of a cross-nationalist axis was not taken by moderate majority nationalism, but by the radical minority wing. The Basque SDLP, that is *mutatis mutandis* the governing PNV, was not able to take an initial, active part in this initiative, since the party was still the most important part of the so-called 'Democratic Bloc' built around the Ajuria Enea Agreement that, as a consequence of the Ermua mobilizations, excluded the possibility of any common initiative with those who supported violence. Furthermore, the recrudescence of terrorism in December 1997 and early 1998, as well as the absence of visible signs of a more critical attitude by HB leaders towards ETA violence, would have been poor politics by any party willing to initiate talks with HB. It was then that the Basque Sinn Féin, Herri Batasuna, made the first step. It was in two parts. In February 1998, immediately after HB's new Ruling Council was elected, the party's spokesmen reissued an idea proposed in September 1997 by the previous Mahai Nazionala now in prison, which invited all political parties, labour unions and other social movements to participate in a so-called 'Ireland Forum' with the purpose of discussing the Northern Irish peace process and its application to the Basque conflict.[76] At the same time, Otegi and the new HB leaders asked the PNV for secret political talks to identify possible points of consensus with a view to a broad national agreement that might serve as a framework for a future ETA ceasefire. The PNV, in the light of inside information about discussions within ETA and increasingly distant from the non-nationalist parties of the Democratic Bloc, given their unwillingness to consider any possibility of a solution to violence based on dialogue, was less reluctant to talk with HB than in 1997. This tendency towards new approaches was encouraged by the categorical rejection of President Ardanza's peace proposal in March 1998. But even before this final crisis of the Ajuria Enea Pact arose, the PNV had already given a positive response to HB's request. The first secret meeting of both parties was held on 26 February.[77]

During the following seven months, PNV and HB met twelve times. There were two main obstacles to an agreement. The first and most complicated was the interference of violence. If the immediate objective of these contacts was to produce a climate of de-escalation and cooperation, and if it was true that ETA agreed and even encouraged this new strategy, why then did the organization continue killing? In May, the spokesman of the right-wing, Navarre-located regionalist party UPN (Unión del Pueblo Navarro)[78] in the town council of Pamplona was shot dead. A few days later, a retired member of the Guardia Civil in Vitoria was killed. Late in June, finally, another PP councillor was assassinated in Renteria. The hypothesis of these crimes as acts committed by ETA dissidents opposed to the new strategy could be ruled out in an organization like ETA known for its strong inner cohesion. Hence, the most probable interpretation of the killings was to consider them extreme tests by which ETA wanted to see how far the PNV was willing to go and how strong the party's eagerness for an *entente* with HB really was.

The PNV passed the test. At the second meeting with HB, the party accepted a proposal by Otegi deciding to 'armour' the talks against external violent interference. Otegi's proposal was another symbolic step towards significant autonomy of the party from ETA. The HB leader emphasized that the party was not ETA and that nobody should blame it for something committed by the paramilitaries. On the other hand, violence and its consequences did not only cause the PNV serious problems, but HB's leadership too, who on several occasions had to defend the continuance of the talks despite what they considered 'police aggression'.[79]

The second obstacle for the PNV–HB talks was the problem of secrecy. The PNV did its very best to keep the talks secret, contracting even a special elite unit of the Ertzaintza with the order to protect the meetings from possible spying.[80] The contacts, however, were soon made public by the media. As a consequence, due to continuing ETA violence, the PNV became the target of tremendous political and media pressure.

For the PNV, the political cost of the talks increased daily and Joseba Egibar, the party's spokesman, admitted that his defence of the talks was jeopardizing his political future.[81] But the PNV persevered because of secret information obtained at a meeting with the ETA leadership, who demanded an intensification of the party's cooperation with HB and assured them that within ETA those supporting a ceasefire and a revaluation of politics were becoming a majority.[82] The fruit of this was a parliamentary *entente* between the PNV, HB, EA and IU[83] on a number of questions more symbolic than practical. Along with other decisions, the new entente rejected a modification of the Basque parliament's guidelines. This modification had been proposed by the socialists in order to fix the duty of any elected deputy to swear an oath of allegiance to the Spanish Constitution. This decision provoked an angry reaction from the Basque socialists, who quit the government, since their two official coalition partners (PNV, EA) had preferred an agreement with a party backing terrorism to a consensus with their socialist ally in the Basque government. 'The coexistence with PNV and EA has become impossible for us', stated Nicolás Redondo, the Basque socialist leader, when announcing his party's decision.[84] Redondo saw the PNV on a path to increasing radicalism and some days later he found more proof of his hypothesis. In the Catalan capital, the PNV signed the so-called 'Declaration of Barcelona' together with the leading nationalist parties from Catalonia and Galicia. In this document the nationalists criticized the lack of recognition of their 'national realities' by the state and implicitly demanded a reform of the Constitution in order to grant the multi-national character of the Spanish state.[85]

While HB, PNV, EA and IU were trying to build the Basque version of the Hume–Adams axis, the Good Friday Agreement was signed in Northern Ireland. The reaction of both ETA and HB was immediate: according to the Argentine daily paper *La Nación*, representatives of ETA had met IRA leaders in Montevideo to get direct information on the Stormont Agreement.[86] The IRA emphasis on politics increased pressure on ETA, since, as the *Irish Times* put it, 'the IRA ceasefire deprived it of a sense of having brothers in arms elsewhere in Europe'.[87] At the same time, HB, after attending the Sinn Féin Conference, recovered an idea already presented months ago, announcing the constitution of the 'Ireland Forum' as a kind of workshop for different Basque parties, unions and other popular organizations. This Forum was formed to analyse the Northern Irish peace process and discuss possible ways of application of the Basque conflict.[88] The first meeting of the Forum took place on 20 June, with the participation of all the nationalist parties, IU, the two nationalist unions, the farmers' union, the peace movement Elkarri and a number of smaller organizations close to nationalist thinking. The idea of the 'third space' and of the 'new majority' had reappeared, pushed by the Irish example. As on previous occasions, ETA was unwilling to leave this new initiative in the hands of the political, social and cultural organizations assembled in the Forum. Only a few days after the Forum's constitution, a bomb killed a PP councillor in Renteria who, a few months earlier, had been substituted for a colleague shot dead by ETA.

However, according to information released later, this new crime, which had generated internal protests within HB, was a tragic accident. The internal debate of the paramilitaries was about to conclude and the decision to declare a ceasefire seemed to be immediate, but this conclusion had not yet been transmitted to the commandos in the underground.[89] This process of transmission was finally committed during July and the absence of violent reactions to the closure of the daily paper *Egin*, on the orders of the Spanish Supreme Court, indicated significant changes within ETA. Yet, the final and definitive decision was not taken until August after a new secret meeting between the PNV and the ETA leadership. This meeting was made public by the paramilitaries after the collapse of the ceasefire and its content became the object of an extremely controversial debate in post-ceasefire *Euskadi*.[90]

The decision for a ceasefire had been taken, the commandos and ETA members living in Latin America were being informed and HB's more flexible approach[91] was gaining the backing of the paramilitaries. Now a means had to be found through which the ceasefire could be interpreted as a fundamental contribution to a future political victory rather than a simple military surrender. The 'Ireland Forum' performed this function with a document issued four days before the ceasefire was announced on 16 September. It was signed by each of the 23 members of the Forum and was later known as the 'Lizarra Agreement'. On 12 September, the Forum met in Estella (or in Basque, Lizarra), a town in the province of Navarre. Its sole objective was to reach a consensus on a draft which reflected the previous work of the Forum. In reality, there was little chance of making major changes to the draft presented by the representatives of HB and PNV Iruin and Egibar. The reason was that ETA did not know the literal text of the draft but only its general outline, on which it had agreed. Since no peace process and no resolution of the Basque conflict was supposed to work without the cooperation and consent of the paramilitaries, it seemed politically unwise to risk this consensus by major changes to the text.[92] The final document, with the first part completely dedicated to the Northern Irish peace process, was further evidence of the deep influence of Northern Ireland on Basque – and especially nationalist – politics.[93]

This declaration based on the Irish experience picks up some of the principles of Ardanza's peace proposal, such as the definition of the conflict as a political conflict, the open and unconditional agenda of the negotiations, the consideration of the Basque people as the sovereign decision-taking subject or the demand for the implicated states to accept the outcome of the negotiation process. There were, however, four remarkable differences. The first was semantic but had an acute political meaning. For Ardanza, an ETA ceasefire prior to political dialogue was an 'absolute necessity'. In the Lizarra document, ETA was not mentioned, but it was envisaged that the negotiations would be carried out in the 'permanent absence of all expressions of violence'. While this was a euphemism for a ceasefire, it could also be applied to what the nationalist left used to refer to as 'state – that is, police – violence'. The second difference was the explicit exclusion of negotiations with ETA in the Ardanza document, against negotiations 'without excluding any of the implicated parties' in the Lizarra Agreement. This might include ETA. The participation of the paramilitaries was, however, conditional because, according to the Lizarra document, the final word rested with the 'citizens of *Euskal Herria*'. The third difference lay in the Lizarra document's specification of the core issues of the future negotiation process, which were considered keys to any sustained solution of the conflict: 'territoriality', meaning the separation of the seven (French and Spanish) Basque territories by political and administrative borders; the recognition of the Basque people as the legitimate decision-maker; and, finally, the acknowledgement of the Basque people's right to 'political sovereignty'. The last was another euphemism not necessarily meaning independence, since a 'sovereign' decision could also be that of a Basque Republic within an Iberian Federation or even that of maintaining the status quo. The *Lehendakari* used in his proposal only very general terms referring to the 'national question' as the principal issue of the negotiations. Furthermore, Ardanza also put emphasis on the point that the negotiation would start with the recognition of the 'currently existing status quo' – a hint looking for the sympathy of the non-nationalist forces – and that there should not be any limits to this negotiation, a sentence aimed at the adherence of the radical nationalists. Finally, the fourth difference concerned the origin and consequences of the conflict. In the Lizarra document it was a conflict between the Basque people and the Spanish and French states, whereas for Ardanza it was also a conflict between different Basque identities.

These differences resulted from the different objectives of the two texts. Ardanza's proposal was that of a (nationalist) president trying to establish the highest possible level of consensus among nationalists and nonnationalists. The Lizarra Agreement, on the contrary, was a document written not exclusively, but predominantly by and for nationalists (including ETA) with the implicit aim of smoothing the way to a ceasefire. It was a political manifesto in the mould of a Basque Hume–Adams document directed towards public opinion but in reality addressed to the local paramilitaries. It was not an institutional declaration, which had to take a Basque Trimble, Paisley or their Spanish allies into account.

Political reactions to the Lizarra Declaration were predictable. The polarization of Basque politics into nationalist and non-nationalist blocs was evident again. Little seemed to have changed since the debate on Ardanza's peace proposal. The Spanish government and the Basque conservatives blamed the PNV, EA and IU for 'breaking the consensus of the democrats' by burying the Ajuria Enea Agreement and adopting an attitude of 'indulgence' towards ETA and radical nationalism. The socialists, anxious about the possibility of losing their non-nationalist voters to the conservatives in the imminent regional elections, used the same arguments as the PP leaders and President Aznar. In this view, the agreement was a capitulation to ETA. One Irish commentator regarded the reactions as a consequence of the impression that in the Basque Country 'democratic nationalists are being seduced by ETA, whereas (...) the SDLP won over Sinn Féin to democracy in Ireland'.[94]

On the other hand, the signatories to Lizarra championed agreement as a first step on the road to peace. The initiative also received official support from the Basque government, which, after the withdrawal of the socialists only consisted of the nationalist PNV and EA. The government also issued a call to ETA to lay down its arms and take notice of what the broad majority of the Basque people were demanding.[95]

When Mari Carmen Garmendia, spokeswoman of the Basque government, issued this statement, she probably knew that this call to ETA was superfluous, since the paramilitaries had already made their decision. On 17 September *Euskadi Información*, successor to the closed daily paper *Egin*, and *Egunkaria*, the daily paper written exclusively in Basque, published the text of a four-sheet-long communiqué written in Basque, in which ETA announced its first ever complete and indefinite ceasefire.[96] The communiqué, signed four days after the Lizarra Agreement, did not actually mention the Agreement. Yet, Lizarra is implicit throughout the text. The first sentence reads: 'After two long decades, now there is once again an open possibility for *Euskal Herria* to take a decisive step towards independence'.

This possibility was the consequence of a 'new political phase' in the history of the Basque people. The most significant feature of this situation was the new consciousness of the political forces, which had traditionally supported the 'dividing autonomism'. According to ETA, these parties now had become aware of the impossibility of moving forward to sovereignty on the path of autonomism. This political shift of the moderate nationalists and the growing conviction of the necessity for dialogue and negotiation as the indispensable tools for a solution of the conflict were in the opinion of ETA the essential factors that had created the new situation. Consequently, for the first time in twenty years it had become possible to 'share efforts and to create a new consensus and meeting point for the common work towards Basque independence'. ETA's answer to the new scenario was the ceasefire. The character of the truce, however, would depend on 'events and steps in the near future'.

In Gernika, the union leader José Elorrieta spoke of the idea of the 'third space' and a 'new peaceful majority' backing Basque sovereignty. According to an Irish commentator, the time was 'ripe' for HB and ETA to enter mainstream politics, but they wanted an 'honourable way' to do so. The PNV 'threw (them) a lifeline',[97] accepting the idea of a pan-nationalist *entente* as the instrument that would kick-start the peace process and be a prime key to the resolution of the conflict. The inter-nationalist party talks, the Ireland Forum and finally the Lizarra Declaration specified the idea of a cross-party nationalist agreement. The negotiation between the PNV and ETA brought the definitive push. Stormont was proof that this strategy was possible. ETA's communiqué fitted perfectly into this inter-nationalist operation, since its message was addressed especially and nearly exclusively to the nationalist community, and not, as usual on previous occasions, to the Spanish government or the 'centralist' parties. On 16 September, the Basque Humes and Adams, seizing the opportunities created by a new political and social framework in which the pressure in favour of an end of violence had become stronger than ever before, achieved their first success. For the first time since the beginning of the violent conflict in the Basque Country, the conditions for a negotiated solution to the problem seemed to be present. After the ceasefire was announced, the Basque–Irish parallels continued. In the regional elections to the Basque parliament on 25 October, the voters rewarded radical nationalism for its new strategic image and its contribution to the achievement of the ceasefire. Herri Batasuna, rebaptised as Euskal Herritarrok, received a substantial peace dividend with 17.94 per cent of the votes. It became the third-largest party in the Basque Autonomous Community behind the PNV (27.97 per cent) and the PP (20.14 per cent), followed by the PSE–EE (17.57 per cent). The party won 57,000 new voters in comparison with the regional elections of 1994 and the total of 223,264 votes was the best result ever obtained by HB.[98] Yet, while HB campaigned for the elections, ETA had already begun to reorganize its commandos. About a year later, the paramilitaries called off the ceasefire. Instead of making politics like their Northern Irish allies, Basque militant nationalism returned to violence and military reasoning. The hope for a peace process vanished and Basque society entered a period of deep political crisis and intense terrorist activity, which surpassed any experience known since Franco's death. The Irish mirror was definitely broken.

9
The End of a Dream

Obviously, since human beings are not mere functional, passive derivations of existing circumstances, a favourable context does not necessarily bring forth favourable results. The history of peace processes is a good example for how a favourable context might change, because the human agency which is engaged in the process commits errors with negative consequences, or certain actors change their mind and end up opposing a process by withdrawing their initial cooperation. The comparison of this frustrated Basque experience with other – for the moment successful – peace processes, especially the Northern Irish one, provides us with interesting data and ideas for the final step of our analysis, in which I shall look for the reasons for the fateful collapse of the Basque attempt at conflict transformation. However, before entering this theoretical debate concerning the causes of the breakdown of what might have become a Basque peace process, we should briefly analyse how this dream for peace became a nightmare of absorbing fear and increasing violence, and how the return of violence impacted on the political system.

9.1 The breakdown of the ceasefire and the escalation of violence

The announcement of the truce in September 1998 raised enormous expectations among the Basque population, which cut across political cleavages. The more political discourse of the new HB leadership was another sign of an apparent willingness to abandon militarism and enter constitutional politics. Yet, behind the public announcement of an 'indefinite' and 'unilateral' ceasefire and the all-encompassing hope for a peaceful settlement of the conflict after so many years of suffering, there was a hidden reality only known to very few of the key actors. This reality did not fit into the new scenario of general expectation and optimism emerging in public opinion, since it was based upon factors which appeared in a new light to make the ceasefire seem the precarious result of secret negotiations with an uncertain outcome.

These negotiations, which only became public knowledge after the breakdown of the truce, were different from prior negotiations in one important

143

aspect, because they were not between the paramilitaries and the state, but between ETA and the democratic nationalists of the PNV and EA. As already indicated above, the Lizarra Agreement and the ceasefire itself were the consequences of the agreement reached in this strand of negotiations, which was carried out in the surprising absence of ETA's political wing Herri Batasuna. The first concrete result of the contacts between the ETA leadership and the PNV was the proposition of an agreement formulated by the paramilitaries, in which, in July 1998, the democratic nationalists were asked to endorse the following basic goals:

1. The creation of a new institution including representatives of all seven (Spanish and French) Basque provinces as a step towards the dissolution of current institutions, as well as towards Basque unification;
2. Cooperation among all organizations 'favourable to the construction of *Euskal Herria*';
3. An end of cooperation with forces intent on 'the destruction of *Euskal Herria* and the construction of Spain (PP and PSOE)'.

As a consequence of this agreement, ETA announced in the fourth point of the text a truce, which in public would be called 'indefinite'. In reality, however, it would be revised after four months in order to ascertain if each of the signatory organizations had or had not kept its word. Furthermore, the truce would exclude 'operations of supply' and possible acts of self-defence.

This proposal was a poisoned chalice. On the one hand, it was the key to an indefinite ceasefire, which never before in the history of ETA had been called and it gave the PNV the opportunity of taking on the role of the party of peace. This peacemaker image was supposed to bring an important political dividend in future elections. However, on the other hand, the clauses of the agreement drafted by the paramilitaries also requested a radical change in the political strategy of moderate nationalism that had obtained since Franco's death and the transition to democracy. This strategy was built upon the principle of cooperation with the non-nationalist parties and the central government in the process of Basque nation-building and the recovery of (partial) self-government by the gradual implementation of the Statute of Autonomy. This principle was to a significant extent a consequence of political necessity, since owing to the impossibility of compromising with the political wing of the terrorists and the loss of the PNV hegemony after the party's split in 1986 no majority could be found within either of the two existing (nationalist and non-nationalist) blocs. Politics had to be done by cutting across the cleavages and this meant a return to the historical alliance between nationalists and socialists, which had been created in 1936 in order to fight against the fascist uprising first within the Basque Country and then for nearly four decades in exile. At the end of the 1990s, this traditional cooperation had already been seriously jeopardized both by the PNV's decision to design a new strategy for peace and self-determination beyond the limits of the Statute of Autonomy and by the socialists' radical rejection of President Ardanza's peace proposal. As a consequence of this divorce, the Basque socialists had quit the regional government in early July 1998. Thus, the PNV had actually fulfilled one of the demands formulated by the paramilitaries already a month before the party received ETA's written proposal. However, the PNV leadership was realistic enough to know that a hypothetical pan-nationalist front, including HB, would not guarantee majorities in all Basque provinces or town halls and that therefore further cooperation with the socialists could not be completely ruled out *a priori*, if the level of political power had to be maintained or even improved upon.

This ambiguous position between the shape of a new pan-nationalist strategy and the limitations resulting from the heterogeneous and pluralistic Basque reality marked the answer given by PNV and EA to the proposal of the paramilitaries. In August 1998, both parties signed the document. Yet their signatures did not mean a total endorsement of the four points, since they added a note on the front page indicating that the 'development of this agreement' could be found on the other side of the sheet. In that attachment, the parties tried to ameliorate the significance of point three, stating that the demand for an exclusion of non-nationalist parties should be understood as a long-term goal and that, 'if the defence of the Basque nation' required this solution, agreements with other parties could be borne in mind to ensure the stability of institutions under nationalist control. Another important point made by PNV and EA in their interpretation of the agreement with ETA referred to point four, adding that 'the ceasefire meant respect for the human rights of all persons'. Obviously, this was an attempt to restrict the meaning of what ETA called 'operations of supply', making sure that the ceasefire would be a real and a total one. Finally, in another document sent by the PNV leadership to ETA, the party reasserts its decision to sign the proposal, while demanding negotiations between the nationalist parties for the specific steps to take and the time-schedules for the implementation of the points agreed upon. Also in this document the possibility of including other (non-nationalist) parties in the government of the Basque institutions is mentioned, although the goal in the long run remains the same, namely, pan-nationalist majorities wherever they are possible.[1]

Was this an agreement or was it not? PNV and EA had signed the proposal, but they had also introduced their particular interpretation about the meaning of the four points. Would ETA agree to this interpretation or would it reject it? For the moment, the former seemed to be the case. A few days after the text of the agreement with the two parties' attachments had been returned to the paramilitaries, the Lizarra Agreement was signed. It was no secret that HB would not have taken part without the paramilitaries' consent. Two weeks later, ETA announced the ceasefire.

Yet, only a few days afterwards, the PNV received a new letter from the underground organization, in which the first serious problems became evident. While still considering the new situation as the 'way to the fulfill-ment of Basque sovereignty' and applauding the PNV's 'political maturity', ETA, however, expressed severe criticism of the party. This was done in two steps. Firstly, the terrorists rejected the party's interpretation of the agree-ment and its four points. And secondly, they criticized the fact that the PNV leaders, and especially the members of the Basque government, were constantly talking about the new political process as if its only ingredient was the truce and its only aim was riddance of violence. The paramilitaries opposed this point of view, stating that 'the political phase that we face is not the phase of "peace" but that of sovereignty. And the period of office in the Vitoria parliament is not going to be that of peace, but the parliament's last period in office. This, at least, is the sense of the agreement.' Furthermore – and this was further proof of ETA's new strategy – the para-militaries warned the PNV leadership that in the new situation created since the summer of 1998 neither the Spanish nor the French government would be taken into account and that the only actors responsible for implement-ing the agreement and leading the Basque Country towards sovereignty were the nationalist parties and the underground organization.

Only a few days after the ceasefire was called, the democratic nationalists already knew that the truce was founded upon very weak groundwork and that there was no reason for any kind of euphoria. They knew that in real-ity the secret agreement, which had opened the door to the ceasefire, was finally only a mutilated one, since ETA had rejected the parties' amend-ments. They were also aware that the paramilitaries did not really bother about the problem of violence and peace, since for them the truce was noth-ing but the derivation of the steps taken in the political process aimed at Basque sovereignty. Thus, already in late September 1998 it was foreseeable that the ceasefire would only last if in the opinion of the underground mil-itants this political process towards sovereignty delivered tangible results.

In view of this scenario, the democratic nationalists' options were quite restricted. Since they embarked upon a secret political agreement with the paramilitaries as a precondition for the ceasefire, the PNV and EA were tied hand and foot. They had to take care that the secrecy of the conversations and the (pseudo-) accord was kept. By refusing to act in public, the politi-cians placed themselves on the same level as the paramilitaries, and there, in the underground, what really counted were weapons and not the demo-cratic legitimacy of the parties obtained in the elections. Hence, ETA played with this advantage when negotiating with the parties, which were aware that any disagreement could put the continuity of the truce at risk. Consequently, in order to impede a premature collapse of the ceasefire, the PNV reacted as if it had not received the letter and as if there was an agree-ment including the party's amendments. This reaction was based on the conviction that the longer the ceasefire lasted, the more difficult it would become to break it. In the meantime, concrete political decisions had to be taken in order to symbolize the strong commitment to the process to Basque sovereignty and, incidentally, to keep the paramilitaries satisfied.

The first steps were taken after the elections to the Basque parliament in October 1998. As already mentioned, the voters applauded the more political discourse of the radical nationalist EH (former HB), granting the party a remarkable peace dividend. However, the usual correlation of political forces was not altered, since the votes, translated into three new seats, won by EH were lost by the moderate nationalist parties PNV and EA. On the other hand, the polarizing effect of the Lizarra Agreement favoured the conservative party PP, which reached its best result in elections to the Basque parliament. In the new parliament, very little seemed to have changed. As before, the nationalist parties held a slight majority of 41 seats, the non-nationalist opposition counted on 34. It was evident that the moderate nationalists had to look for a partner, if they wanted to appoint the PNV candidate Juan José Ibarretxe new president. Since in July 1998 the socialists had already quit the government and the secret pact with ETA demanded the rupture with the political forces 'aimed at the destruction of *Euskal Herria'*, Ibarretxe knew that a return to the traditional coalition with the Basque socialists was not possible, if the ceasefire and the hope of a peaceful settlement of the conflict was to be consolidated. In December, the negotiations with EH enabled the election of the PNV candidate as new Basque *Lehendakari*. Finally, in May of the following year, this pan-nationalist cooperation created an important, new result, when the *Lehendakari* signed a formal pact with the EH spokesmen, in which the radical nationalists manifested their commitment to support the PNV–EA government with their votes. The text of the agreement included a clause expressing the willingness of the signatories to work for a solution of the conflict 'by exclusively political and democratic means' and to aim for 'the total disappearance of all actions and expressions of violence'. Even if no explicit condemnation of ETA and its armed struggle could be found, for most of the democratic nationalists the acceptance of this clause by the political wing of the paramilitaries was another sign confirming the gradual transformation of the Liberation Movement and its willingness to enter civil politics. With the party backing a nationalist government rooted in the Statute of Autonomy, which had always been rejected by radical nationalists, the paramilitaries were unlikely to take up arms. This, at least, was the reasoning of PNV and EA nationalists, who consequently were able to sell the agreement with EH as an 'important stepping stone to peace, coexistence and national construction'.[2] This statement could not be reduced to a mere product of nationalist propaganda. Even *El País*, the most important Spanish daily paper close to the Socialist Party and radically opposed to Basque nationalism, published an editorial with a surprisingly optimistic touch. Referring once again to the Northern Irish example, it was argued that ETA and EH might have reached the same conclusion as the IRA and SF, being more and more convinced that it was not necessary to 'wait for independence before starting to work for the fatherland'. If this impression was correct, the agreement might be a valid tool for a peaceful settlement, since – as demonstrated both by the Northern Irish peace process and the German Green Party – 'the integration of the anti-system parties nearly always goes through a process of power sharing with them'.[3]

With this agreement, the governing nationalists had taken an important step towards the implementation of points three and four of the secret pseudo-accord with ETA. The elections to the European parliament, the provincial parliaments and the town councils of June 1999 confirmed both the impermeability of the two political blocs of nationalists and non-nationalists, and the strategy of moderate nationalism to break its ties with the socialists, while approaching the radical EH. As in October 1998, these second elections during the truce had not changed the political landscape in favour of nationalism. On the contrary, the PNV lost its majority in the provincial parliament of Alava and in the capital Vitoria. San Sebastián, the capital of the most nationalist province of Gipuzkoa, again voted for a socialist mayor, as did other larger towns in Gipuzkoa and Bizkaia. This was the second occasion on which the expectations of moderate nationalism were frustrated, since the peace dividend given by the voters was to the radicals to the detriment of the governing nationalists. Furthermore, the political polarization initiated in the summer of 1998 was not only failing to produce more nationalism, on the contrary, it was contributing to a spectacular empowerment of the most radical opponent of Basque nationalism. Indeed, in both elections the conservative Partido Popular had obtained excellent results, which only a few years ago had still been unthinkable. In 1999, the Basque followers of President Aznar were governing in the Diputación of Alava and the council of Vitoria, and what was still more worrying for the PNV, the party had made enormous progress in Bizkaia and its capital Bilbao, where traditionally the PNV had ruled nearly without opposition.

Yet, despite this somewhat frustrating reality, the PNV leadership did not see any reason to introduce major changes in the party's political strategy, and this strategy was determined both by the party's programme demanding in the long run Basque sovereignty, and by its willingness to consolidate the ceasefire and the peace process by implementing the points of the secret pact with ETA. A new product of this strategy came in February and September 1999 with the foundation of a new institution, which corresponded to the 'united and sovereign institutional structure' including all Basque territories as expressed in point 1 of the secret agreement. After the first general assembly of about 700 nationalist councillors in Pamplona, this new initiative was formalized in a new meeting held in Bilbao, in September. In Bilbao, 1,778 nationalist councillors constituted Udalbiltza as the first political institution with delegates from town councils located in each of the seven Basque territories on either side of the Spanish–French border. Of the delegates, 1,483 came from the Basque Autonomous Community, representing a total of 56 per cent of all councillors in that region; 271 came from Navarre (15 per cent of the total number of councillors in that province), and only 24 from the French Basque Country. Among the Basque capitals, only that of Bilbao had voted – with a slight majority of a single vote – the formal adhesion to Udalbiltza. Neither the Basque President, nor the president of the Basque parliament were present during the founding meeting. PNV president Arzallus was keen to make it clear that the new institution would not 'infringe any legality' and that its function would be to symbolize 'the image of a people' without 'substituting any other institution'. EH leader Otegi, however, had no doubt that Udalbiltza had 'inaugurated a new period' and that this period would conclude with a 'new juridical and political status'. The foundation manifesto did not specify the future programme of the new institution, stating in rather vague terms that Udalbiltza had been created in order to display publicly the 'existence of *Euskal Herria* as a nation' and to lay the groundwork for a future political and institutional unification of the seven territories as a result of increasing cooperation between their town councils.[4]

The controversies concerning the spirit and the objectives of this new Assembly of Basque municipalities reflected the complicated situation of moderate nationalism very well thanks to the secret negotiations with the paramilitaries. On the one hand, since PNV and EA had never abandoned the idea of a future unification of all Basque territories on either side of the border as a political objective in the long run, this new initiative fitted well into the nationalist ideology. Furthermore, Udalbiltza – an initiative agreed upon in the secret pact – was supposed to be an important tool favouring the consolidation of the ceasefire. On the other hand, however, the PNV was the party which, from the establishment of the autonomy, controlled the Basque government and many of the other important institutions (province governments, town councils). Owing to this experience of autonomous self-government accumulated over years, the party was realistic enough to know that any change in the status quo by an enlargement of Basque political power had to be a gradual and negotiated process, and that the idea of bringing an end to all institutions linked to the Statute of Autonomy within only a few years was completely absurd. Thus, the task of moderate nationalists was a double one. ETA and the radicals had to be satisfied by playing the game of a political actor strongly committed to the struggle for Basque self-determination. At the same time, the party leadership had to make sure that this new initiative, which was carried out hand in hand with the pro-ETA radicals, was not understood as a frontal attack against the autonomous government controlled by its own people. Such an interpretation would not only undermine the authority of the *Lehendakari*. It would also unleash a loss of confidence on the Basque business community and in general on all sectors of society not identified with the politics of self-determination or independence.

In the end, the moderate nationalists were not able to accomplish either the first or the second task, since in reality both were incompatible. As I shall analyse below, the increasing cooperation with the radicals, the frequent questioning of the autonomy by PNV leaders, and the promotion of controversial initiatives like Udalbiltza were factors that contributed to the shaping of the most serious crisis of the Basque political system since democracy had been restored. Yet, all these gestures symbolizing willingness to go beyond the limits of the regional autonomy performed precisely by the party that years before had struggled most for the devolution of autonomy, were not enough to satisfy the paramilitaries. Eventually, as prisoner of an impossible double strategy and motivated by the will to impede a return to terrorism at any price, moderate PNV nationalism came under fire from both sides.

Since September 1998, the PNV had known that ETA was not at all willing to transfer the management of the political process to the parties. It would continue monitoring it, reducing the role of HB to that of a mere manager of previously adopted decisions. The party's absence in the secret conversations was a clear sign of the hierarchy established within the Liberation Movement. During the months following the announcement of the ceasefire, the paramilitaries issued several public communiqués and gave interviews with a clear message directed at the governing nationalists. This message can be summed up as follows.

The Lizarra Agreement had created a new political situation, which for the first time in history has made a strategy towards Basque self-determination possible. The first steps on this way have been taken and this made armed struggle superfluous for the moment. The final success of this new policy, however, depended on a deepening and specification of the general strategy, which had to be translated into tangible measures and decisions. This, however, would not be possible, unless the PNV gave up all its links with the autonomous institutions and the 'Spanish' parties. Most of the communiqués included an implicit or explicit warning for the PNV and its leaders, who were blamed for their temptation to slow down the process leading to Basque freedom.

Indeed, contrary to prior experiences, in its public media performances, ETA focused its analysis nearly exclusively on the activity of governing nationalism, omitting with very few exceptions references to the Spanish or French governments. As a consequence of the new strategy aimed at the accumulation of nationalist power as an indispensable tool to break the state's resistance against the Basque struggle for self-determination, the paramilitaries did not attach great importance to negotiations with the Spanish government. During the 14 months of the truce, only one single meeting between the ETA leadership and delegates of the Aznar administration took place, and it was the Spanish president, and not the underground organization, who had put forward the initiative to organize this meeting. Already in November 1998, Aznar had publicly authorized contacts with the paramilitaries in order to 'check' their willingness to lay down their arms and embark upon a peace process. This meeting was held in May 1999 in Zurich. Its contents were leaked to the media a month later and can only be regarded as a complete disagreement. While the paramilitaries, chaired by the head of the political office Mikel Albizu ('Mikel Antza'), introduced political and constitutional issues (recognition of the right of self-determination; Basque unification) on to the agenda, the Spanish delegation, led by the General Secretary of the Presidency Javier Zarzalejos, was only willing to debate security issues (prisoners, refugees). Both sides agreed on meeting again, but nobody seemed to be really interested in keeping these contacts alive. The imprisonment of Kantauri, one of the ETA leaders who had done an important job in preparing the Zurich meeting, and then later that of Belén González Peñalva, who had participated in the meeting, were considered by the underground group to be open aggression. The remaining confidence vanished, when the name of the Basque Bishop Uriarte as mediator was leaked to the press, and on this occasion not only the radical nationalists blamed the Spanish Minister of the Interior Mayor Oreja for this sabotage of the dialogue. On the other hand, the total lack of flexibility shown by the paramilitaries during the conversation, their insistence on political negotiations, and their strategic decision to play the cards of the nationalist power accumulation were reasons enough to cancel the contacts, as was finally announced in August 1999. ETA accused Aznar and his government of manipulating the information about the contacts for 'electoral purposes' and of destroying any attempt to create a climate of confidence by an attitude of 'intoxication'.[5]

A month before, in a new secret meeting with PNV and EA delegates, ETA had increased its pressure on the governing nationalists. According to the paramilitaries, the steps taken to implement the agreement of the summer of 1998 had not been sufficient. In their opinion, this was due to the agreement's lack of concreteness and to the laxity of both parties, which had started back-pedalling instead of engaging in the alteration of the political and juridical framework. Consequently, ETA cancelled the previous agreement and presented a draft for a new one as a means of defining the precise strategy and of enabling a way out of the impasse. This new proposal consisted basically in the call for elections in all Spanish and French Basque territories to create a 'National parliament', which would be in charge of drafting the text for a Basque Constitution. This National parliament, together with the already existing Udalbiltza and another new chamber representing the different Basque regions, would make up the future administrative structure of the independent Basque Country. The implementation of this new proposal would lead to the end of the armed struggle.

Two things emerged from the contents of the proposal: firstly, the enormous gap existing between Basque reality and the imagined microcosm of the underground activists; and secondly, the terrorists' feeling of superiority towards the democratic nationalists, which were supposed to be unable to reject any proposal made by ETA, since they needed for their own political success the continuance of the ceasefire and, furthermore, had to avoid by all means the publicity of their secret negotiations with the paramilitaries. Yet, already during the meeting PNV and EA branded the proposal as 'Utopian, unrealistic, fantasy and counter-productive for the national construction'. However, the nationalists were well aware that a new lack of agreement would destroy the momentum initiated in the summer of 1998 and that the return of terror hung over the parties like the sword of Damocles. To keep the contacts alive, PNV and EA promised to study the proposal and send a written answer before September. We know the wording of the PNV letter dated in August and received by the ETA leadership in early September. For the party it was impossible to agree with the proposal. In the letter, the arguments forwarded in the secret meeting were repeated. The PNV considered it impossible to organize the national elections demanded by ETA without previously 'do(ing) tremendous pedagogical work and gain(ing) the support of the citizens'. While rejecting the idea of the national elections as premature, the PNV drafted another proposal in more general terms, assessing the Basque right for self-determination, the party's commitment to a political process aiming at the definition of a new institutional structure and its promise to struggle for the implementation of this structure after having received the democratic support of the Basque people. The letter ended with the invitation to talk about this proposal at a later meeting.[6]

This was the end of the dream. The rude awakening came late in November 1999, when ETA announced in a long communiqué its decision to reactivate the armed struggle. The arguments were already known: PNV and EA were 'sticking to the Autonomy Statute of the Moncloa [residence of the Spanish President], giving more importance to their usual management than to the initiatives designed for the construction of a new political and juridical framework'. As a consequence, according to the interpretation of the paramilitary leadership, the political process initiated in the summer of 1998 was 'suffering from a blockade and obvious rottenness'. In this new context, ETA assured people that it had no alternative but to take up arms 'in response to its commitment to the defence of *Euskal Herria*'.[7]

What followed was a dramatic translation from words into deeds. In December, the police intercepted two vans on the way to Madrid carrying about 2,000 kilograms of dynamite. This material was part of the eight tons stolen by a commando in France during the truce. In January 2000, in Madrid a member of the Spanish military became the first victim assassinated by ETA since the collapse of the ceasefire. This was the beginning of a bloody nightmare caused by more and more indiscriminate violence against nearly everybody opposed to ETA and its ideology. Never before in the history of violent nationalism has the spectrum of real and possible targets of violence been as widespread as after the collapse of the ceasefire. It would be beyond the scope of this study to display the details of this return to terror, which so far (by March 2003) has killed 44 persons, caused massive costly destruction by car-bombs, and forced several hundreds of persons to move under the protection of bodyguards and/or organize their lives according to special rules of self-protection (looking under the car; not repeating the daily itinerary to work; not frequenting certain places, etc.). Yet, a couple of facts should be pointed out in order to manifest the dramatic change the collapse of the ceasefire meant for the Basque people (and many others outside the Basque Country):

- The (former) Spanish Minister of the Interior was right when assessing the ceasefire as a 'trap ceasefire' (*tregua trampa*). ETA itself agreed with this definition, stating that it was a 'trap for the Spanish and the French states, as well as for the strategy of submission to Spain carried out previously by PNV and EA'.[8] Indeed, although the paramilitaries stopped killing for 15 months, they used this time for a complete reorganization of the group's clandestine structure, integrating a large number of young and still 'legal', e.g. unknown by the police, militants into new commandos. According to information provided by the news agency Vasco Press, the average age of ETA militants has dropped from 35 years in 1993 to 28 years after the collapse of the ceasefire. In the summer of 2002, nine out of 19 'wanted terrorists' on the list published by the Spanish Ministry of the Interior were aged under 28 (the average of all 19 ETA members was 30.74 years).[9] In many cases, these new members had been socialized in violence and radical nationalist thinking in the groups of the street-guerrillas and the youth organization of the Liberation Movement. As a consequence, this new post-ceasefire generation of ETA terrorists is politically less prepared than the previous ones and extremely coldblooded when acting.
- Consequently, never before in the history of ETA was it so difficult to detect strategic political reasoning behind the group's violent activity. Apparently, a demonstration of military power has become more important than the fulfilment of political objectives. This absolute predominance of military activism has brought with it a remarkable enlargement of the list of targeted persons, which now includes all politicians from the conservative and socialist parties; all members of the army and police forces, including the Basque *Ertzaintza*; all employers unwilling to pay the 'revolutionary tax'; all judges located in the Basque Country; all Spanish judges dealing with terrorism or street violence; a large number of intellectuals, university teachers and journalists; moderate politicians from the PNV and EA.[10] In fact, ETA seems to have converted those, who still

in the summer of 1998 were considered new allies, into political enemies, who deserve the same treatment as the other enemies of *Euskal Herria*. This became evident in the spring of 2000, when the paramilitaries leaked to the press most of the documents dealing with the secret contacts between ETA and the democratic nationalist parties. As forecast, this produced a real political and media thunderstorm against both parties and their leaderships.

- Since the end of the ceasefire, the increasing pressure of terrorism has forced many persons to abandon the Basque Country.
- The return of violence produced not only a tremendous problem of security. It also affected the Basque political system, which entered a period of acute crisis. Actually, this crisis, which had never since Franco's death reached similar dimensions, can be considered the only victory of violent nationalism so far, because polarization made a democratic and massive response to the challenge of terrorism nearly impossible. One of the preconditions for any democratic response to the threat of political violence is a 'consistent, clear and credible policy based – if possible – upon a broad consensus'.[11] Why was it, in the post-ceasefire *Euskadi*, so difficult to reach this consensus?

9.2 The agony of normal politics

After studying different ways and methodologies to put an end to civil wars, William Zartman concluded that 'at best, internal conflicts are simply subsumed back into normal politics'.[12] Fortunately, the situation in the post-ceasefire Basque Country is far from being a civil war, because the notion of war as applied to the conflict is nothing but a unilateral invention defended by a minority underground group. Yet Zartman's statement does make sense in *Euskadi*, as it does in Northern Ireland. Since its very beginnings, the Northern Irish peace process was rooted in the objective of bringing militant republicanism back into politics by convincing the IRA and SF that violence had become more a liability than an asset in the fulfilment of the Republicans' political goals. In the Basque case the core idea, which pushed the moderate nationalists into secret negotiations with ETA and into alliance with the political wing of the paramilitaries was not very different, because the perspective of a new political majority favouring Basque self-determination required the silencing of the guns. Once a ceasefire was consolidated, the hope for a lasting peace would shape a new situation, which was supposed to bring a peace dividend to the nationalist parties by a gradual, but massive adhesion of many of the Basque citizens, who had traditionally been opposed or, at least, indifferent to nationalist politics. As a result of this process, two birds would be killed with one stone: violence was transformed into normal politics, and a democratic process leading to self-determination was kick-started.

However, while in Northern Ireland this strategy was apparently successful, in the Basque case the collapse of the ceasefire produced exactly the opposite result, and this in a double sense. Firstly, violence was not subsumed back into normal politics. Instead, it returned more vigorously and indiscriminately than ever before; and secondly, and this was no less pernicious, normal politics entered a period of extreme tension and polarization. The political parties were aligned along two blocs, the nationalists and the non-nationalists (or Spanish nationalists). Since neither of the two blocs was able to reach sufficient majorities in the institutions, and cross-bloc agreements became more and more impossible, neither the Basque government, nor the parliament or any other institution was able to do its usual business. From varying political standpoints, the media contributed to increasing the tension and to highlighting the situation of permanent public political rioting. The political elite engaged in completely superfluous dialectic, grandiloquent combats; the institutions seemed to be anaesthetized, unproductive and degraded to mere platforms for the parties' clashes; the return of terrorism carried out both by the new ETA commandos and the violent street-gangs jeopardized once again the state's monopoly of violence, introducing the sensation of threat and fear as a daily experience into the life of large communities. In other words, the breakdown of the ceasefire in November 1999 plunged the Basque political system into its deepest crisis since the restoration of democracy.

What made this crisis so acute and difficult to resolve was the fact that the highly passionate controversy about violence and its victims was constantly mixed up with the legitimate discussion of different political projects and expressions of identity. Basque politics became extremely emotional, while the space for more rational, transverse policy-making, cutting across the established fronts, became narrower and narrower. Among the principal actors on stage, none seemed to be aware of the risk linked to a script which determined a fatal end of the scene they all were playing, or, at best, none of them was able or willing to rewrite it and imagine a new, more optimistic outcome. The democratic nationalists, including the *Lehendakari* Ibarretxe, needed too much time to analyse the new situation after the cancellation of the ceasefire and to draw pertinent conclusions. Ibarretxe was in office and governing thanks to the votes of ETA's political wing EH. When in January 2000 his new allies rejected the condemnation of the paramilitaries' first killing after the collapse of the ceasefire, the *Lehendakari* 'suspended' the pact with EH, as if he was convinced that the radicals only needed time and a new opportunity to manifest their commitment to democracy. Only a month later, when ETA used a car bomb to assassinate the Basque socialist leader, deputy in the Basque parliament and former Minister of Education in the regional government, Fernando Buesa, together with his bodyguard, a member of the Basque police force Ertzaintza, Ibarretxe decided to break its agreement with EH. According to the Basque president, this decision was necessary, since 'it has not been possible for Basque society to confirm the clear manifestation of rejection and disapproval of ETA's strategy',[13] which the parliamentary agreement with EH was based upon. Responding to this decision, EH gave further proof of its complete lack of political autonomy from the paramilitary leadership, recovering its previous strategy of anti-system resistance, announcing in March its partial, and then in September 2000 its total withdrawal from the autonomous parliament. Despite this new blow[14] against the PNV and EA, now governing in minority and constantly out-voted by the opposition parties, the democratic nationalists still continued for weeks and months cancelling their agreements with EH in other institutions, especially the town councils and Udalbiltza, which split into an Assembly made up exclusively of EH politicians, and another organization including PNV and EA councillors. Contradictory statements about the 'death' of the Lizarra Agreement, its 'failure' or the 'endurance of its principles' contributed to the doubts on which the new political strategy of the governing PNV was based.[15] Declarations like those published by PNV president Arzallus, who suggested that the major disagreement between his party and ETA was about the means of the struggle, but not about the final objective, which was self-determination and independence, were not precisely helpful in resolving the confusion. Indeed, for the first time since 1906 the PNV approved its first programme: in its National Assembly of January 2000, the 400 delegates passed nearly unanimously a new programme, with an explicit reference to the right of self-determination as the supreme aspiration of the party's political strategy. On previous occasions, the principal political goal had been ambiguously described as that of the restoration of the old *Fueros*, abolished in the nineteenth century, which could be understood both as a claim for independence or of autonomy. Yet nothing was said about what a hypothetical implementation of the right of self-determination might suppose and why the party was demanding it. Was it a mere euphemism for independence or did it include the possibility of other autonomous or federal models? While ambiguity was not completely ruled out as far as the political objective in the long run was concerned, several preconditions were formulated to create the scenario, within which the process for self-determination would be triggered. These conditions served the purpose of pointing out the difference between the PNV programme and that of violent nationalism and to silence the voices criticizing the increasing tendency of the moderate nationalist leadership to embrace the discourse of the radicals. According to the programme adopted in early 2000, a few days before ETA killed its first victim after the suspension of the ceasefire, the process towards self-determination and Basque unification requested a previous 'definite cessation' of violence; the existing institutions and legal prescriptions were its starting-point, which had to be respected and reformed by democratic means; the final step was a referendum to be held by Basque citizens on the new political project and its proposals for institutional change.[16]

While the *moderate* nationalists accentuated their *radical* pro-sovereignty profile, confirming also in the 2000 programme its confidence in the 'nationalist collaboration' as the methodological basis of the political process, the Basque and Spanish non-nationalist parties started to emphasize the radical anti-nationalist dimension of their discourses. Only a few weeks after the cancellation of the ceasefire, it was President Aznar himself, who designed the political message, which would be repeated by PP or PSOE politicians and by the anti-nationalist media in one or another form over the next few months. Its polemical centrepiece was the thesis that, after all, there was no real difference between PNV and ETA nationalism, since both agreed on Basque independence as their supreme political goal. Nationalism was the same as terrorism, and, as a consequence, the fight against moderate nationalism was an indispensable precondition, if the fight against terrorism was to be successful. In December 1999, Aznar started his campaign with two extremely harsh and hurtful statements concerning the PNV, which at that time was still formally the Spanish government's ally in parliament and as such requested to vote for the budget for the year 2000 together with the other (Catalan and Canary) parties allied with Aznar. Celebrating the day of the Spanish Constitution, the President declared that the PNV was trying to push the Basque Country towards the 'Europe of Kosovo', meaning a Europe based on 'exclusion, imposition, ethnic cleansing and the annihilation of the opponent'. According to Aznar, while appeasing ETA and giving ideological succour to it, the PNV was playing exactly the same role as Chamberlain and Daladier did when they signed the Munich Agreement of 1938 with Hitler, consenting to the annexation of the Sudetenland as the only means of preventing war. Only two days before, in a meeting with the German chancellor Schröder in Berlin, Aznar had already issued a similar statement, denouncing the fact that 'the PNV is willing to agree partially with ETA, despite the terrorists' decision to keep on killing'.[17] During the following months, Aznar and his party colleagues continued with this strategy of labelling the democratic nationalists as pro-terrorists. The enemy to fight was no longer only ETA. It was also the PNV and its leaders, who were 'a fundamental and serious part of the Basque problem'. The Spanish president was joined by most of the Spanish and Basque socialist leaders, who renounced presenting a different discourse. Facing the Basque problem, the two largest opposition and governing Spanish parties joined up with one another in the bloc of the 'constitutionalist' forces, which were supported by a massive campaign orchestrated by the bulk of the Spanish media and many intellectuals. The common aim was to discredit the Basque government and the nationalist parties, to force the *Lehendakari*'s resignation and to call new elections in order to substitute for the nationalist government a 'constitutionalist' one. There were no limits to rhetorical polemics, if these were supposed to contribute to the achievement of the political aim. Within a very few months, in the mirror of the Spanish media, the PNV had lost its democratic and anti-fascist tradition adopting a new profile as a poorly disguised ally of totalitarian terrorism. Opinion-makers wrote articles with significant titles like 'The Basque President and Death', in which the *Lehendakari* was invited to break all contacts with HB and to 'join the democrats', because otherwise he and his party would be considered 'one of those "willing executioners"' identified by Daniel Goldhagen in Nazi Germany. The sociologist Ruiz Olabuenaga has pointed out the highly emotional, 'and therefore aggressive' character of this mass media campaign, as well as its 'simplistic, absurd and reductionist' ingredients.[18]

The words were followed by deeds. In January 2000, a few days after the first ETA victim was killed since the breakdown of the ceasefire, the leaders of the Conservative Party announced their decision to boycott all meetings with the Basque president and to renounce any contact with him. The Basque parliament entered a period of total blockade. The government was in a minority and was permanently outvoted by the constitutionalist opposition. However, lacking the sufficient number of deputies, PP and PSE were unable to win a motion of censure and to push the *Lehendakari* and his government out of office. This was ETA's real victory, because the democratic institutions of the Basque autonomy, which had been rejected by militant nationalism since they had come into existence, were now politically castrated and the party system was strongly polarized by the crude confrontation of the democratic parties aligned to one of the two blocs.

Under the fire of both the constitutionalist opposition and the militant nationalists, the democratic nationalists had to face enormous difficulties in their attempts to find a way out of the crisis. Firstly, they had to pay for the errors committed in 1998 and 1999, which had undermined, or even destroyed, the confidence of the non-nationalist parties; secondly, their slowness to break with their new allies after ETA's return to violence, the incapacity to transmit unconditional solidarity to the victims, and the problems (or unwillingness) to differentiate their ambiguous programme of Basque self-determination clearly from that expressed by ETA – all these were factors, which contributed to increasing and consolidating the polarization of the Basque political system. The final, formal remaining link with the Spanish government was broken in December 1999. In response to President Aznar's harmful declaration about the PNV's proximity to totalitarian terrorism and its procedures for ethnic cleansing, the nationalist party leader Arzallus announced the end of the alliance with the conservative government in the Cortes, adding that his party would now explore a common strategy with the radical HB nationalists aimed at Basque self-determination.[19] Yet, as already mentioned above, this intention was aborted when about a month later ETA returned to the scene, killing its first victim after the cancellation of the ceasefire.

As a consequence of all these clashes and conflicts, in the spring of 2000 Basque democracy was seriously jeopardized. Indeed, despite a completely different historical context, the factors challenging democracy in the Basque Country at the end of the twentieth century frequently appear in the literature written by scholars interested in the development of democratic systems and the reasons for their breakdown. First of all, the recommencement of ETA killings and street-gang violence, as well as the enormous problems facing the Spanish, French and Basque police forces in dismantling the commandos demonstrated the terrorists' success in the daily undermining of the state's monopoly of the legitimate use of physical force.[20] Scholars who have worked with this Weberian definition of a modern state have concluded that a state, which was incapable of exercising this monopoly of violence, would lose its legitimacy and enter into a crisis. Among the factors contributing to the outset of a crisis in democratic regimes, Juan Linz highlights the citizens' rational calculation concerning the regime's basic functions of efficacy and efficiency. According to Linz, efficacy is the 'capacity of a regime to find solutions to the basic problems facing any political system', while 'effectiveness' refers to the capacity of implementing the policies agreed upon in order to resolve the problems. If neither efficacy nor efficiency is granted, the citizens are likely to lose their confidence in the political elite, withdraw their legitimacy and push the regime into a deep crisis.[21]

The Basque panorama following the breakdown of the ceasefire apparently seemed to match this theoretical framework. First, neither the Spanish central government nor the Basque one was able to 'find solutions to the basic problems'. How could they, if they were not even capable of establishing a common diagnosis of the nature of those 'basic problems'? Was it only terrorism, as the Spanish government and the constitutional parties argued? Or was it, besides terrorism, also a political conflict about the relationship between the Spanish state and the Basque Country, as claimed by the nationalists? Without a shared diagnosis, no policy of conflict resolution was likely to be agreed upon and, less still, to be implemented. Spanish and Basque politics were lacking a minimum of efficacy and efficiency.

Yet, *Euskadi* was not Weimar. Despite this agony of normal politics and the increasingly bad reputation of the political parties in the opinion polls, democracy in the Basque Country was not completely lost. The impulses for its recuperation came from civil society, which had been less contaminated by the crisis of the political system than one might have expected. During the months after the collapse of the truce two core ideas appeared with vigour in plenty of public rallies held usually in the aftermath of lethal ETA activities. The first was the unconditional rejection of violence from a moral and political standpoint; and the second was the claim for the unity of all democrats as an indispensable precondition for any solution to the problem. This image presented by thousands of anonymous citizens, many of whom used to show self-made posters with inscriptions like 'Unity' or 'ETA no!', while joining in silent protest meetings or demonstrations organized by the peace groups or the parties, contrasted remarkably with the attitude displayed by the party leaders, who were not even able to walk side-by-side behind one and the same banner. The culmination of this grassroots' pressure was popular mobilization after the killing of the Catalan socialist and former minister Ernest Lluch in Barcelona. In the family's address to the people, read in front of ten thousand demonstrators with many high-ranking policy-makers among them, the idea of peaceful dialogue and democratic unity was described as the political legacy of the victim and that any politician willing to honour the memory of the victim should respect and practise this principle, instead of blocking any possibility of a settlement because of the predominance of short-run, blind and egoistic party-interest.

This popular message, repeated on several occasions, was received with distrust and criticism by the central government and the conservatives of President Aznar, who insisted on his strategy of publicly blaming Basque nationalists as a whole for the existence of terrorism and of consequently considering the struggle against nationalism as an indispensable precondition for the fight against terrorism. There was no reason for altering this strategy, since opinion polls indicated that this anti-nationalist toughness was generating political support and votes in most of the Spanish regions. On the other hand, for the democratic nationalists in the Basque Country the popular claim for dialogue and unity became a sort of life-jacket. It permitted not only the survival of a political thunderstorm organized by the paramilitaries, the constitutionalist parties and the dominant mass media; it also helped the nationalists to recover at least part of the political initiative lost after the frustration of the Lizarra experiment. Under the leadership of the Basque *Lehendakari* Ibarretxe, Basque democratic nationalism started a timid and gradual, but at the same time constant and visible modification of its strategy, amending some of the errors committed during the period of the Lizarra Agreement and its final demise. After dissolving the Basque parliament and calling for new elections as a means of putting an end to the situation of political blockade provoked by the lack of majorities in parliament, Ibarretxe campaigned for the votes with a very simple programme, in which the core ideas expressed in the popular mobilizations achieved a central significance. The programme contained a triple commitment to the defence of human rights and the rejection of violence, the principle of unconditioned dialogue between all political actors as the only methodology likely to enable a settlement of the conflict, and thirdly, the respect and implementation of any decision taken democratically by Basque society. This third point, more than a commitment, was a demand directed to the Spanish government and a *politically correct* circumlocution of what on other occasions used to be addressed as the Basque right to self-determination.[22]

During the campaign, President Ibarretxe made it clear that, if he were the winner of the elections, he would by no means govern with the support of the militant EH nationalists, unless they clearly and definitely condemned ETA violence. While performing a new sensitivity towards the victims and their families, as well as a stronger commitment of the Basque police force to the persecution of political crime, the *Lehendakari* took care not to abandon his discourse of moderation and reconciliation. By doing so, he managed to create a public image of an honest person who would not only talk about the unity of the democrats against terrorism, but tried to practise it by putting forward concrete proposals, inviting his political opponents to a round table and by refusing to respond to the caustic and frequently hurtful criticisms pronounced by the conservatives, the socialists and the Spanish media during the most mobilized and controversial electoral campaign ever organized in the Basque Country – and throughout Spain – since democracy had been re-established.

When the ballot boxes were opened on 13 May 2001, most of the polls agreed that the only doubt to be resolved by the voters was if the PP–PSE *entente* would win with a simple or an overall majority. Yet, electoral surveys are not an exact natural science, but an extrapolation and correlation of different kinds of information in a process which is not completely neutral, but to some extent exposed, like all social sciences, both to personal values, opinions and interests, and to the somewhat anarchic reluctance of the analysed human collective to behave according to statistical predetermination. In other words, what happened in the Basque elections of May 2001 was a tremendous surprise for everyone, nationalists and non-nationalists. The triple message of the Basque voters was clear and expressed with authority, since never before had the participation in any kind of election in Spain been so high (80 per cent). Firstly, the voters supported the discourse of dialogue and peace defended by President Ibarretxe, pushing democratic nationalism up to 600,000 votes and 42.73 per cent, to its best electoral result in the history of post-Francoist Spain. Secondly, the radical and highly polemical campaign of conservatives and socialists, rather than bringing a political dividend, returned like a boomerang on the constitutionalist parties, which were left far from their aim of reaching an overall majority. And thirdly, the voters manifested their increasing disapproval and disgust for terrorism, punishing the militant nationalist EH for the party's abandonment of politics and its subordination to military thinking with an authentic electoral annihilation. The party lost half of its seats in parliament, being reduced from 14 to seven.

It was illusory to expect that the elections of May 2001 meant a drastic turning-point in the crisis of the Basque political system. ETA continued killing as if nothing had happened; despite his electoral triumph, Ibarretxe had no majority in parliament and the parties in the opposition could veto any governmental initiative if they voted together; President Aznar's conservative government insisted on the strategy of confrontation instead of testing new ways of cooperation with the democratic nationalists. Yet, the surprising result of the elections shaped new opportunities for a gradual return to normal politics. This was true in a triple sense. Firstly, elections put an end to the previous period of political vacuum provoked by the extreme

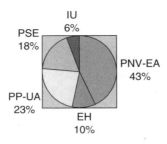

Graph 9.2.1 Elections to the Basque parliament (13 May 2001)
Source: *El Diario Vasco*, 14 May 2001.

weakness of a government, which was unable to govern Basque affairs. Now, the *Lehendakari* Ibarretxe had received visible popular support for his policy of dialogue, peace and self-government and nobody could cast any doubt on his legitimacy of leading Basque politics towards democratic normalization. Secondly, the more open-minded leaders of militant pro-ETA nationalism became aware that the continuance of violence and the party's dependence on the strategy of the more and more unpopular paramilitaries would necessarily jeopardize the political future of radical nationalism. And thirdly, the Basque socialists had to learn that their unconditional alliance with the conservative PP neither produced votes nor contributed to resolving the deep political crisis of democracy in the Basque Country. This was an invitation to design a more autonomous political profile without excluding ways of cooperation with the democratic nationalists, if a minimum consensus made cooperation possible.

Thus, after May 2001, Basque politics entered a period of new opportunities. The problems, however, were old. Yet the *Lehendakari* Ibarretxe had the advantage of being able to reflect *ex post* on a very recent experience to resolve these problems, which had been promoted by his party and had dramatically failed. Such a reflection might help to avoid errors and to do things better than had been done in the summer of 1998. But what are these errors? Why did the ceasefire break down? Why does ETA continue killing? In the final chapters I shall try to formulate some possible answers to these questions. The comparison with other peace processes, especially the Northern Irish one, and theoretical approaches to ethnic violence and nationalism might provide some ideas and suggestions.

9.3 Why didn't it work? Or: how not to tackle a peace process

Among the different peace processes initiated during the 1990s, the Basque attempt to find a peaceful accommodation for the violent conflict has dramatically failed. Fortunately, the consequences of this failure do not amount to the level of bloodshed and open warfare reached by the other prominent case of a frustrated settlement. In fact, both the terrorist escalation and then the military aggression against the Palestine territories ordered by the Sharon administration have buried any hope of a gradual settlement of the Israel–Palestinian conflict in the short run. In the spring of 2002, within a scenario dominated by unfettered violence, political resolutions as proposed by the Madrid Framework (1991) or the Oslo Agreements (1993, 1995) have become wishful thinking. In the Basque Country, even less time was necessary to proceed from a mood of euphoric expectation to a state of depressive frustration. In the summer of 1998, the impression that the cycle of political violence was coming to an end and that an opportunity for a negotiated solution to the conflict had been opened, was dominant in large parts of Basque (and Spanish) society, cutting across different political and ideological sectors. Every month of the indefinite and unilateral ceasefire, which never before in the history of ETA had been called, contributed to strengthening this feeling. Yet, as I have already pointed out, after the collapse of the truce and the return of increased terrorist violence, the Basque political system was challenged by its deepest crisis since Franco's death, and only a shift in the strategy of moderate nationalism and, especially, the dynamics of civil society, prevented Basque democracy from falling into the yawning chasm by recovering the rules of normal politics little by little.

Since that painful transformation of hope for peace into fatalist desperation and acid political confrontation too little time has passed to establish comprehensive theoretical assertions concerning the reasons for this frustrating experience, which is generally summed up as the 'strategy of Lizarra' in reference to the pro-nationalist rapprochement preceding the ceasefire of the summer of 1998. Moreover, the current political polemics between the parties do not at all facilitate a better understanding of the errors committed during the design and the implementation of that strategy. For the constitutionalist parties, 'Lizarra' has become an etymological *passe-partout* for the description of nationalist imperialism, the selling-out of democracy to terrorism, ethnic cleansing or the nationalist holocaust against non-nationalist Basques. The moderate nationalists, on the other hand, tend to avoid the debate about Lizarra, or, when this is impossible, to put emphasis on their humanitarian and ethical desire to put an end to violence when initiating the process. Finally, pro-ETA radical nationalists claim that a return to Lizarra is the only possible way forward to peace and democracy in the Basque Country.

Within this context characterized by the lack of temporal distance and political calm, the following reflections can only be regarded as a preliminary, modest contribution to a necessary academic debate with evident political implications. I shall organize my thoughts basically around two fundamental questions. Firstly, I shall try to isolate the factors, which made the experiment of the summer of 1998 fail, asking about the missed chances and the errors committed. Secondly, in the following chapter I shall discuss several theoretical approaches, which might explain the continuance of terrorist violence, before advancing my own explanation.[23]

As to the first question, I propose considering two different areas of analysis: firstly, the attitude of the principal actors involved in the aborted peace process; and secondly, the main instrument designed for the implementation of the process, e.g., the nationalist *entente*. For the discussion of both issues, the comparison with the Northern Irish peace process might help to reveal some of the problems attached to the Basque case.

The veto holders: (a) the Spanish government

Among the principal actors involved we have to consider first the so-called veto holders with the capacity to bring down any attempt at peaceful conflict settlement both by their active opposition or their passive inhibition. Darby and Mac Ginty argue that the 'most recent peace processes have included those who were in a position to prevent a settlement – the veto holders', because 'a lasting agreement is impossible unless it actively involves those with the power to bring it down by violence'.[24] While this is true concerning the paramilitaries, it is also evident that no agreement is likely to be successful, let alone implemented, without the active support of the leading political force, which in a parliamentarian democracy is usually the government. After overcoming an initial reaction of incredulity and confusion, and despite President Aznar's support of direct contacts with ETA, the Spanish government's attitude during the ceasefire can at best be called fudged, if not obstructionist. Joaquín Navarro, a High Court judge in Madrid, blames the conservative administration for losing 'the best opportunity which had ever existed to achieve a definitive peace'.[25] Even if in the light of the information, which will be discussed later, this statement seems quite exaggerated and unilateral, serious doubts can be cast on Aznar's commitment to a process, which had taken him by surprise, was out of his control and challenged the future of his political project in the Basque Country. Why, if not in order to block the process, did the Spanish government leak the name of the mediator in the government's contacts with the paramilitaries (the Basque bishop Uriarte)? Was it really necessary and politically opportune to capture and imprison one of the ETA interlocutors present in the secret meeting held in Zurich? Why did the Aznar administration practically renounce the application of any significant measure of confidence-building as a means of putting pressure on the paramilitaries and public opinion, in order to make the return of violence more difficult? The prison policy might have been an interesting playground for such measures, since, as we have seen, the policy of distributing the ETA prisoners throughout Spanish prisons far away from their and their families' homeland, was strongly opposed not only by ETA, but by a large majority of Basque society. Except for the transfer of several prisoners from the Canary Islands to the peninsula, the measures taken by the conservative government and publicly announced as acts of goodwill aimed at consolidating the truce, in reality were not much more than political propaganda. It has to be remembered that all of the ETA prisoners released during the ceasefire were released according to the law, because they suffered from an incurable sickness or had served three-quarters of their sentence. In this case the confidence-building measure seemed to consist only in the active implementation of a law and its requirements, in opposition to the tendency of obstructing this implementation whenever possible during the pre-ceasefire period. In the same sense it should also be stated that the invitation to former ETA militants now in exile to return to Spain was another trick of political marketing, since it only affected former terrorists with no penal charge, who could return to Spain anyway, if they wished to.

This attitude of passivity and obstruction stands in sharp contrast to the active one performed by the British government(s) in the early stages of the Good Friday Agreement. Based upon an overall 'rethinking of the conflict', both the Conservative and the Labour governments gradually abandoned their security-guided interpretation of the Northern Irish conflict while articulating a new 'strategic political approach' to Northern Ireland. As a consequence, the idea of inclusive talks was put forward, the agenda of political and constitutional issues to be discussed was open-ended, and concrete measures of confidence-building – including the transfer of long-term Republican prisoners in English prisons to jails in the Republic of Ireland – were announced. Later, the release of the prisoners, whose para-military organizations continued respecting and implementing the terms of the Agreement, became one of the strongest points of attraction in the Good Friday document for all those who might be tempted to consider a return to the practice of political violence.[26]

But there was (and still is) another politically more relevant criticism against the conservative Spanish government and its attitude to the cease-fire. This criticism was shared by Basque nationalists of all political *couleur* and started to appear in the publications of ETA at a time when the IRA's real commitment to the decommissioning of arms became more and more evident. Confronted by the risk of definitely losing their only 'brothers in arms' remaining in Western Europe and encouraged by the necessity to defend not only the return to, but the intensification of the armed struggle against the will of the immense majority of Basque society, ETA recovered the reference to the Northern Irish example in order to legitimate the group's violent strategy. Offering its own interpretation of the IRA's decision to actively cooperate in the process of decommissioning, the ETA bulletin *Zutabe* explained this decision as the result of the 'long struggle carried out by the Republican movement' leading to the recognition of the right of self-determination as formally granted by the Irish and British governments in the Downing Street Declaration signed in December 1993. On the contrary, in the Basque Country this right has not yet been recognized either by the Spanish or the French government and, consequently, there was no reason for laying down their arms: 'Peace and freedom will only reach the Basque Country if the democratic rights of *Euskal Herria* are respected.'[27]

While it is true that the statement of Basques' right to self-determination has so far been rejected by Madrid (and Paris), this parallelism between the Northern Irish and the Basque cases deliberately omits the profound differences between both situations, due to which a Spanish version of the Downing Street Declaration could hardly be expected even during the truce. More specifically, I would suggest considering the following points. First of all, the Downing Street Declaration was a bilateral agreement between the UK Prime Minister John Major and the Irish *Taoiseach* Albert Reynolds, in which both governments abandoned part of their historical claims in order to build up a consensus. Thus, Major agreed that 'it is for the people of the island of Ireland alone, by agreement between the two parts respectively, to exercise their right to self-determination on the basis of consent, freely and concurrently given, North and South, to bring about a united Ireland, if that is their wish'. But in return he achieved the Irish renunciation of their constitutional claim for a unified Ireland, which was expressed in the text as the willingness to look for a 'balanced constitutional accommodation' by the introduction of 'proposals for change in the Irish Constitution which would fully reflect the principle of consent in Northern Ireland'.[28] This policy of *do-ut-des* was important to calm both leaders' constituencies and protect the agreement from critical voices denouncing the selling-out of Britain's or Ireland's 'national interests'. In Spain, however, a similar Declaration would necessarily have been unilateral, since there was no second government representing the nationalists, who were divided. The involvement of the Basque government would probably have been contested by ETA and radical nationalists due to the exclusion of Navarre and the French Basque Country. And what would have happened with the non-nationalist half of the Basque citizens who feel comfortable being part of Spain? Even if such a unilateral Declaration might receive majority support in the Basque Country, in the rest of the Spanish state it might easily have been looked upon as an attitude of giving in to terrorism with negative electoral consequences for the government. The prospect of an end to terrorism linked to a hypothetical Spanish Downing Street Declaration might not be enough to silence such Spanish nationalist criticisms, since the pressure of violence and the amount of people directly and daily suffering from it is far lower in the rest of Spain than in the Basque territories.

But there is still a second, even more important difference between the Basque and the Northern Irish cases consisting in the completely different political and administrative starting-points. When Major and Reynolds signed their document, both politicians were aware that sooner or later the situation of discrimination suffered by the Republican community in Northern Ireland had to be brought to an end, if the violent conflict was to be resolved. This required a restoration of some kind of political and administrative autonomy as an institutional channel granting the political participation of both communities, the formation of democratic majorities and the implementation of democratically accorded policies. On the contrary, in the Basque Country – except for the French part – autonomous institutions had already been established and received the popular support of the citizens in a referendum. These institutions had already been working for more than two decades and had managed, as we have seen in an earlier chapter, to reach an important level of self-government, which was significantly higher than the one defined in the Good Friday Agreement.[29] These institutions apparently count on a high degree of legitimacy, because in none of the different elections to the Basque parliament did the pro-ETA nationalists of HB, which since the establishment of autonomy has been the only political force openly opposed to it, receive a result that might have seriously undermined the legitimacy of the autonomous institutions. It was evident that no Spanish president could make a *tabula rasa* either with the popular support for autonomy formally expressed in the referendum or with two decades of effective autonomous policy. Only, if in the Basque Country a new democratic and broad majority favouring a new political and administrative framework beyond regional autonomy were visible, might a Spanish President respond to this new situation recognizing the right to self-determination. This means, in other words, that in the Basque Country a hypothetical formal recognition of that right could not be the result of a simple government declaration. It had to be the outcome of a previously negotiated political process carried out by all the participants involved, including the Basque people and their political representatives.

This takes us to a third difference, which has already been alluded to above. Whereas the Northern Irish society is quite clearly separated in two more or less homogeneous communities, whose members are bound together in each community by shared national identities, myths, history, public culture and even territory, Basque society is probably more heterogeneous. In the Basque cities, there is no separation of the quarters along ethno-cultural lines. People still live, work, marry or celebrate together. The big football clubs like Athletic Club de Bilbao, despite a certain nationalist bias in its history, attract people from both Basque and Spanish ethno-cultural backgrounds and from all political affiliations. Many Spanish-speaking parents send their children to Basque schools, while it is no exception to find Basque-speaking adults voting for non-nationalist parties. The consequence of all this is the difficulty of defining the subject with any precision. Is the Basque population that which lives in the seven historical regions in Spanish and French territory? Or the Basques of the four provinces on the Spanish side of the border? Or is it the population of the three provinces of the Autonomous Community of *Euskadi*? And in this latter case, what would happen if the citizens of Alava, where the non-nationalists parties are a majority, decided to demand their proper right to self-determination and separate from *Euskadi*? In a hypothetical referendum on the issue of self-determination, what kind of majority could be considered sufficient to proceed towards an alteration of the current political and administrative status quo? Would the support of 55 per cent of the voters in the Basque Autonomous Community be enough? This is the score normally reached by the nationalist parties in the elections to the Basque parliament. Would this be enough to alter or substitute the Statute of Autonomy, which in 1979 had been backed by more than 90 per cent of the voters?

In conclusion, it is not necessary to refer to President Aznar's Spanish nationalist ideology or his strategy of confrontation with Basque nationalism for his own electoral purposes when asking for the reasons that made a Spanish Downing Street Declaration during the ceasefire highly improbable. Owing to the completely different situations of both cases, the text and the procedure of Downing Street could not serve as a model for Moncloa.[30]

The veto-holders: (b) the ETA paramilitaries

After spelling out the doubts about the Spanish government's commitment to consolidate the momentum of the truce, we have to add immediately that the attitude of the other veto-holder, the ETA paramilitaries, did not contribute at all either to raising confidence in the government or to facilitating any progress towards a peaceful settlement of the conflict. In communiqués and interviews given after the collapse of the ceasefire, the spokesmen of the underground group manifested their willingness to continue monitoring the political process in the Basque Country, making it clear at the same time that they never had in mind anything similar to a peace process, peace being, in their opinion, nothing but a mere consequence of the conquest of Basque sovereignty. ETA assumed both the definition of the specific measures to be taken in the process towards sovereignty and the *tempo* of the process. Thus, a settlement could only be engineered after a full implementation of the ETA programme. Any deviation from this programme was reason for a return to armed struggle, and as we have seen above, this is exactly what happened when the moderate nationalists refused to put into practice the paramilitary proposal to hold elections in all (French and Spanish) Basque provinces and create a new 'national' parliament as a substitute for the autonomous institutions. Furthermore, the history of the months following the cancellation of the ceasefire has evidenced that the paramilitaries used the time of the truce for the logistical and operational strengthening of their organization, creating a large number of new commandos, achieving and testing new arms and consolidating the links with the legal groups acting as street-guerrillas. It is obvious that no peace process in the world is likely to progress, if one of the veto-holders is completely unwilling to negotiate any point of its maximalist programme. In contrast to what happened with militant Irish Republicanism, within ETA no 'rethinking of the conflict' took place. The traditional military reasoning was not reassessed and challenged by a 'more sophisticated and political approach'.[31] Hence, one of the basic preconditions for any peace process was missing.

The errors of moderate nationalism

It is probably true that the moderate nationalists of the PNV and EA were convinced that they were creating the conditions that would help the paramilitaries to abandon the armed struggle when engaging in the secret negotiations of the summer of 98 and implementing the pan-nationalist coalition expressed in the Lizarra Agreement. Yet, despite this honourable intention, the moderate nationalists committed at least two serious errors with fatal consequences. First, we might ask how it was possible that a party like the PNV and its leaders, who are usually quite well informed about ETA's internal affairs, could reach the conclusion that ETA was ready to lay down its arms and to take up politics, when evidently this was not the case.[32]

Still more serious was the second error. Consenting to direct political negotiations on constitutional issues with ETA, moderate nationalists accepted the paramilitaries' pretension to monitor the process, thereby granting them a legitimacy they actually did not have. One of the most outstanding differences in the peace processes in Northern Ireland and in the Basque Country is in the role played by the radical nationalist party as the political wing of the armed group. Whereas in Northern Ireland Gerry Adams and Sinn Féin started secrete contacts with John Hume and the Social Democratic and Labour Party to pilot the IRA step-by-step towards politics, during secret negotiation between moderate nationalists and ETA, HB was not even present. Although there is not much inside information about the relationship between the political and the armed wings of the Basque Movement for National Liberation, it seems that a strict top-down hierarchy from the military centre to the political executor is still in place. On the other hand, in Northern Ireland Sinn Féin has apparently gained more political autonomy from and ascendancy over the military wing. This might also be related to the personality and charisma of a leader like Gerry Adams. A similar personality cannot be found within the Basque Liberation Movement. Whatever the reasons for this difference, it seems to be clear that in a democratic political system, a successful peace process is hardly imaginable without the transfer of the political mandate from paramilitaries to the only agencies with legitimacy to speak on behalf of the people: the political parties.

The defective instrument: the nationalist *entente* as an exclusive political front

The main instrument for the political implementation of the politics decided by the nationalist *entente* was the Lizarra Agreement, which, as we have seen, cannot be understood without considering the previous (semi-)accord between ETA and PNV/EA concerning the cancellation of all kinds of cooperation with the 'Spanish' political forces or the creation of a new 'national' assembly with representatives from all Basque territories. As explained earlier, the agreement of September 1998 was drawn up based upon the experience offered by the 'Irish mirror' and drafted according to the conclusions formulated by a parallel workshop on the Northern Irish peace process. The text contained the main traditional nationalist claims and ideas, identifying the roots of the conflict as a contention between the Basque people and the Spanish and French states, while arguing that the keys for any settlement were the unification of all Basque territories ('territoriality') and the recognition of the Basque people's right of self-determination. The process of negotiations leading to the implementation of this programme would in its second phase ('Resolution phase') permit the silencing of the guns. Despite a reference to the 'plurality' of Basque society, Lizarra was a typically nationalist platform and, except for the left-wing Ezker Batua, no major non-nationalist group could be found among the signatories.

Yet, the problem was not the nationalist design of the agreement, but its conditioning by the previous secret (semi-)accord reached with the paramilitaries. As will be remembered, ETA had linked the ceasefire to a total break with all kind of political cooperation between the moderate nationalists and the 'enemies of *Euskal Herria*', meaning the socialists and conservatives. In the light of this petition and despite the different interpretations given to it by the paramilitaries and the parties, we might ask what the reference to the 'plurality' of Basque society could really mean, if the parties representing the second half of this society were excluded from a political process supposed to facilitate a peaceful settlement of the conflict. This was, in my opinion, one of the major differences from the Northern Irish process, which was said to be the model for the Basque one. In Northern Ireland, the nationalist *entente* was the tool that silenced IRA arms and, as a consequence, smoothed the way for the Stormont negotiations. The core idea was the strengthening of the Republican movement as a necessary strategy prior to negotiations with Unionists and the British government. Neither the SDLP, nor the SF, and probably not even the IRA, imagined any settlement of the Troubles without an agreement with the Unionists. On the other hand, in the Basque case the strategy was an exclusive one, not only because ETA continued monitoring and conditioning the process, but also because the Lizarra Agreement did not preview, let alone develop, any mechanism that might have helped to tackle the problem of how to bring the constitutionalist parties into the process. Instead of offering them an opportunity to participate, these parties 'were forced onto the ropes' in a situation of 'subordination and off-side'. These are words published in one of the very few serious analyses of the Lizarra experience written by one of the signatories of the Agreement. The author is affiliated to Zutik, a left-wing group close to the Liberation Movement, but critical of the armed struggle. According to this auto-critical interpretation, written after the cancellation of the ceasefire, while sidelining the constitutionalists, the supporters of Lizarra were unable to correct the public image attached to their initiative, which was looked upon not as a possible way to a settlement of the conflict and peace, but as a nationalist and exclusivist front in the struggle for self-determination and independence.[33]

When the democratic nationalists became aware of these problems and recognized that, instead of leading and controlling the process, they were following guidelines laid down by ETA and the radicals, and that, moreover, the errors made them lose votes and power, it was too late. The constitutionalists and most of the media had already joined in an anti-nationalist front; any communication between the blocs was broken; the political system was challenged by the deepest crisis since the restoration of democracy; and, if this was not problematic enough, ETA had returned to armed struggle carrying out a campaign of terror which personally affected and threatened more citizens than ever before in the history of the paramilitary group. In the words of the underground organization, the decision to cancel the ceasefire was a response to the group's 'commitment to defend *Euskal Herria*'.[34] This argument might have been somewhat convincing in 1968, when the first policeman was shot dead by an ETA activist during Franco's dictatorship. Thirty-one years later, however, it has lost its plausibility. This raises a serious theoretical problem: how can the continuance of political violence in the Basque Country at the beginning of the twenty-first century be explained, if it is possible to explain at all?

9.4   The perpetuation of Basque violence: testing theories and learning lessons

> *They no longer believe in God. The new religion is nationalism. The peoples no longer go to church. They go to national clubs.*
> (Graf Chojnicki commenting on the decay of the Austro-Hungarian Empire in Joseph Roth's novel *Der Radetzkymarsch*, 1932)

In a recent review of different conceptual and theoretical approaches to nationalism, Anthony D. Smith has questioned the classical dichotomist distinction between *ethnic* and *civil* (or *organic* and *voluntarist*) types of nationalism. According to Smith, this typology is firstly more normative than sociological, and secondly unable to explain the complex reality of the phenomenon, since 'so many nationalisms change "character" over time and so often partake of elements of both types, that the original analytic distinction loses much of its practical value'. His example concerning the treatment of the Jews by the French Republic, the 'home' of civic nationalism, is quite eloquent in this sense, showing that 'even such a pared-down version of nationalism may produce quite illiberal, xenophobic policies'.[35]

The same observation may apply to the analysis of political violence. Causes, character and performance of violent groups change together with the changing historical context within which they evolve. However, while the debate on the causes of political violence, let alone ethnic conflict, has for many decades been one of the classical issues addressed by historians and social scientists,[36] the problem of the evolution in time of groups who practise armed struggle has been investigated far less. Whereas a number of alternative theoretical approaches concerning the roots of political violence and terrorism are available, we don't know too much about how, when and why armed underground groups change their strategy, their organization or their repertoire, or, on the contrary, why they do not change even if the surrounding circumstances do. Cynthia Irvin has drawn attention to the discrepancy between the large number of studies focusing on the causes of political violence and the small number of studies dealing with the question 'under what circumstances armed insurgent organizations adopt alternative, non-violent strategies'.[37] Her excellent comparative book on militant nationalism in Ireland and in the Basque Country is one of these scarce studies about this under-researched issue. From another point of view, Jennifer Holmes has not tackled the problem of the origin of political violence in Spain, Peru and Uruguay, but that of its consequences for democracy. She concludes that of the three cases the Spanish case has managed to reach the highest level of democratic stability. According to Holmes, this 'improvement in support for democracy' was a consequence of the fact that 'the Spanish state did not violently and repressively react to the terrorist violence'.[38] But why then does violence in Spain continue at the beginning of the new century? Shouldn't we expect a decline in terrorism as a response to the consolidation of democracy? The answer to these questions was of course beyond the scope of Holmes's book, and we won't find it in most of the publications on ETA violence either. None of the theoretical approaches towards violent nationalism in the Basque Country – predominantly elaborated by Anglo-Saxon writers – offers a satisfying explanation of this problem. This, in my opinion, is due to the somewhat static character of the theories, which in most of the cases focus only on a certain period of nationalist violence or, if generalizing their hypothesis, do not take sufficiently into account the profound transformation of the historical framework within which ETA activity evolves and which I have analysed in this book. Despite these deficiencies, the published literature offers some hints which, in addition to more general theoretical considerations concerning political violence and terrorism, might be helpful in finding some possible responses to our question concerning the *why* of ETA's continuance.

What then are the theoretical explanations available to understand violent insurrection in the Basque Country? The problem is that nearly all of them deal with the Francoist period and don't make a clear differentiation between dictatorship and democracy. There is a broad consensus among most of the authors concerned with Basque violence who agree with the thesis that Francoism created the context in which ETA could arise: Franco was ETA's father. However, the arguments differ when explaining why in the Basque region a historical conflict of ethnic identity and political power became violent, whereas in other regions like Catalonia it remained a purely political conflict. Clark, Jáuregui or Moxon-Browne emphasize the high degree of political repression and the 'reaction to the stagnation and sense of futility experienced by younger nationalists within an established party, and against an atmosphere of repression under Franco'.[39] Conversi blames the lack of a 'shared core value' like language in the Catalan case for the fact that in the Basque Country violence could perform this attractive function within the nationalist movement. The 'structural conductiveness model' presented by Díez Medrano is based on the empirically not very correct assumption that the weakness of the bourgeoisie within the nationalist movement and absence of organizational alternatives outside the PNV opened the door to radical and violent schisms within mainstream nationalism. Waldmann, on the contrary, argued that it was the 'lack' of a moderate nationalist force – in reference to the PNV's lack of operational politics during the dictatorship – which triggered radical and violent nationalism. On the other hand, however, the German sociologist argues in a similar vein to Díez Medrano, explaining ETA violence as lower-class violence, since in his opinion during Francoism the middle and upper classes lost control of the nationalist movement. Zirakzadeh for his part criticizes 'the modernization interpretation of Basque political violence, which emphasizes the psychological pain created by rapid modernization and explains violence in terms of the political channelling of the pain'. He instead stresses the instrumental dimension of violence and its dependence on the workings of a broader context characterized by the confluence of various factors, especially the existence of economic problems, the influence of local political and social struggles and the informing role of formal ideologies like Marxism or anti-colonialism.[40]

Among all these studies Irvin's book deserves special attention. It is the most sophisticated and the only approach towards Basque violence focusing explicitly on the more recent (pre-ceasefire) situation and tackling our central problem concerning the permanence of violence in a democratic context. She tries to combine structural elements ('instrumental approach': rational choice) and other factors stressed by the 'behavioural models' of social mobilization, placing them into a new framework inspired by the political-process theory, and attempting to demonstrate that 'a militant nationalist movement's choice of strategy and structures can best be understood as the outcome of a process of debate and coalition-building among three distinct subgroups of activists: ideologues, radicals, and politicos. The relative size and influence of each group within the organization are held to be affected by external conditions and strategic situations in the political environment. Which strategy dominates, is determined by the relative strength and interactions of different subcoalitions of activists.' Her conclusion is that 'in periods characterized by high levels of state repression, revolutionary nationalist organizations are most likely to attract ideologues and radicals, who will prefer a strategy focused primarily on an armed confrontation with the state, while politicos are most likely to enter during periods of greater regime openness'.[41]

The application of all these different approaches to explain the causes of insurgent violence in the post-ceasefire Basque Country generates a series of methodological problems. Let us consider the basic arguments presented by the different authors.

To start with Irvin's point, it seems to me that while her argument might have a *prima facie* plausibility, it loses power when contrasted with the empirical reality of Spanish and Basque history over the last 25 years. Or, to put it another way, despite the imperfection of Spanish democracy (and of all democracies) I cannot find evidence for the thesis that the continuance of ETA violence might be a result of 'state repression'. On the contrary, from a historical perspective I have tried to argue in this book that due to the consolidation of Spanish democracy and the increasing implementation of Basque self-government, never before in the contemporary history of the Basque nation had the process of nation-building made such important progress as during the last 25 years. Since the first democratic elections of 1977, the Basques are asked every couple of years to express their political opinion by voting for one of the parties, ranging within the political spectrum from parties favouring independence to Spanish-nationalist right-wing parties. Plurality, participation and political choice: aren't these the core elements, which indicate a high level of 'regime openness'? And if so, why then are the politicos so weak within ETA and the Liberation Movement? The data offered by Irvin are highly selective and do not actually corroborate her thesis. Social scientists should be careful when evaluating both information on 'state repression' facilitated by militants or their media, and statistical data on detentions or 'increasingly more coercive'[42] anti-terrorist policy. Those figures should at least be objectified by placing them in the historical context of growing self-government, more and more indiscriminate ETA violence and the increasing rejection of that violence both by Spanish and Basque society. In Irvin's analysis, however, Basque autonomy – with all its political, economic and cultural consequences, highlighted in previous chapters – does not deserve more attention than merely one or two casual references in a narrative focused on the repressive dimension of 'regime responsiveness'. What about Conversi's point concerning language? Again, his thesis might be helpful in understanding the origins of political violence, but not its current continuance. One of my arguments so far has consisted in pointing out that regional autonomy has been especially beneficial to the Basque language. There is now a broad consensus among nationalists and non-nationalists that *Euskara*, as one of the outstanding elements of the Basque culture, has to be protected and sponsored, even if the controversies about the specific policies needed to achieve this goal are permanent. Hence, we could suggest that at the beginning of the twenty-first century the language has indeed become one of the 'core values' of Basque society and that, as Van Amersfoort and Mansvelt Beck put it, 'the role of language in education is no longer a source of contention' and that instead the problem is the 'politicization of language'.[43]

Is relative deprivation, caused by economic problems, a factor fuelling the current political violence? In section 7.3, 'Violence and the economy', my response to this question was negative basically for two reasons. Firstly, I have argued that during the 1990s the Basque economy managed to surmount the industrial crisis and to become one of the most prosperous industrial areas in Spain enjoying a high percentage of economic growth. While ETA continues its post-ceasefire offensive, in the spring of 2002 *Euskadi* has become the most prosperous of all Spanish regions in terms of per capita income. According to the Basque Institute of Statistics, in *Euskadi* the average annual income rate is 18,755 euro, which lies 20 per cent above the Spanish average and has also already surpassed the European average.[44] My second argument was the lack of correlation between the regional or local intensity of street violence and rates of unemployment. Mansvelt Beck has tabled a similar argument. Looking for a specific environment that forms a particular 'biotope' for radical nationalism, this geographer's ecological analysis of HB's electoral implantation does not show any correlation between the radical nationalist vote and unemployment.[45]

Can continuing nationalist violence be explained in terms of class-analysis? Is the middle and upper-class's loss of control of the nationalist movement, and the consequent lack of moderate influence, still an argument to take into account? The answer has to be twofold. Firstly, after more than a century of history, Basque nationalism has become a cross-class movement with an important presence both within the working class and big business. In early 2002, it was precisely due to the pressure of the Basque business community that the regional government dropped its claim for a direct Basque presence in the decision-taking EU institutions. This was done in order to facilitate an agreement on the new law regulating the specifics of Basque financial autonomy ('Conciertos Económicos') with the Spanish central government, which refused to sign any agreement unless that claim was dropped. On the other hand, focusing exclusively on the radical and pro-ETA nationalist sector attached to the Liberation Movement, and despite the presence of small and middle-scale entrepreneurs especially in the most nationalist province of Gipuzkoa, this influence of business interests is far smaller, if not absent. However, there is only very scarce statistical data both concerning the social background of ETA activists and the social structure of the Liberation Movement, its organizations and its voters, which might support the thesis of lower-class violence. As already mentioned, at least for an analysis of HB's electoral implantations, cleavages like rural/urban or ethnically Basque/Spanish seem to be more significant than those of class-structure.

Finally, the argument of the 'instrumental dimension' of political violence and its strategic determination by cost–profit calculation has to be discussed. In fact, in September 1998 ETA argued that a new opportunity of progressing towards Basque self-determination had been created when announcing the ceasefire. As analysed above, the nationalist *entente* of Lizarra was a powerful coalition with real possibilities of forging political majorities for the achievement of radical nationalist goals. Such a favourable opportunity structure had never existed before in the history of radical Basque nationalism. But this was also true in November 1999 when the terrorists called off the ceasefire. This opportunity was destroyed not because the moderate nationalists refused to engage in a completely absurd and unrealistic political project (elections in all seven Basque territories), but because ETA politically castrated HB, provoked a popular revolt of disgust and rejection of terrorist violence among Basque citizens, and forced the breakdown of all cooperation with democratic nationalism, which for ethical and political reasons had to distance itself from a party, which had lost all its political autonomy with respect to the paramilitaries. As a consequence, after the collapse of the ceasefire radical nationalism attached to ETA has become politically weaker than ever before in its history. A situation of extraordinary power has been substituted by a panorama of weakness and confusion, which according to analysts like the anthropologist Juan Aranzadi might end up with the 'political suicide' of militant and left-wing nationalism, unless the latter is able to recover some of its autonomy from the underground group.[46] Even if we admit our lack of detailed information about the interior life of the group, it is hardly imaginable that this political and social decay could have been the intended result of a decision (the end of the ceasefire) based on a rational choice and with instrumental purposes. If the purpose was to force the democratic nationalists to adopt ETA's claims, assume all of its proposals and remain (at least temporarily) compliant towards violence, it is not necessary to be a political scientist to be aware of the remarkable lack of 'rationality' in this decision, based on an unrealistic premise (the decisive power of violent coercion on democratic nationalists) and a still more unrealistic prospect (the achievement of self-determination by force and sidelining Basque society).

In concluding this brief outline of the main theoretical explanations of political violence in the Basque Country, it seems that none of them offers a satisfactory hypothesis when applied to the problem of continuance and intensification of violence in the framework of a parliamentary democracy at the beginning of the twenty-first century. If we discard socio-psychological interpretations of violent militants and their behaviour as a pathological deviation from democratic normality,[47] where then should we look for theoretical clues likely to cast some light on our problem? I suggest considering the following arguments.

First, we should abandon the idea that democracy is a perfect antidote to violence and terrorism. On the contrary, according to Waldmann, democracies offer quite favourable circumstances for terrorist activity because, among other reasons, given the freedom of the press and of expression, paramilitaries can expect to find a considerable public echo for their violent activities.[48] Thus, in the opinion of the German sociologist, in democratic systems terrorists will always find one of the important elements that make for a favourable 'opportunity structure' for their activities. Without mentioning it, this opportunity structure was also in Joseba Arregi's mind (for many years he was nationalist Councillor for Culture and government spokesman, and is now one of the most outstanding, intellectually prepared dissidents in his party, PNV) when in one of his recent books he made his party's leaders partially responsible for the persistence of terrorism. According to Arregi, the PNV leaders helped to create a favourable opportunity structure for ETA activists, outlining four reasons: (1) for simplifying the analysis of ETA as a mere consequence of an unresolved political problem, without recognizing the totalitarian character of the organization; (2) for sharing the political aims of the violent radicals (self-determination, independence); (3) for requesting and offering a 'dialogue without limits' as the only possible way to resolve the conflict, forgetting that within a democratic system any dialogue between democrats and totalitarian activists has to be carried out within the limits and rules established by democratic norms and institutions; (4) for discrediting and undermining the Statute of Autonomy backed in the 1979 referendum by a broad majority of Basque voters, including those of the PNV.[49] Some of these arguments seem reasonable and helpful for a better understanding of continuing violence in the Basque Country. They have already been alluded to in my own analysis when referring to the PNV's surprising lack of information concerning ETA's situation and intention at the beginning of the secret negotiations or to the error of negotiating directly constitutional issues with the paramilitaries. I have also underlined the positive effects of Basque autonomy for the process of nation-building, while criticizing any hasty underestimation. Arregi's second point, however, is more questionable. Is it really true that the fact that a democratic party shares a certain political aim, in this case self-determination, with the terrorists helps to create a favourable opportunity structure by encouraging them to continue with the armed struggle? I think that it would be far more encouraging for terrorists to see that their activity can generate such a decisive impact on the political system so that even governing parties are forced to change their programme. By doing so, the democratic parties would deliver a kind of power of veto to the underground group, which could interfere in democratic politics in a much more drastic manner than it already does with its violent activities. In conclusion, whereas a democratic party with a programme of self-determination or independence will always be a challenge to and competitor of the paramilitaries, a (temporary) renunciation of these aims would give the terrorists the key to political business, by placing them, moreover, in the favourable position of being the only reference for all the citizens who share these aims. In other words, democrats should not reject democracy when tackling the problem of political violence.

A further argument to explain current Basque violence is related to the particular evolution of what we could call group-dynamics within armed underground organizations with a long life-cycle. In the Basque case, we might differentiate two aspects, the dynamics with respect to the evolution of the in-group, and those that define the relationship between the group and the exterior. Concerning the internal evolution of ETA, it is known that both the decision to call for and to cancel the ceasefire provoked debate and controversy within the Executive Committee of the paramilitaries. As we have seen, at the end violence returned and was now carried out by the hardliners, who were keen to 'restrict internal communications, inhibit participation in political debates, and perhaps restore group cohesion and solidarity'.[50] In a similar sense, Heywood suggests that greater emphasis placed on political negotiation might provoke 'the adoption of more radical stances by hard-line activists'.[51] This is exactly what happened. The breakdown of the ceasefire aborted any attempt to articulate an autonomous political discourse of HB–EH and even those leaders, who had generally been considered 'politicos', returned to a discourse which was (is) determined by military logic and reasoning. Furthermore, as Martha Crenshaw points out, violence also has an important function for the recruitment of new militants. Recruitment is frequently carried out by 'initiation rites that involve violation of taboos, or "bridge-burning acts" that create guilt and prevent the convert's return to society'.[52] Indeed, most of the young ETA activists captured after the end of the ceasefire had been socialized in the use of violence, participating in the activities of the street guerrilla gangs before joining the underground group.

As to the second point, in relation to the external context, scholars of political violence and terrorism have underlined the tendency of terrorist groups to endure even if 'objective' circumstances change. The specific microcosm in which terrorists live is based on extreme security measures and very high in-group solidarity. This lifestyle separates the activists from their environment, making them unable to perceive any feature of reality not corresponding to their own one-dimensional perception. As Martha Crenshaw puts it, this would be the last step of a 'gradual growth of commitment and opposition', at the end of which the violent struggle becomes 'a self-generating phenomenon'. Armed activity would be aiming almost exclusively at the reproduction of their own group structures and producing a constant reminder of the state's inability to exercise a monopoly in the use of coercive force. For group outsiders, however, it becomes increasingly difficult to recognize any rationality and concrete purposiveness beyond these actions.[53] Waldmann argues in a similar sense, maintaining that 'the longer a terrorist group exists, the greater the tendency for mere self-regeneration'.[54] At the end of this development, and as a result of the growing distance between the paramilitary group and society, a strong decline in the level of the group's legitimacy even among its followers is likely to occur, because – according to Guelke – firstly, instead of emphasizing the ends, the group places much more value on the means, and secondly, the means employed in the advancement of those (fudged) ends are no longer considered in any way proportionate to the objectives sought.[55] The increasing mobilization of the peace movement and the electoral debacle of pro-ETA nationalism in May 2001, when EH lost half of its seats in the Basque parliament, seem to corroborate this thesis.

Yet ETA is far from being a mere Baader-Meinhof phenomenon. Despite the obvious loss of legitimacy and the evident demise of its political power, the group is still covered by a broad organizational network and thousands of followers, ranging from teenagers engaged in violent street gangs to passive voters (143,000 in 2001). As a third theoretical argument for the explanation of continuing violence and enduring (relative) popular support, I suggest considering this kind of nationalism as a political religion. A detailed discussion of this concept is beyond the scope of this book. Since Durkheim's famous analysis in *The Elementary Forms of the Religious Life*,[56] the functional similarity of religion and the idea of a nation have become important issues addressed by the theory of nationalism. On the other hand, based on the writings of Max Weber about the process of secularization, various scholars have applied the thesis of the endurance and transformation of religious thinking in the secularized world to explain the rise of totalitarian movements like fascism and Stalinism.[57] The complex universe of nationalism requires a differentiated application of these conceptual and theoretical tools. While rejecting, contrary to Steven Grosby's thesis, a general identification of the concepts of religion and nationalism,[58] I do agree with those interpretations of nationalism which underline the ambiguous and volatile frontier between the two phenomenona, since nationalism has incorporated core elements of evident religious origin like the idea of chosenness, the glorious resurrection of the nation, the attachment to a sacred territory, the shared memories of golden ages, the cult of the glorious dead, the symbolic celebration of the nation, and others. Anthony D. Smith, while describing the nation as a 'political form of the sacred community', emphasizes the three dimensions of all nationalisms. They are at the same time political ideologies, public cultures and political religions celebrating their nations characterized by the 'sacred properties' mentioned above. Smith adds, however, that not all nations were (or are) 'suffused by all of these sacred properties', because the impact of 'secular materialism and individualism' tends to undermine 'the central beliefs in a community of history and destiny'.[59] Hence, we might conclude by formulating the hypothesis that nationalism is always more than a mere political movement and ideology, and that – taking its phenomenological and functional relationship with religion for granted – it might have very different faces according to the higher or lower impact of secular thought, individualism, pluralism and democracy on it. It should thus be possible to establish a typology of nationalist movements reaching from nationalisms which combine their claims for the collective rights of the nation with an active defence of civil society and democracy, to movements which reject all interference of liberal and democratic thought, promote a 'transfer of sacredness' from religious thinking to political life and substitute the devotion to the nation for that to God. This would be the case of the classical 'political religions' from the revolutionary French Republic to Hitler's National Socialism.

Returning to our problem of Basque violence, the anthropologist Joseba Zulaika presented in 1988 an attempt to go beyond the common cognitive or interest-based models of explanation by the introduction of ideas attached to a framework of anthropological and cultural gestation and representation.[60] He insisted that in the Basque case violence could not exclusively be understood in terms of rational and purposive behaviour, instead its 'magic' and 'ritual' ingredients were the essential factors for the durability of violence. Zulaika recognized a direct relationship between the 'desacramentalization' of religious symbols and rites on the one hand, and the 'resacramentalization' of society on the other. According to this thesis, this sacramental engagement in the political arena would be symbolized by the sacrifices offered by ETA activists and their readiness to 'offer' their own life as a supreme act of worship dedicated to the new god, that is, the Basque nation. Zulaika's case study is located in a small village and his findings seem to corroborate one of the theses put forward in the studies of the classical political religions, according to which in small-scale localities a high level of social control can be established by small social and cultural networks and the political discrimination of outsiders and dissidents. Thus, the reproduction of sectarian thinking and collective behaviour (political religions) can be enacted more easily than in a large city. A decade after the publication of Zulaika's book, Mansvelt Beck established a clear correlation between political support for ETA and the scale of the city: 'The stronger HB is represented, the smaller the municipality.'[61] In 2002, the problems for the non-nationalist parties of finding candidates for the municipal elections in small towns, where the pressure of violent groups and terrorists against the enemies of the nation is unbearable, confirm this thesis. Other elements highlighted by scholars as constitutive elements of a political religion might be mentioned here in order to support the thesis of violent Basque nationalism as a form of political religion, namely, the military element and its cult of blood and death, present not only in all ETA activities but also in HB meetings (the worship of ETA and its priests, who are the dead 'soldiers' – the *gudariak* – and the prisoners), which in some sense might be described as Sironneau's 'sacred ceremonies'.[62] Furthermore, in any communiqué of ETA's we can find plenty of evidence for its total *faith*, understood as a 'complete, authentic and exclusive consent to a belief',[63] which is the belief in the Basque nation, in the validity of their own interpretation of the nation, its wishes and its rights, and in the legitimacy of the means used to implement these rights – including the physical elimination of all 'enemies of the nation'. If we add as a final element the strictly hierarchic top-down functioning of the Liberation Movement, where the political party is apparently unwilling or unable to maintain a certain level of autonomy with respect to the paramilitary head, the thesis concerning the transformation of violent nationalism into a political religion becomes plausible.[64] A recent study of the Basque National Liberation Movement's discourse has also put forward the explanation of militant nationalism as a political religion.[65] Religions are cultural systems of transcendental belief helpful in creating identity and making sense of one's existence in the world, and as such they are able to evolve with certain autonomy from their political or economic context. This is what Waldmann means when stating the 'immunization against empirical evidence'[66] as a characteristic feature of armed underground groups with a long life-cycle. The Basque paramilitaries' unwillingness – or inability – to recognize the plurality of the Basque nation, the progress in the process of nation-building reached during post-Franco democracy, and the people's desire to stop the killing, is a good example of this immunization and its fatal consequences.

10
Epilogue: the Basque Contention in the Age of Globalization: Old Problems, New Opportunities

Experience proves that it is possible for one nationality to merge and be absorbed in another: and when it was originally an inferior and more backward portion of the human race the absorption is greatly to its advantage. Nobody can suppose that it is not more beneficial to a Breton, or to a Basque of French Navarre, to be brought into the current of the ideas and feelings of a highly civilised and cultivated people – to be a member of the French nationality (...) – than to sulk on his own rocks, the half-savage relic of past times, revolving in his own little mental orbit, without participation or interest in the general movement of the world.

(J. S. Mill, 1863)

The very fact that historians are at least beginning to make some progress in the study and analysis of nations and nationalism suggests that, as so often, the phenomenon is past its peak. The owl of Minerva which brings wisdom, said Hegel, flies out at dusk. It is a good sign that it is now circling round nations and nationalism.

(E. Hobsbawn, 1990)

The fact that neither a scientific nor an eclectic version of global culture could have much popular resonance and durability suggests that the conditions for a postmodern supersession of nationalism have not yet been realized, and that globalization, far from leading to the supersession of nationalism, may actually reinforce it.

(A. D. Smith, 2001)

When John Stuart Mill published his famous studies *Utilitarianism, Liberty* and *Representative Government*, Basque nationalism had not yet emerged. Yet, on either side of the Spanish–French border, there already existed a Basque problem. In France, politics under the Empire of Napoleon III and then, especially, during the Third Republic, continued the nationalist work of the revolutionaries aiming at the consolidation of the Unitarian French nation-state. This task required the elimination of particular cultures like the Basque one. Applying the words of E. Weber, Basque peasants, who 'were said to have no sympathy in common with the rest of France', had to be transformed into Frenchmen.[1] In Spain, the reputation of the Basques was not really any better, since it was in the Basque territories where the traditionalist and reactionary Carlist movement had its bastion. Consequently, for the Spanish liberals the precondition for the destruction of Carlism and the consolidation of the Spanish nation-state was the abolition of Basque self-government. Thus, both in France and in Spain, state-led nationalism was at odds with Basque particularism, but whereas in France this process of French nation-building was quite successful, the weak Spanish nationalism was unable to assimilate Basque culture and political tradition. On the contrary, the mobilizing effect of socio-economic modernization triggered the rise of a powerful nationalist movement struggling for the recuperation of lost freedom. Ever since then, for longer than its century-old history, Basque nationalism has survived all adverse situations, including nearly 50 years of dictatorship. It has proved resistant to different political, economic and cultural circumstances and its recent evolution seems to suggest that Hobsbawm's desire concerning the last flight of Minerva's owl as a symbol for the expected end of the history of nationalism, is not likely to be satisfied in the near future. The hope, or rather conviction, that the progress of markets, the economy and civilization would convert nations and nationalisms into those 'half-savage relic(s) of past times' mentioned by Mill, had already been formulated by Basque socialists at the beginning of the twentieth century. A century later, the relic, far from vanishing, has achieved a political and social power as never before in its history. Moreover, scholars concerned with the relationship between globalization and nationalism, like Anthony D. Smith, have reached the opposite conclusion, arguing that globalization apparently reinforces national (regional, local) identities, because, as Manuel Castells puts it in 'The Information Age', when the world is becoming too big to be controlled, the social actors try to reduce it once again to their own scale. When the networks dissolve time and space, people anchor themselves in their places and recall their historical memory.[2]

Notwithstanding this longevity of the Basque contention for identity and home-rule, in this book I have emphasized the deep changes this contention and its main actor, Basque nationalism, have witnessed during the twentieth century. Among other features, I have highlighted the making of the Basque nation as a democratic and pluralistic society, in which different patterns of identity (Spanish, Basque, 'More Basque than Spanish', etc.) coexist; the remarkable progress in the process of nation-building following the restoration of democracy and the implementation of regional autonomy, a process which nationalists frequently tend to undervalue; the split of the Basque problem into two parts, which are the democratic struggle for self-determination on the one hand, and the activity of violent nationalism with its own dynamic; and finally, the most important initiative for a peaceful settlement of the conflict at the end of the 1990s, as well as its errors and the reasons for its dramatic collapse.

Despite democracy, autonomy and pluralism, at the beginning of the twenty-first century, after more than a hundred years of both peaceful and violent contention, the twofold Basque conflict with its external dimension (*Euskadi* versus Spain) and its internal implication (nationalist Basques versus non-nationalist Basques; democratic versus violent nationalists) seems far from a democratic and peaceful settlement. Nonetheless, the new century might open up new opportunities for conflict de-escalation and peaceful accommodation, if certain circumstances are met and the lessons of history understood. In particular, I invite the reader to consider some ideas, which I regard as really crucial for the Basque future. Yet, before going into detail, I would like to forward a more general reflection. It seems to me that any strategy of conflict settlement and violence de-escalation in the Basque Country, if it aims to be successful in the near future, has to combine – much more than has been the case so far – practices of traditional contemporary peace-making and measures aimed at intensifying young people's education and socialization in the values of peace, democracy and pluralism. As we have seen, the problem of violence is not exclusively a problem of the paramilitary commandos; it is at the same time a microsociological problem generated by a culture of violence. This culture of violence is reproduced within a broad social network of organizations, groups, initiatives or media through rituals, rites of passage, symbols, and belief systems which convey transcendent meaning. Since this process affects young people especially, effective peace politics have to focus more decisively on education as one of the most powerful means of socialization likely to foster democratic values and behaviour, as well as to prevent totalitarian thinking. The first steps have already been taken. In this sense, recent initiatives by peace groups like Elkarri or Gesto por la Paz in cooperation with the Basque government, consisting of the drawing up of special teaching units dedicated to issues like peace or tolerance, have to be mentioned. To conclude, politics of conflict settlement and, as one of its core ingredients, strategies of peacemaking in the Basque Country of the twenty-first century will only be successful in the long run if they are built upon this complementary axis of socialization and education, while taking into account the following suggestions:

1. Any solution to the conflict has to be based upon democratic and peaceful dialogue, i.e., dialogue both between the Basques and the Spanish government, and dialogue among the Basques themselves. This dialogue is unthinkable, if many of those, who are supposed to take part in it, have to live under the permanent threat of terrorism. Thus, the democratic nationalists must be particularly interested in an end to violence, since no democratic progress towards a higher level of self-determination is likely to be reached unless the basic precondition, namely, the cessation

of violent activities, is established. On the contrary, the popular mobilization following the assassination of the young councillor Blanco in the summer of 1997 suggests that the further continuance of nationalist violence tends to undermine the popularity of Basque nationalism in general and jeopardize its political power.

2. This evident impact of violence should also encourage those leaders of militant nationalism, who still are able to think in terms of democratic politics instead of paramilitary logic, towards a rethinking of their strategies and aims, if the separatist and leftist option of Basque nationalism is to survive. In the not too distant future, the lack of political initiative and the blind submission to the ETA paramilitaries' directives is likely to end with the political suicide of this militant branch of Basque nationalism.

3. The return of militant nationalism to democratic politics, if it should happen, will probably be the result of the pressure articulated by Basque society in terms of a growing opposition to ETA terror. It was not by chance that the first splits within the Liberation Movement since the times of transition were carried out after the disastrous results of the regional elections in May 2001, when EH lost half of its seats in the Basque Parliament.[3] This increasing loss of legitimacy expressed by the people it claims to represent, as well as in the aftermath of 11 September probably more intensive and effective measures of policing, will be the only way to change ETA paramilitaries' minds, even if the group's dynamic for self-preservation and its attachment to politico-religious mysticism hinders realistic perception of such impulses coming from civil society. On the contrary, strategies based exclusively upon repressive policing, instead of contributing to conflict de-escalation are likely to provoke the opposite result. The new Spanish 'Law of Parties', which has been promoted by the conservative government and has been passed by a broad majority of the Cortes in the very moment I am writing these lines (June 2002), has been designed as a legal tool for the outlawing of Batasuna,[4] based on the argument that the party is an essential element of the ETA terrorist network. The banning of Batasuna as further proof of the government's toughness in the struggle against terrorism will probably produce an important political (electoral) dividend for Aznar's conservative party in the rest of the Spanish state. In the Basque Country, however, it is likely to short-circuit the political decline of pro-ETA nationalism by a wave of solidarity. Besides the juridical problems of the law, in terms of political opportunity one might ask how far the banning of a political party, which despite its spectacular decline in the elections of 2001 was voted for by more than 140,000 Basques, is supposed to generate any kind of benefit in the struggle against terrorism. In short, from the point of view of democracy and peace in the Basque Country, I do not exaggerate when characterizing this law as one of the most serious political errors committed in Spain since Franco's death.

4. The banning of Batasuna is a grave error also for another reason. If my hypothesis is correct that, as in Northern Ireland, the only way of settling the Basque conflict is through dialogue and the absence of violence, somebody has to represent those 10–15 per cent of the Basque voters close to militant nationalism. In this book I have analysed the fatal consequences of the governing nationalist parties' experience of negotiating political issues with those, who in a democratic system do not have any legitimacy to do so, namely the paramilitaries. Outlawing a party which represents a significant sector of society, and thus is invested with the right to speak on behalf of that community, in the end means doing the terrorists a political favour.

5. If the presence of militant nationalism at any future negotiating table is necessary, the same is obviously true for the non-nationalist sectors of society. One of the most important lessons to be learned from the Lizarra experience is that within the framework of a pluralistic Basque society no unilateral initiative is likely to be successful. A pan-nationalist agreement might kick-start a process, but from the beginning it has to include reasonable offers for the non-nationalist forces to join the process without abandoning their basic principles. This, however, will only be possible if both parts renounce their maximum claims, try to find the lowest common denominator and find a democratic meeting-ground.

6. Yet this exercise in democratic self-limitation requires the democratic nationalists to make a previous effort to define their political goals more precisely both in the short and in the long run. This is absolutely necessary, since in a peace process 'the negotiations (have to) address the central issues in dispute'.[5] This book has underlined the programmatic ambivalence of the PNV as one of the most significant features in the history of moderate nationalism since its genesis at the end of the nineteenth century. The party's politics oscillated like a pendulum between ideological (separatist) radicalism and a more pragmatic *Realpolitik* aimed at the gradual conquest of regional autonomy. The Agreement of Lizarra symbolized a new swing of the pendulum towards a more radical position characterized by the claim for a higher degree of self-government beyond regional autonomy. Yet, it has not been explained either what kind of benefit such a new political status is supposed to produce, or what the constitutional model of that new status should look like (an independent state? A federal state within Spain? An autonomous region with broader political rights? and so on). So far, the only precision of the political programme consists in the defence of the *Basque people's right to decide their future*, which is a pleasant-sounding euphemism for self-determination, and the proposal of calling a referendum in order to facilitate that decision. Unless this ambiguity is substituted by precise and tangible political proposals, the non-nationalists' reluctance to engage will hardly diminish, since from their standpoint behind every nationalist claim for a revision of the status quo lurks the phantom of secession.

7. This nationalist haziness is not only a legacy left by the party's history. To a certain extent, it is also a reflection of the process of globalization,

its multiple consequences and its impact on nationalist theory and practice. As Montserrat Guibernau has pointed out, globalization has opened new opportunities for nations without states, because the traditional nation-state is surrendering certain aspects of its sovereignty to supranational institutions. At the same time, however, globalization is creating new dilemmas for stateless nations like that of an 'increasing internal diversity' due to 'the transnational circulation of people, culture and financial resources'.[6] The consequences of this development for nationalist politics seem evident in the Basque case also. First, the transformation of society requires a new concept of the nation. Classical ethnicity-based concepts rooted in nineteenth-century reality, like that formulated by the PNV founder Sabino Arana, are no longer valid as a tool for democratic politics aiming at a nation-building that understands the coexistence of identities not as an obstacle, but as an asset. Indeed, applying David Miller's typology, the Basque one is a society in which the category of 'nested nationalities' (Basque and Spanish/French at the same time) coexists with that of 'rival nationalities', whose members have 'mutually exclusive national identities' (only Basque/Spanish/French).[7] The second consequence of globalization is the erosion of the classic concept of sovereignty, which is no longer the exclusive sphere of the nation-state. That means that the solution for stateless nations keen to protect their culture and to increase the degree of self-government and welfare can hardly be a return to a state model that is becoming more and more outdated by twenty-first-century reality. Instead, democratic nationalists should abandon the utopia of a completely independent and sovereign state and proceed to the elaboration of alternative concepts based upon what Michael Keating calls 'unpacking sovereignty', so that 'functions and responses to specific types of demand can be divided and distributed among the three levels of minority nation, state, and transnational regime'. 'So an individual could be a member of the broad Basque nation for some purposes, a citizen of the smaller Basque Autonomous Community for others, a citizen of Spain, and a European'.[8] Owing to these deep changes in society and politics, at the beginning of the twenty-first century democratic Basque nationalism is at the crossroads. The future of the Basque nation depends not only on the management and of the hoped-for end of political violence. It also depends on the nationalists' ability to adapt their ideology and politics to the changing context.[9] For more than 100 years they have survived other kinds of challenges. To survive this new one and to smooth the progress of a democratic, peaceful, wealthy and civic Basque nation, an attentive and patient reading of Robert Musil's lesson about the human being's multiple identities which is the epigraph to this book might be helpful.

Notes

1 Introduction: the History of This Book

1 H. L. Nieburg, *Political Violence: the Behavioral Process* (New York: St Martin's Press, 1969), p. 13.
2 E. Zimmermann, *Political Violence, Crises, and Revolutions: Theories and Research* (Boston, MA: G. K. Hall, 1983), p. 346.
3 P. Waldmann, *Terrorismus. Provokation der Macht*, 2nd edn (München: Gerling Akademie Verlag, 2001), pp. 12–13.

2 Why It Began: a Strong Periphery within a Weak State

1 J. Linz, 'Early State-Building and Late Peripheral Nationalisms against the State: the Case of Spain', in: S.N. Eisenstadt and St Rokkan (eds): *Building States and Nations: Analyses by Regions*, Vol. II (Beverly Hills: Sage Publications, 1973), pp. 32–116, quotation p. 33.
2 L. González Antón, *España y las Españas* (Madrid: Alianza 1997), p. 9; H. Schulze, *Staat und Nation in der europäischen Geschichte* (München: Beck, 1994), p. 139 (my translation); B. Jenkins and S. Sofos, 'Nation and Nationalism in Contemporary Europe: A Theoretical Perspective', in: B. Jenkins and S. Sofos, (eds): *Nation and Identity in Contemporary Europe* (London: Routledge 1996), pp. 9–32, quotation p. 10.
3 J. M. Jover Zamora, *La civilización española a mediados del siglo XIX* (Madrid: Espasa-Calpe, 1992), p. 100.
4 A. Morales Moya, 'Los orígenes de la administración pública contemporánea', in: A. Morales Moya and M. Esteban de Vega, (eds): *La historia contemporánea en España* (Salamanca: Universidad de Salamanca, 1996), pp. 53–72, quotation p. 57.
5 For this, and other possible concepts of 'nation' see P. Alter, *Nationalismus* (Frankfurt a.M.: Suhrkamp, 1985), especially p. 23. For the famous definition of the state, see M. Weber, 'Die rationale Staatsanstalt und die modernen politischen Parteien und Parlamente (Staatssoziologie)', in: M. Weber, *Wirtschaft und Gesellschaft*, 5th edn (Tübingen: Mohr, 1980), pp. 815–68, especially p. 824.
6 An overview of this debate with an extensive bibliographical 'state of the art' can be found in L. Mees, 'Der spanische "Sonderweg": Staat und Nation(en) im Spanien des 19. und 20. Jahrhunderts', in: *Archiv für Sozialgeschichte*, 40, 2000, pp. 29–66.
7 G.L. Mosse, *The Nationalization of the Masses: Political Symbolism and Mass Movements in Germany from the Napoleonic Wars through the Third Reich* (Ithaca, New York: Cornell University Press, 1977).
8 For the theoretical background, see Ch. Tilly, 'Western State-Making and Theories of Political Transformation', in: Ch. Tilly (ed.): *The Formation of National States in Western Europe* (Princeton: Princeton University Press, 1975), pp. 601–38.
9 A.D. Smith, *The Ethnic Origins of Nations* (Oxford: Blackwell, 1986).
10 The *fuerismo* would be the Basque protonationalist equivalent to the 'phase A' in Miroslav Hroch's model of the evolution of smaller nationalist movements in

nineteenth-century Europe. Contrary to Hroch's typology, however, protonationalism was in the Basque Country not only cultural, but from its very beginnings also political. See M. Hroch, *Social Preconditions and National Revival in Europe: A Comparative Analysis of the Social Composition of the Smaller European Nations* (Cambridge: Cambridge University Press, 1985). Concerning *fuerismo* and Carlism, see B. Clavero, *Fueros vascos: Historia en tiempo de Constitución* (Barcelona: Ariel, 1985); J. Extramiana, *Historia de las Guerras Carlistas*, 2 vols, (San Sebastián: Luis Haramburu, 1979); V. Garmendia, *La ideología carlista (1868–1876): En los orígenes del nacionalismo vasco* (San Sebastián: Diputación Foral de Guipúzcoa, 1984); J. Fernández Sebastián, *La génesis del fuerismo. Prensa e ideas políticas en la crisis del Antiguo Régimen (País Vasco, 1750–1840)*, (Madrid: Siglo XXI, 1991); J. Juaristi, *El linaje de Aitor: La invención de la tradición vasca* (Madrid: Taurus, 1987); M.C. Mina, *Fueros y revolución liberal en Navarra* (Madrid: Alianza, 1981).

11 J. Alvarez Junco, 'La nación en duda', in: J. Pan-Montojo (ed.), *Más se perdió en Cuba: España, 1898 y la crisis de fin de siglo* (Madrid: Alianza, 1998), pp. 405–75. See also S. Balfour, *The End of the Spanish Empire (1898–1923)* (Oxford: Clarendon Press, 1996).

12 M. González Portilla, *La formación de la sociedad capitalista en el País Vasco*, 2 vols, (San Sebastián: Luis Haramburu, 1981); M. Gárate, *El proceso de desarrollo económico en Guipúzcoa* (San Sebastián: Cámara de Comercio de Guipúzcoa, 1976).

3   How It Began: the Evolution of Basque Nationalism until the Civil War (1876–1939)

1 The best biography is that of J. Corcuera, *La patria de los vascos: Orígenes, ideología y organización del nacionalismo vasco, 1876–1903* (Madrid: Taurus, 2001). See also J.J. Solozabal, *El primer nacionalismo vasco: Industrialismo y conciencia nacional* (Madrid: Túcar, 1975); J.-C. Larronde, *El nacionalismo vasco: su origen y su ideología en la obra de Sabino Arana-Goiri* (San Sebastián: Txertoa, 1977); S. Payne, *Basque Nationalism*, (Reno: University of Nevada Press, 1975).

2 Ch. Tilly, *From Mobilization to Revolution* (New York: McGraw-Hill Publishing Company, 1978), p. 146. The text in parentheses is mine.

3 Ibid.

4 L. Mees, *Entre nación y clase: El nacionalismo vasco y su base social en perspectiva comparativa* (Bilbao: Fundación Sabino Arana, 1991); S. De Pablo/L. Mees, 'Historia social del nacionalismo vasco (1876–1937). Teoría y práctica de un movimiento social interclasista', in: J. Beramendi/R. Máiz/X.M. Núñez Seixas (eds), *Nationalism in Europe: Past and Present*, Vol. II (Santiago de Compostela: Universidad de Santiago de Compostela, 1994), pp. 247–74.

5 S. De Pablo/ L. Mees/ J.A. Rodríguez Ranz, *El péndulo patriótico: Historia del Partido Nacionalista Vasco*, Vol. I (Barcelona: Crítica, 1999).

6 Hroch, *Social Preconditions*. The phase of the 'mass movement' is Hroch's 'phase C' in the evolution of nationalist movements.

7 L. Mees, 'Das baskische Labyrinth. Sozialgeschichtliche Implikationen, kulturelles Umfeld und politische Artikulation des baskischen Nationalismus 1876–1937', *Archiv für Sozialgeschichte*, 32 (1992), pp. 33–55.

8 L.L. Bonaparte, *Carta lingüística del Príncipe Louis-Lucien Bonaparte, publicada en el número 116 (tomo IX) de la revista bascongada 'Euskal-Erria'* (San Sebastián:

J. R. Baroja, 1883) (first edn: London: 1863); L. Velasco y Fernández de la Fuente, *Los Euskaros en Alava, Guipúzcoa y Vizcaya. Sus orígenes, historia, lengua, leyes, costumbres y tradiciones* (Bilbao: Amigos del Libro Vasco, 1983) (first edn: Barcelona 1879), pp. 474–90; W. von Humboldt, 'Ankündigung einer Schrift über die Vascische Sprache und Nation, nebst Angabe des Gesichtspunctes und Inhalt derselben', in: ibid., *Gesammelte Schriften*, Vol. III (Berlin: B. Behr, 1904), pp. 288–99, quotation p. 292; M. de Unamuno, *Obras Completas*, Vol. IV (Madrid: Escelier, 1968), pp. 237–48.

9   In Spain, people conserve the surnames of the father (first), mother (second), grandfather (third), grandmother (fourth), and so on.

10   See especially M. N. Zald and J. D. McCarthy, *Social Movements in an Organizational Society* (New Brunswick: Transaction, 1987).

11   L. Castells, 'El nacionalismo vasco (1890–1923): ¿una ideología modernizadora?', *Ayer*, 28 (1997), pp. 127–62.

12   After the reunification of the two nationalist parties, which had split in 1921, the party recovered in 1930 the traditional name of 'Partido Nacionalista Vasco'.

13   L. Mees, *Nacionalismo vasco, movimiento obrero y cuestión social (1903–1923)*, (Bilbao: Fundación Sabino Arana, 1992); J. L. de la Granja, *Nacionalismo y II República en el País Vasco. Estatutos de Autonomía, partidos y elecciones. Historia de Acción Nacionalista Vasca: 1930–1936* (Madrid: CIS/Siglo XXI, 1986).

14   For the history of the nationalist union see L. Mees, 'Social Solidarity and National Identity in the Basque Country: The Case of the Nationalist Trade Union ELA/STV', in: P. Pasture and J. Verberckmoes (eds), *Working-Class Internationalism and the Appeal of National Identity: Historical Debates and Current Perspectives* (Oxford and New York: Berg, 1998), pp. 43–81.

15   E. J. Hobsbawm, *Nations and Nationalism since 1780: Programme, Myth, Reality* (Cambridge: Cambridge University Press, 1990), p. 140.

16   M. Keating, 'Do Workers Really Have no Country? Peripheral Nationalism and Socialism in the United Kingdom, France, Italy and Spain', in: J. Coackley (ed.), *The Social Origins of Nationalist Movements: The Contemporary West European Experience* (London: Sage, 1992), pp. 62–80, quotation pp. 78–9.

17   B. Anderson, *Imagined Communities: Reflections upon the Origin and Spread of Nationalism* (London and New York: Verso, 1991).

18   E. J. Hobsbawm and R. Ranger (eds.), *The Invention of Tradition* (Cambridge: Cambridge University Press, 1983); J. L. de la Granja, 'La invención de la historia: Nación, mitos e historia en el pensamiento del fundador del nacionalismo vasco', in: J. G. Beramendi/R. Máiz/X. M. Núñez Seixas (eds), *Nationalism in Europe: Past and Present*, Vol. II, (Santiago de Compostela: Universidad de Santiago de Compostela, 1994), pp. 97–139; J. Juaristi, *El linaje de Aitor: La invención de la tradición vasca* (Madrid: Taurus, 1987).

19   According to its creator, red symbolized the people, while the green cross was green in allusion to the colour of Basque freedom symbolized by the Oak Tree of Gernika and to the green cross of Saint Andrew, since on that day (30 November) of the year 888, according to the legend recovered by Sabino Arana, the Basques had fought an important battle against the Spanish invaders defending their independence (the 'Battle of Arrigorriaga'). Hence, green represented the Basque tradition of self-determination, while the white cross was a copy of the cross in the traditional shield of Bizkaia as a symbol of Catholicism. See Corcuera, *Patria*, p. 241.

20   L. Mees, 'El nacionalismo vasco y España: reflexiones en torno a un largo desencuentro', *Espacio, Tiempo y Forma: Historia Contemporánea*, Serie V, IX (1996), pp. 67–83.

21 Owing to their criticism against the confessional and clerical bias of the reunified PNV, some dissidents created a new party, Acción Nacionalista Vasca (ANV) in November 1930. It was a moderate nationalist, liberal and non-confessional organization, which defended Basque autonomy within the Republic and was committed to a development to the left during the last months before the beginning of the Civil War. As a result of this development, ANV joined the Popular Front in the elections of 1936. The best study of ANV and of nationalist history during the Second Republic is the book of J. L. De la Granja, *Nacionalismo y Segunda República en el País Vasco* (Madrid: Centro de Investigaciones Sociológicas/ Siglo XXI, 1986).

22 J. P. Fusi, *El problema vasco en la II República* (Madrid: Turner, 1979); J. L. de la Granja, *República y Guerra Civil en Euskadi* (Oñati: IVAP, 1990); C. Garitaonaindia and J. L. de la Granja (eds), *La Guerra Civil en el País Vasco: 50 años después* (Bilbao: Universidad del País Vasco, 1987). In English, there is quite a rich bibliography about the Second Republic and the Civil War in Spain. One of the latest and best comprehensive studies, with plenty of bibliographic references, is that of G. Esenwein and A. Shubert, *Spain at War: The Spanish Civil War in Context, 1931–1939* (London: Longman, 1995).

23 For this contrast between the backward interior and the mobilized coast see S. de Pablo, *La Segunda República en Alava: Elecciones, partidos y vida política* (Bilbao: Universidad del País Vasco, 1989); J. A. Rodríguez Ranz, *Guipúzcoa y San Sebastián en las elecciones de la II República* (San Sebastián: Fundación Social y Cultural Kutxa, 1994); M. Ferrer, *Elecciones y partidos políticos en Navarra durante la Segunda República* (Pamplona: Gobierno de Navarra, 1992); E. Majuelo, *Lucha de clases en Navarra, 1931–1936,* (Pamplona: Gobierno de Navarra, 1989); J. Chueca, *El nacionalismo vasco en Navarra (1931–1936)* (Bilbao: Universidad del País Vasco, 1999).

24 F. de Meer, *El Partido Nacionalista Vasco ante la Guerra de España (1936–1937),* (Pamplona: EUNSA, 1992).

25 M. Blinkhorn, 'The Basque Ulster: Navarre and the Basque Autonomy Question under the Spanish Second Republic', *The Historical Journal,* 17/3 (1974), pp. 595–613.

26 According to Sabino Arana's orthography, this neologism was initially spelt with a 'z'. After the process of language standardization, the official spelling is now with 's': *Euskadi.*

27 H. Southworth, *Guernica! A Study of Journalism, Diplomacy, Propaganda, and History* (Berkeley: University of California Press, 1977); M. Tuñón de Lara (ed.), *Gernika: 50 años después (1937–1987): Nacionalismo, República, Guerra Civil* (San Sebastián: Universidad del País Vasco, 1987).

4 Dictatorship and Exile: the Shape of the New Nationalism

1 One of the best studies on Francoism and its leader is the biography written by P. Preston, *Franco* (London: HarperCollins, 1993). The most recent and comprehensive research on the history of Basque nationalism during the Civil War, Francoism and democratic transition is S. de Pablo/L. Mees/J. A. Rodríguez Ranz, *El Péndulo Patriótico: Historia del Partido Nacionalista Vasco, vol. II: 1936–1979* (Barcelona: Crítica, 2001).

2 This odyssey was described by Aguirre himself in his book *De Gernika a Nueva York pasando por Berlín,* which was translated into English under the title *Escape via Berlin* (New York: Macmillan, 1944). Recently, an unpublished diary written

during his escape from fascism has been discovered in the Library of Congress in Washington. See J. A. de Aguirre y Lecube, *Diario de Aguirre* (Tafalla: Editorial Txalaparta, 1998).

3   J. C. Jiménez de Aberasturi (ed.), *Los vascos en la II Guerra Mundial: El Consejo Nacional Vasco en Londres 1940–44 (Recopilación documental)* (San Sebastián: Sociedad de Estudios Vascos, 1991).

4   In 1938, Irujo had resigned from his office in the republican government headed by Negrín in protest against the president's centralist policy in Catalonia. Later, in 1945, Irujo returned to the new government formed in exile until his definitive resignation in 1947. See M. Irujo, *Un vasco en el Ministerio de Justicia*, 3 vols (Buenos Aires: Ekin, 1976–79).

5   K. San Sebastián, *Crónicas de postguerra 1937–1951* (Bilbao: Idatz Ekintza, 1985); J. C. Jiménez de Aberásturi, *De la derrota a la esperanza : políticas vascas durante la Segunda Guerra Mundial (1937–1947)* (Oñati : IVAP, 1999).

6   In 1947, after the crisis of the government chaired by Llopis, Martínez Barrios, the president of the Spanish Republic in exile, even offered Aguirre the presidency in the new government. The offer was rejected by the *Lehendakari*.

7   J. M. Garmendia and A. Elordi, *La Resistencia vasca* (San Sebastián: Haranburu, 1982); J. C. Jiménez de Aberasturi and K. San Sebastián, *La huelga general del 1. de mayo de 1947. (Artículos y documentos)* (San Sebastián: Sociedad de Estudios Vascos, 1991).

8   In a meeting of the 'Political Commission' of the PNV in exile in France, Antón Irala, secretary to *Lehendakari* Aguirre, explained to his colleagues his interpretation of the Marshall Plan in these terms: 'Now we are at the most favourable stage to chuck out Franco, but this stage will be a long one. This Marshall Plan, if it is carried out, will mean a real revolution in all the spheres of the world. The Marshall Plan has got a material and a spiritual content. The fact that Franco has been excluded from this plan already implies an attack against him. The continuity of Franco, even if they prefer that to any other dubious solution, has started to bother the Americans.' See the record of the meeting ('Reunión del EBB (Axpe) con la Comisión Política', 27 August 1947), Archivo del Nacionalismo, EBB, K 120, C 2.

9   Quoted in the editor's introduction to Aguirre's diary mentioned in a previous note. Galíndez's fascinating biography has been the object of several novels. Even today, and after some research has been done, there are still open questions concerning his disappearance in March 1956, when he was kidnapped on Fifth Avenue in New York. The most likely hypothesis concerning the authors of the kidnapping refers to Dominican agents in the service of the dictator Trujillo, who captured Galíndez with the complicity of the American Secret Service, and took him to the Dominican Republic, where he was tortured and then thrown from an airplane into the Caribbean. See I. B. Urkijo, *Galíndez: la tumba abierta. Los vascos y los Estados Unidos* (Vitoria-Gasteiz: Gobierno Vasco, 1993).

10 Record of the meeting of the 'Comisión Política' (23 March 1948), Archivo del Nacionalismo, EBB, K 120, C 2 ('El Gobierno de la República y todo lo que gira a su alrededor ha terminado para mí. (...) Si se trata de echar a Franco, hoy sólo hay una postura seria. Apoyar a la monarquía.')

11 Ibid. (22 September 1952).

12 R. P. Clark, *The Basque Insurgents. ETA, 1952–1980* (Madison: University of Wisconsin Press, 1984); J. M. Garmendia, *Historia de ETA* (San Sebastián: Haranburu, 1995); P. Ibarra, *La evolución estratégica de ETA* (San Sebastián: Kriselu, 1987); G. Jauregui, *Ideología y estrategia política de ETA. Análisis de su evolución entre 1959 y 1968* (Madrid: Siglo XXI, 1981); F. Letamendia, *Historia del nacionalismo*

vasco y de ETA, 3 vols (San Sebastián: R & B, 1994); C. E. Zirakzadeh, *A Rebellious People: Basques, Protests, and Politics* (Reno: Nevada University Press, 1991); J. Sullivan, *ETA and Basque Nationalism: The Fight for Euskadi 1890–1986* (London: Routledge, 1988); A. Elorza *et al.*, *La historia de ETA* (Madrid: Temas de Hoy, 2000).

13   P. Waldmann, *Militanter Nationalismus im Baskenland* (Frankfurt: Vervuert, 1990), p. 71.

14   A. Gurruchaga, *El código nacionalista vasco durante el Franquismo* (Barcelona: Anthropos), p. 213.

15   L. C. Núñez, *Clases sociales en Euskadi* (San Sebastián: Txertoa, 1977), pp. 157–71; J. Ruiz Olabuenaga and M. C. Blanco, *La inmigración vasca. Análisis trigeneracional de 150 años de inmigración* (Bilbao: Universidad de Deusto, 1994); the following figures concerning the decay of *Euskara* are taken from L. C. Núñez, *Opresión y defensa del euskera* (San Sebastián: Txertoa, 1977), pp. 26–8.

16   L. Mees, 'Zwischen Mobilisierung und Institutionalisierung. Der baskische Nationalismus 1953–1995', in: H. Timmermann (ed.), *Nationalismus in Europa 1945–1995* (Berlin: Duncker & Humblot, 2001), pp. 221–62; S. Tarrow, *Power in Movement: Social Movements, Collective Action and Politics* (Cambridge: Cambridge University Press, 1994); B. Tejerina, *Nacionalismo y lengua* (Madrid: CIS/Siglo XXI, 1992).

17   F. Sarrailh de Ihartza (pseudonym: F. Krutwig), *Vasconia: Estudio dialéctico de una nacionalidad* (Buenos Aires: Norbait, 1973; first: 1963), pp. 12 and 44.

18   See Gurruchaga, (1985), pp. 292–309.

19   X. M. Núñez Seixas, *Los nacionalismos en la España contemporánea (siglos XIX y XX)*, (Barcelona: Hipòtesi, 1999); L. Mees, 'De spanische "Sonderweg"'; J. L. de la Granja/J. Beramendi/P. Anguera, *La España de los nacionalismos y las autonomías* (Madrid: Síntesis, 2001).

20   P. Waldmann, *Ethnischer Radikalismus: Ursachen und Folgen gewaltsamer Minderheitenkonflikte am Beispiel des Baskenlandes, Nordirlands und Quebecs* (Opladen: Westdeutscher Verlag, 1984). Waldmann, using also data supplied by Clark (1984, pp. 143–6) analysed the information concerning only 81 prisoners. The recent study of Domínguez includes 1,118 cases. See F. Domínguez Iribarren, *ETA: Estrategia organizativa y actuaciones 1978–1992* (Bilbao: Universidad del País Vasco, 1998), pp. 43–77.

21   D. Conversi, *The Basques, the Catalans, and Spain* (London: Hurst, 1997), p. 263.

22   T. R. Gurr and B. Harff, *Ethnic Conflict in World Politics* (Boulder: Westview Press, 1994), p. 85.

23   G. Giacopucci, *ETA-pm: el otro camino* (Tafalla: Txalaparta, 1997); the lawyer Juan Mari Bandrés was one of the politicians who on behalf of ETA p-m participated directly in the negotiations. See his memoirs R. Castro, *Juan María Bandrés, memorias para la paz* (Majadahonda: HMR, 1998).

5   The Transition towards Democracy and the Basque Problem

1   R. Gunther/H.-J. Puhle/P.N. Nikiforos (eds), *The Politics of Democratic Consolidation: Southern Europe in Comparative Perspective* (Baltimore and London: Johns Hopkins University Press, 1995), p. 4.

2   This is a translated quotation taken from one of the most recent comprehensive studies on processes of transition and democratic consolidation. See W. Merkel and H.-J. Puhle, *Von der Diktatur zur Demokratie: Transformationen, Erfolgsbedingungen,*

Entwicklungspfade (Opladen: Westdeutscher Verlag, 1999), p. 244. See there also the extensive bibliography (pp. 251–61). More information about the Spanish transition and its comparison with other cases can be found in the following books: R. Gunther/G. Sani/G. Shabad, *Spain after Franco: The Making of a Competitive Party System* (Berkeley: University of California Press, 1986); D. Share, *The Making of Spanish Democracy* (New York: Praeger, 1986); J. Linz and A. Stepan, *Problems of Democratic Transition and Consolidation: Southern Europe, South Africa, and Post-Communist Europe* (Baltimore: Johns Hopkins University Press, 1996); S. P. Huntington, *The Third Wave: Democratization in the Late Twentieth Century* (Norman: University of Oklahoma Press, 1991); J. M. Maravall, *Regimes, Politics, and Markets. Democratization and Economic Change in Southern and Eastern Europe* (Oxford: Oxford University Press, 1997); J. Tusell and A. Soto (eds), *Historia de la transición 1975–1986*, (Madrid: Alianza, 1996); A. Soto, *La transición a la democracia. España 1975–1982* (Madrid: Alianza, 1998).

3 D. Share and S. Mainwaring, 'Transition through Transaction: Democratization in Brazil and Spain', in: W. Selcher (ed.), *Political Liberalization in Brazil* (Boulder: Westview Press, 1986), pp. 175–215.

4 The important role of Juan Carlos has been highlighted by different scholars. See e.g. the studies written by Ch. T. Powell, *El piloto del cambio: el rey, la monarquía y la transición a la democracia* (Barcelona: Planeta, 1991); J. Tusell, *Juan Carlos I: La restauración de la monarquía* (Madrid: Temas de Hoy, 1995).

5 For the construction of the 'state of autonomies', its origins and current problems see the recent study – with further bibliographical notes – of E. Aja, *El Estado Autonómico: Federalismo y hechos diferenciales* (Madrid: Alianza, 1999).

6 Gunther/Puhle/Diamandourus, p. 11.

7 This is the thesis of A. Rivera, 'La transición en el País Vasco: un caso particular', in: J. Ugarte (ed.), *La transición en el País Vasco y España. Historia y memoria* (Bilbao: Universidad del País Vasco, 1998), pp. 79–91.

8 J. Corcuera, *Política y derecho. La construcción de la autonomía vasca* (Madrid: Centro de Estudios Constitucionales, 1991), p. 117.

9 For the evolution of Basque nationalism during the Transition see, besides the book of Corcuera, *Política*, G. Jáuregui, 'La cuestión nacional vasca y el Estatuto de Autonomía', *Revista Vasca de Administración Pública*, 1, (1981), pp. 79–109; De Pablo/Mees/Rodríguez Ranz, *Péndulo, II*, pp. 325–79.

10 Corcuera, *Política*, p. 80; J. P. Fusi and J. Palafox, *España: 1808–1996: El desafío de la modernidad*, 4th edn (Madrid: 1998), p. 376.

11 Document reproduced in S. de Pablo/J. L. de la Granja/L. Mees, *Documentos para la historia del nacionalismo vasco: De los Fueros a nuestros días* (Barcelona: Ariel, 1998), pp. 155–7.

12 Years later, the communist representative in the constitutional commission, Jordi Solé Tura, considered the exclusion of the PNV as a grave political error. See J. Solé Tura, *Nacionalidades y nacionalismos en España: Autonomías, federalismo y autodeterminación*, (Madrid: Alianza, 1985).

13 The party's official communiqué in *Deia*, 19.11.1978.

14 See the text of the so-called 'K.A.S. Alternative', signed in August 1976 by several parties of the radical nationalist left and by ETA, reproduced in De Pablo/Granja/Mees, pp. 153–5.

15 Results from Catalonia in J. L. de la Granja/P. Anguera/J. G. Beramendi, pp. 214–16; for the Basque Country, see J. Linz *et al.*, *Atlas electoral del País Vasco y Navarra* (Madrid: Centro de Investigaciones Sociológicas, 1981), pp. 88–93; http://www.euskadi.net.

16   Corcuera, *Política*, p. 138.
17   English version of the Statute in Internet, http:www.euskadi.net.
18   See De Pablo/Mees/Rodríguez Ranz, *Péndulo* I and II.
19   For the evolution of the radical nationalist left during the transition and the first
       years of democratic consolidation see the testimony of one of HB's principal lead-
       ers, the former M.P. Francisco Letamendia: F. Letamendia, *Historia del nacional-
       ismo vasco y de ETA*, especially Vol. II, pp. 221–493 ('ETA en la Transición').
20   The complex organizational network of the 'Liberation Movement' is studied by
       J. M. Mata, *El nacionalismo vasco radical: Discurso, organización y expresiones*
       (Bilbao: Universidad del País Vasco, 1993).
21   English version of the KAS document in R. P. Clark, *Negotiating with ETA: Obstacles
       to Peace in the Basque Country, 1975–1988* (Reno: University of Nevada Press,
       1990), p. 82.
22   However, the demand for 'complete political independence' and for the 'achieve-
       ment of an independent and reunified Basque state', as well as the 'execution of
       the socialist revolution' were already integrated in the introductory paragraph of
       the original KAS manifesto published in August 1976. See the text in De Pablo/
       Granja/Mees, pp. 153–5.

6   Democracy, Autonomy and Violence

1   The three elected presidents of the Autonomous Basque Community (Carlos
      Garaikoetxea, José Antonio Ardanza, Juan José Ibarretxe) are all members of the
      PNV.
2   J. M. López de Juan Abad, *La autonomía vasca: Crónica del comienzo (El Consejo
      General del País Vasco)* (San Sebastián: Txertoa, 1998); Corcuera, *Política* (1991).
3   In Table 6.3 the figures for 1990/91 do not total 100, since 1 per cent of the pupils
      went to special schools without any language model, mostly for children of
      foreigners and other inhabitants without a regular residency in the Basque
      provinces; referring to Table 6.4, there is no figure for the model B and the
      age between 16 and 19, because in that education level only the models A and D
      are offered.
4   All the figures are taken from Universidad del País Vasco. Vicerectorado de
      Euskara, Situación actual de la docencia bilingüe en la UPV (Bilbao: Universidad del
      País Vasco, 1998).
5   See *El Diario Vasco*, 2 January 1998 (interview with Josune Ariztondo, the head of
      the Department for Language Policy in the Basque government).
6   J.M. Torrealdai, *XX. Mendeko Euskal Liburuen Katalogoa (1900–1992)* (Donostia:
      Gipuzkoako Foru Aldundia, 1993), especially pp. XIV–XV; more information
      about the evolution of the Basque language in the different areas can be found
      in J. Intxausti, *Euskera, la lengua de los vascos* (San Sebastián: Elkar, 1992).
7   See Arana's letter to Engracio Aranzadi, reproduced in De Pablo/De la Granja/
      Mees, pp. 44–6.
8   See the Manifiesto in *El Diario Vasco*, 21 October 1999.
9   On the problem of national identities in Navarre, see M. J. Izu Belloso, *Navarra
      como problema: Nación y nacionalismo en Navarra* (Madrid: Biblioteca Nueva, 2001).
10   In Navarre, there is no mixed model B. The model G refers to education exclu-
       sively in Spanish.
11   See the classical study of E. Weber, *Peasants into Frenchmen: The Modernization of
       Rural France 1870–1914* (Stanford: Stanford University Press, 1976); see also

B. Jenkins, *Nationalism in France: Class and Nation since 1789* (Savage-Maryland: Barnes & Noble, 1999).

12 F. Etxeberria Balerdi, *Bilingüismo y educación en el País del Euskara* (San Sebastián: Erein, 1999), p. 99. Model X refers to schools in the French Basque Country with exclusively French education.

13 The best study of nationalism in the French Basque Country is that of J. E. Jacob, *Hills of Conflict: Basque Nationalism in France* (Reno: Nevada University Press, 1994), quotations pp. 8, 40 and Weber, *Peasants*, p. 99.

14 In 1996, 73 per cent of the 2,428,000 inhabitants of *Euskal Herria* were living in the Autonomous Community of the Basque Country, 18 per cent in Navarre and 9 per cent in the French part. See Etxeberria, p. 93.

15 J. I. Ross, 'Structural Causes of Oppositional Political Terrorism: Towards a Causal Model', *Journal of Peace Research*, Vol. 30, 3 (1993), pp. 317–29.

16 M. Miralles and R. Arques, *Amedo: el Estado contra ETA*, 3rd edn (Barcelona: Plaza & Janes, 1989); A. Baeza, *GAL, crimen de Estado* (Madrid: ABL, 1996); S. Morán Blanco, *ETA entre España y Francia* (Madrid: Editorial Complutense, 1997).

17 As an example, see the anthropological study of a small rural area in Gipuzkoa written by J. Zulaika, *Basque Violence: Metaphor and Sacrament* (Reno: Nevada University Press, 1988); see also C. J. Watson, *Sacred Earth, Symbolic Blood: A Cultural History of Basque Political Violence from Arana to ETA* (Ann Arbor: UMJ, 1996).

18 I. L. Horowitz, 'The Routinization of Terrorism and Its Unanticipated Consequences', in: M. Crenshaw (ed.), *Terrorism, Legitimacy, and Power: the Consequences of Political Violence* (Middletown/Connecticut: Wesleyan University Press, 1986), pp. 38–51.

7 'The times, they are a-changin''

1 J. Darby and R. Mac Ginty (eds), *The Managment of Peace Processes* (Palgrave Macmillan: London, 2000), pp. 7–8.

2 R. P. Clark, *Negotiating*, p. 3.

3 Statement of Iñaki Albistur, quoted in G. Giacopuzzi, *ETA p-m. El otro camino* (Tafalla: Txalaparta, 1997), p. 225.

4 See the text discussed in the 'Conferencia de cuadros' in ibid., pp. 209–10.

5 After its unification with the majority sector of the Basque Communist Party, in March 1982 the coalition EE was transformed into the political party Euskadiko Ezkerra–Izquierda para el socialismo (EE–IPS).

6 R. Castro, *Juan María Bandrés*, p. 215.

7 Clark, *Negotiating*, p. 107. The new president of the government after the resignation of Suárez was Leopoldo Calvo Sotelo. His governing party, UCD, had already entered its final crisis. After the elections of October 1982, which brought the socialists to power, the party practically vanished from the political life.

8 Arzallus rejected that accusation, arguing that his trip to the French side of the Basque Country was only a reaction to a request by the *poli-milis*, inspired by the need of being informed about what was happening. According to the PNV leader, he never encouraged the paramilitaries to continue the armed struggle. In his recent biography, however, Bandrés repeats the same charge against Arzallus and the most 'conservative and traditionalist' sectors of the party, who 'dislike an ending of the armed struggle, because that would diminish their capacity of negotiation'. See Castro, p. 251.

9 Clark, *Negotiating*, p. 109, mentions the number of 200; Bandrés himself calculates 'from 250 to 300' persons with individual pardons (Castro, 216).
10 Ibid., p. 265.
11 J. M. Irujo and R. Arques, *ETA: la derrota de las armas. Todas las sombras, secretos y contactos de la organización terrorista al descubierto* (Barcelona: Plaza & Janes, 1993), p. 78; previous quotation from Clark, *Negotiating*, p. 165. See also C. Fonseca, *Negociar con ETA: De Argel al Gobierno del PP* (Madrid: Temas de Hoy), 1996 and, from a pro-ETA point of view, I. Egaña and G. Giacopucci, *Los días de Argel: Crónica de las conversaciones entre ETA y el Gobierno español* (Tafalla: Txalaparte, 1992).
12 Inside information about the negotiations can also be found in A. Pozas, *Las conversaciones secretas Gobierno–ETA* (Barcelona: Ediciones B, 1992). Pozas was at that time communications adviser attached to the Spanish Minister of the Interior. The newest and most complete analysis of the talks in Algeria is a chapter of a book written by F. Domínguez Iribarren, *De la negociación a la tregua. ¿El final de ETA?* (Madrid: Taurus, 1998), pp. 64–80.
13 See Domínguez Iribarren, *Negociación*, pp. 73–4.
14 See Irujo and Arques, pp. 201–3, quotation p. 201.
15 In June 1987, ETA placed a bomb in a Barcelona supermarket killing 21 persons and injuring another 39; in December of the same year, a car bomb against the police barracks in Zaragoza killed 11 persons, five of them being young children; in February 1988, the industrialist Emiliano Revilla was kidnapped. After 249 days and a payment of 500 million pesetas, he was released.
16 Domínguez Iribarren, *Negociación*, p. 64.
17 Clark, *Negotiating*, p. 201.
18 See De Pablo/Mees/Rodríguez Ranz, *Péndulo*, vols I and II.
19 A certain exception might be that of the small party Acción Nacionalista Vasca, which in 1936 adopted a leftist programme.
20 The following figures are taken from the web page issued by the Asociación de Víctimas del Terrorismo (http://www.avt.org/eta).
21 This figure is obviously somewhat artificial, since some of the kidnappings overlapped.
22 B. Delgado Soto and A.J. Mencía Gullón, *Diario de un secuestro: Ortega Lara, 532 días en un zulo* (Madrid: Alianza, 1998).
23 M. A. Iglesias (ed.): *Ermua, 4 días de julio: 40 voces tras la muerte de Miguel Angel Blanco* (Madrid: El País-Aguilar, 1997).
24 M. Castells, *The Information Age: Economy, Society and Culture*, Vol. I: *The Rise of the Network Society* (Cambridge, Mass.: Blackwell, 1996).
25 J. Seaton, 'Why do we think the Serbs do it? The new 'ethnic' wars and the media', *Political Quarterly*, 70, 3, (1999), pp. 254–70, quotation p. 260.
26 An English version of the 'Democratic Alternative' can be found on the web page of *Euskal Herria Journal* (http://www.contrast.org/mirrors/ehj). The following quotations are taken from this text.
27 *Oldartzen. Oinarrizko Txostena. Egoeraren azterketa eta ildo politikoa*, December 1994, Ms.
28 *El País*, 9.12.1997.
29 *Egin*, 30.12.1997.
30 *El País*, 13.1.1997.
31 As an example, see the communiqués of ETA and KAS in *El País*, 3, April 1997. The acronym KAS stands for Koordinadora Abertzale Sozialista (Patriotic Socialist Coordinating Council), which is an illegal organization created to coordinate the

strategy of the political and the armed wings of the Movement. ETA-m is a full member of KAS, a fact that provides real decision-making authority to this Council. Towards the end of the 1990s and the beginning of the new decade, according to an investigation carried out by the Spanish National High Court, ETA decided to substitute KAS by another organization called Ekin, which was supposed to perform the same function of coordination between the underground group and its political wing, being however less exposed to the growing police pressure. Yet, the judge Garzón declared Ekin illegal and imprisoned several of its leaders.

32   *Actitudes hacia la violencia en el País Vasco*, Mayo 1997 (Ed.: Gobierno Vasco. Presidencia, Gabinete de Prospección Sociológico'), Ms, p. 12.

33   K. Aulestia, *HB. Crónica de un delirio* (Madrid: Temas de hoy, 1998), p. 11.

34   Ibid., p. 223.

35   M. Arriaga, *Y nosotros que éramos de HB: sociología de una heterodoxia abertzale* (San Sebastián: Haranburu, 1997).

36   The text of the sentence in *El País*, 2 December 1997.

37   A detailed study of the evolution of the French attitude towards the ETA problem in Domínguez Iribarren, *Negociación*, pp. 258–300.

38   As a brief analysis of the most important dimensions of the crisis and a source for statistical data see the article 'A pesar de ETA', in: *Cambio 16*, 27 October 1997.

39   Domínguez Iribarren, *ETA: estrategia organizativa*, pp. 263–71, quotation p. 265. Concerning the nuclear plant at Lemoniz, however, we could question if the dismantling and its costs can be exclusively and totally atributed to ETA violence. Even without terrorism, it was forseeable that the government's decision to construct a nuclear plant only a few kilometres away from the most populous Basque region, that is, Bilbao and its industrial hinterland, would provoke the protest of the affected population, who obviously would not consent to such a high risk for its health and safety. In fact, ETA only started acting against Lemoniz when a strong anti-nuclear social movement had already been set up. Thus, the very decision to build the nuclear plant in that context, taken by some politicians who apparently did not bother too much about problems like health and security, was equally responsible for the high costs generated by the paralysis of the construction.

40   Ibid. and *El País*, 28 January 1998.

41   See the figures for the EU in http://www.europa.eu.int/comm/eurostat.

42   El País, 17 January 1998. The situation in the province of Navarre with an unemployment rate of 9.72 per cent is better. See *El País*, 6 January 1998.

43   In Spain, different and quite contradictory statistics of unemployment rates are available. I have chosen only data proceeding from statistics methodologically based on the standard criterion suggested by the International Organization of Labour, and thus valid and meaningful in an international context.

44   *Landeia*, 59, enero 1998, p. 22.

45   *Plan de Actuación del Gobierno para el desarrollo de los valores democráticos y fomento de actitudes de solidaridad, tolerancia y responsabilidad en los adolescentes y jóvenes vascos* (ed. Gobierno Vasco), Vitoria (1997), Ms, p. 16.

46   Ibid., p. 33.

47   During the ceasefire of 1998/99, HB created a new electoral platform called 'Euskal Herritarrok' (EH).

48   *El Diario Vasco*, 10 April 1997.

49   *El País*, 28 January 1998.

50   The statement of Mr Uriarte (Banco Bilbao Bizkaia) in *El País*, 19 June 1997.

51 Interview with J. M. Korta and J. M. Ruiz Urchegui (14 November 1997), tape-document.
52 *El País-Negocios*, 29 September 1996.
53 *El País*, 23 September 1996.
54 See the report on the agreement in *El País*, 18 January 2000. In winter 2002, in a second round of negotiations between the Basque and the Spanish administrations, no agreement could be reached on the Basque claim for a direct presence in those European institutions, where decisions affecting the Basque tax system are taken. Madrid rejected this claim, arguing that according to the Constitution all kinds of international relations were an exclusive domain of the central government. Yet, still more important than this formal argument was the fear that a direct Basque presence in Brussels would be another step towards Basque independence.
55 See the interview with Zubia in *El Diario Vasco*, 9 May 1999.
56 See the quotation in the article 'El "boom" turístico vasco', in *El País*, 26 October 1998.
57 For more details see the article 'Euskadi recibió en 1999 un millón y medio de visitantes, cifra histórica para el turismo vasco', in *El País*, 21 January 2000.
58 The presentation of the report and the press-conference in *El Diario Vasco*, 13 May 1997.
59 These were Emilio Ybarra, president of the major Basque bank BBV; Iñigo Oriol, the president of the electricity company Iberdrola, and Baltasar Errazti, the predecessor of Knörr as head of Confebask.
60 See the report about this encounter in *El País*, 23 April 1999, with the significant title 'The Basque businessmen ask Aznar to consolidate the peace by means of dialogue'.
61 See the interview with Zubia in *El Diario Vasco*, 9 May 1999.
62 Darby and Mac Ginty, p. 241.
63 F. Llera, *Los vascos y la política* (Bilbao: Universidad del País Vasco, 1994), pp. 103 and 104.
64 Quoted in Domínguez Iribarren, *Negociación*, p. 241.
65 This is the metaphor used in the title of one of the most recent and solid studies about the Basque peace movement. See M. J. Funes, *La salida del silencio: Movilizaciones por la paz en Euskadi 1986–1998* (Madrid: Akal, 1998). Also Domínguez Iribarren, *Negociación*, p. 240, refers to 'the long stage of silence, during which only minority groups of citizens had dared to face up to terrorism'.
66 *El País*, 20 July 1997.
67 See the report 'Crónica de Documentación y Actualidad', quoted in Domínguez Iribarren, *De la negociación a la tregua*, pp. 243–4.
68 *El País*, 20 January 1998.
69 During the months preceding the ceasefire, several cases of violent aggression against persons wearing the symbol of the blue ribbon were recorded.
70 Interview with Xabier Azkazibar, Bilbao 9 June 1997 (tape document).
71 More information about the organizational structure and the discourse of these peace groups can be found in B. Tejerina/J. M. Fernández Sobrado/X. Aierdi, *Sociedad civil, protesta y movimientos sociales en el País Vasco: Los límites de la teoría de la movilización de recursos* (Vitoria: Gobierno Vasco, 1995), pp. 39–44, 83–9, 131–2.
72 'The Basque Conflict' (report prepared by Elkarri, 1995, Ms), p. 26.
73 'Elkarri, el trayecto de una idea', Ms (1997), report elaborated by the group (no pagination).

74 In 2001 the leadership of Gestoras was put into jail by the judge of the Spanish High Court Baltasar Garzón on a charge of being members of the terrorist organization ETA.

75 'The Basque Conflict', p. 26.

76 See the statement of Bakea Orain in *El Diario Vasco*, 19 July 1997. In September, a member of the same group talked about the 'recent dissolution of the Maroño-groups'. See *El País*, 29 September 1997.

77 El Diario Vasco, 10 June 1997.

78 The data and Elzo's statement in *El País*, 24 November 1997.

8 Give Peace a Chance: On the Way to the Ceasefire

1 Among Tilly's rich bibliography on theoretical and empirical problems related to the model of the political opportunity structure, see especially his already classic book *From Mobilization to Revolution* (New York: McGraw-Hill, 1978); S. Tarrow, *Power in Movement: Social Movements, Collective Action and Politics* (Cambridge: Cambridge University Press, 1994); S. Tarrow, *Democracy and Disorder: Protest and Politics in Italy 1965–1975* (Oxford: Clarendon Press, 1989).

2 M. Von Tangen Page, *Prisons, Peace and Terrorism: Penal Policy in the Reduction of Political Violence in Northern Ireland, Italy and the Spanish Basque Country, 1968–97* (London: Macmillan Press – now Palgrave Macmillan, 1998), p. 141.

3 *El Diario Vasco*, 13 June 1997.

4 Von Tangen Page does not give any evidence for his thesis that 'the social reinsertion legislation has also proved to be a very effective way to encourage members of the ETA-m to renounce violence and return to normal life' (Von Tangen Page, p. 161). Not even the spokesmen of the Spanish conservative government argue with the hypothetical success of this penal policy when legitimating its continuity. They rather point out that a transfer of the prisoners to jails near or in the Basque Country would make the control of the prisoners by the ETA leadership even easier than it is now.

5 *Texto del Plan de Acercamiento de Presos a Cárceles Próximas al País Vasco aprobado por el Parlamento Vasco*, Vitoria-Gasteiz, Febrero de 1997, Ms, p. 9.

6 *Egin*, 25 April 1997.

7 See both the text of the law and of the EP resolution in the appendix of the *Texto del Plan de Acercamiento*.

8 *El Diario Vasco*, 6 June 1997; *El País*, 7 June 1997.

9 Cf. L. Mees, 'Mobilisierung'; De Pablo/Mees/Rodríguez Ranz, *Péndulo, II*, pp. 325–79.

10 The text of the agreement is reproduced in *El País*, 13 January 1998.

11 See the editorial ('Diez años') of the HB-attached daily paper *Egin*, 11 January 1998.

12 The announcement of the 'mini' ceasefire by ETA in June of 96 was more imaginary than real, since at the same time ETA still held as a hostage the prison-worker Ortega Lara. The parties of the 'Democratic Bloc' rejected this 'offer', linking the start of talks to several preconditions (liberation of Ortega Lara, unlimited ceasefire, acceptance of the Basque society's pluralism and of the majority will democratically expressed by the people).

13 There have been rumours that the origin of the leak was the conservative Spanish Minister of the Interior or the Secret Services interested in aborting the initiative, giving it no time to mature.

14 Owing to their minority background, their dogmatic and extremist bias and the evident incapacity of forging any consensus, I don't consider 'serious' either the so-called 'KAS Alternative', nor its substitute the 'Democratic Alternative' defended by ETA and HB.

15 *Para un acuerdo entre los Partidos de la Mesa sobre el 'final dialogado': Documento de Trabajo*, Ms, Vitoria-Gasteiz, 17 March 1998.

16 Conversation with the author, Vitoria-Gasteiz 12 March 1998.

17 On the Northern Irish peace process, see J. Darby and R. Mac Ginty, 'Northern Ireland: Long, Cold Peace', in: Darby and Mac Ginty, pp. 61–106.

18 Interview with J. Egibar, 15 May 1997 (tape document).

19 Interview with J. Mayor Oreja, *El País*, 19 December 1997. This interview was given a very few hours after another Basque PP councillor (Luis Caso of Renteria) had been killed.

20 For the results of the different opinion polls, see *El País*, 4 March 1998; *El Diario Vasco*, 29 March 1998; ibid., 20 May 1998.

21 See *El Diario Vasco*, 24 January 1998.

22 See the interview in *El Diario Vasco*, 5 April 1998.

23 See the article 'Apaciguamiento y tregua' by A. Surio, in *El Diario Vasco*, 2 March 1998.

24 In declarations to the media, Arzallus blamed the Spanish Secret Service for leaking the document to the press and trying to 'torpedo' the peace proposal by that 'manipulation'. See his statements and the information about the record in *El Diario Vasco*, 18 March 1998.

25 The quotation contains a sequence of the 'Manifesto for the Democracy in Euskadi' issued by the radically anti-nationalist 'Forum of Ermua' on the day of its foundation in February 1998. See the complete text in *El País*, 14 February 1998.

26 See Ardanza's statement in *El Diario Vasco*, 24 March 1998.

27 J. M. Ollora, *Un futuro para Euskadi* (San Sebastián: Erein, 1994).

28 Figures according to the statistics published in *El Diario Vasco*, 14 May 2001.

29 One of the last victims, a town councillor in Renteria, had just a few months before substituted another colleague killed by ETA in the same town.

30 For the history of the nationalist labour movement in the Basque Country, see L. Mees, 'Social Solidarity'; on the history of LAB, see E. Majuelo, *LAB sindikatuaren historia: Langile Abertzaleen Batzordeak (1975–2000)* (Tafalla: Txalaparta, 2000).

31 In January 2002, this number had nearly reached the historic record of 100,000.

32 There are no official figures, but it is known and admitted by Elorrieta himself that the unrest especially of many Basque policemen members of the union, forced quite an important number of *ertzainak* to quit the union.

33 See *El Diario Vasco*, 18 March 1997.

34 See their declarations to the press in *El Diario Vasco*, 16 July 1997.

35 *El Diario Vasco*, 2 October 1997.

36 *El Diario Vasco*, 10 October 1997.

37 Javier Villanueva, 'Puesta de largo del soberanismo vasco', *HIKA*, 1997ko azaroa, p. 28.

38 The text of the conference in *HIKA*, 1997ko azaroa, pp. 22–3.

39 See the interview in *El Diario Vasco*, 26 October 1997.

40 See Arregi's article 'Lágrimas por el "tercer espacio"', in *El Diario Vasco*, 18 December 1997.

41 See for instance the interview with Elorrieta quoted above and the meeting held by Fernández in Tolosa, *El Diario Vasco*, 18 December 1997.

42　The first programme of the PNV, adopted in 1906 and valid until post-Francoism, defined the 'recovering of the old Fueros' previous to the first abolition law of 1839 as the supreme political aim of nationalist politics. This formula permitted the integration of separatists and autonomists in the party, avoiding its split.

43　A. Arteta, 'La gran infección', in: A. Arteta/D. Velasco/I. Zubero, *Razones contra la violencia: Por la convivencia democrática en el País Vasco*, Vol. II (Bilbao: Bakeaz, 1998), pp. 13–94, especially 88–92.

44　R. Zallo, *Euskadi o la Segunda Transición: Nación, cultura, ideologías y paz en un cambio de época* (San Sebastián: Erein, 1997).

45　See the comment of Alberto Surio ('La foto borrosa') in *El Diario Vasco*, 19 October 1997.

46　See the interviews with Elorrieta in *Egin*, 17 December 1997, and Fernández, in *El Diario Vasco*, 15 December 1997.

47　The text of the communiqué, completely written in *euskara*, was published by *Egin*, 19 December 1997.

48　See the different statements in *Egin*, 20 December 1997 ('Los aludidos respondieron a ETA').

49　Quotation in *El Diario Vasco*, 30 December 1997 ('HB y LAB salvan al "tercer espacio" de sus críticas a la "tercera vía" ').

50　This opinion is quoted in *El Diario Vasco*, 13 December 1997.

51　See the weekly chronicle titled 'Encuentros en el tercer espacio' in *Egin*, 22 December 1997.

52　I. Gurruchaga, *El modelo irlandés: historia secreta de un proceso de paz* (Barcelona: Península, 1998); R. Alonso, *La paz de Belfast* (Madrid: Alianza, 2000); R. Alonso, *Irlanda del Norte: una historia de guerra y la búsqueda de la paz* (Madrid: Editorial Complutense, 2001).

53　A. Ugalde Zubiri, *La acción exterior del nacionalismo vasco (1890–1939): Historia, pensamiento y relaciones internacionales* (Bilbao: Universidad del País Vasco, 1996); X. M. Núñez Seixas, 'El mito del nacionalismo irlandés y su influencia en los nacionalismos gallego, vasco y catalán (1880–1936)', *Spagna Contemporanea*, 2, 1992, pp. 25–58; X. M. Núñez Seixas, 'El espejo irlandés y los reflejos ibéricos', *Cuadernos de Alzate*, 18, 1998, pp. 169–90.

54　S. de Arana Goiri: 'Los nacionalistas de Irlanda', *Bizkaitarra*, 19, 20 January 1895.

55　M. Ugalde, *Mujeres y nacionalismo vasco: Génesis y desarrollo de Emakume Abertzale Batza. 1906–1936* (Bilbao: Universidad del País Vasco) 1993; Mees, *Nacionalismo*, pp. 325–30; J. Juaristi, *El bucle melancólico: Historias de nacionalistas vascos*, 5th edn (Madrid: Espasa Calpe, 1998), pp. 207–68.

56　'The links between the Basque separatist movement and Republicans date back to the early 1970s when ETA provided the IRA with handguns (...). In the 1980s, the IRA passed on car-bomb technology to the Basque guerrillas, while ETA is believed to have provided logistical support for IRA operations against British interests in Germany and the Netherlands.' See *The Irish Times*, 21 September 1998 ('Adams urges ETA to seek dialogue').

57　P. Waldmann, *Ethnischer Radikalismus*; E. Moxon-Browne, 'La política étnica: estudio comparativo de los católicos norteirlandeses y los vascos españoles', *Revista de Estudios Políticos*, vol. 63, 1989, pp. 83–105; C. L. Irvin, *Militant Nationalism: Between Movement and Party in Ireland and the Basque Country* (Minneapolis and London: University of Minnesota Press, 1999); M.K. Flynn, *Ideology, Mobilization, and the Nation: The Rise of Irish, Basque and Carlist National Movements in the Nineteenth and Early Twentieth Centuries* (New York: St. Martin's Press – now Palgrave Macmillan, 2000).

58   Darby and Mac Ginty, *Management*, p. 64.
59   See the definition of this concept as a modification of the more common one of the 'political opportunity structure' in D. Rucht, *Modernisierung und neue soziale Bewegungen: Deutschland, Frankreich und USA im Vergleich* (Frankfurt a.M.: Campus, 1994), pp. 303–23.
60   Tarrow, *Power*, p. 191.
61   *The Irish Times*, 31 October 1998 ('Basque leader sees peace process as way forward').
62   See the references and quotations from this document in *El Correo Español*, 21 July 1997 and *El Mundo*, 22 July 1997.
63   See *El País*, 12 July and 16 July 1997; *El Diario Vasco*, 15, 16, 17 and 21 July 1997.
64   José Luis Alvarez Santa Cristina/Kepa Pikabea Ugalde/Roxario Pikabea Ugalde, 'Abertzaleon estrategiaz', 1997ko abuztua (MS), p. 2.
65   Joseba Urrosolo Sistiaga: 'Irlandakoak balio al du Euskal Herrirako? Irlanda – Euskal Herria', *Egin*, 23 December 1997.
66   Iulen de Madariaga: 'De la manifestación abortada del 13 de diciembre y otras cosas', *Egin*, 20 January 1998.
67   See the ETA documents published in *El País*, 2 and 3 November 1998.
68   *El País*, 2 November 1998.
69   Quoted in *Egin*, 27 January 98.
70   See the interviews in *El Diario Vasco*, 2 February 1998 and *El País*, 9 February 1998.
71   See e.g. Arzallus' statement in *El Diario Vasco*, 19 January 1998.
72   Garaikoetxea, leader of EA, criticized the 'lack of courage' that in *Euskadi* was impeding the negotiation; Arzallus praised Tony Blair, contrasting his example with the Spanish politicians who defended the 'military means' as the only way of fighting against ETA; HB's new leader Arnaldo Otegi confirmed that 'Euskadi is going to experience the same process as Northern Ireland does'. See *El País*, *Egin* and *El Diario Vasco*, 13 April 1998.
73   This statement of Iturgaiz and the following ones of Redondo, Huertas and Iturgaiz can be found in *El Diario Vasco*, 12 April 1998 ('Los partidos vascos discrepan sobre la aplicación en Euskadi de la vía irlandesa').
74   *El Diario Vasco*, 16 July 1998.
75   Here are only four examples from the enormous bulk of press articles dedicated to this question: Imanol Zubero, 'Irlanda y País Vasco, odiosas comparaciones' (*El País*, 14 April 1998); Antonio Elorza, 'De Stormont a Euskadi' (ibid., 17 April 1998); Miguel Herrero de Miñón, 'Método de Stormont' (ibid., 18 April 1998); Manuel Castells, 'El Estado red' (ibid., 20 April 1998).
76   *El Diario Vasco*, 17 February 1998.
77   This at least is the date published later by *El País*, 2 November 1998.
78   UPN is the governing party in the Autonomous Community of Navarre. It is anti-nationalist and allied with Aznar's PP.
79   See *El Diario Vasco*, 6 and 24 June 1998.
80   In April, HB discovered that all the telephones of the party's office in Vitoria were tapped by the Spanish Secret Service CESID. Later it was known that the office in Bilbao had been spied on with microphones and cameras at least since 1995.
81   *El País*, 20 September 1998.
82   *El País*, 2 November 1998. The newspaper does not specify the names of the interlocutors, nor the exact date, nor the source of the information, which later was not denied by the PNV. By the end of April, ETA issued a communiqué requesting the PNV to break with its 'Spanish' allies, announcing 'profound changes' for the future of the Basque Country.
83   IU and EA had also held a number of previous separate meetings with HB.

84 *El País*, 1 July 1998.
85 See the text of the 'Declaration of Barcelona' in *El Diario Vasco*, 17 July 1998.
86 Information published by *El Diario Vasco*, 27 April 1998.
87 See the comment of Paddy Woodworth in *The Irish Times*, 30 October 1998 ('Basques expect a new impetus to peace process').
88 *El Diario Vasco*, 23 April 1998.
89 Information published by *El País*, 20 September and 2 November 1998.
90 I shall come back to this meeting and the following polemics in Chapter 9.
91 At the beginning of September 1998, HB decided to participate in the regional elections to the Basque parliament to be held in October under the name of Euskal Herritarrok (Basque Citizens). This new denomination was registered both to prevent a possible banning of HB and to open the new electoral coalition to sectors purged in previous phases or simply discontented with the extreme military bias of HB politics.
92 Information according to *El País*, 5 October 1998.
93 This declaration was signed by:
   a. political parties or coalitions: AB: Abertzaleen Batasuna, HB: Herri Batasuna, EAJ-PNV, EA: Eusko Alkartasuna, Izquierda Unida, Batzarre, Zutik;
   b. Trade unions: ELA, LAB, EHNE, ESK-CUIS, STEE-EILAS, Ezker Sindicala, Hiru;
   c. Other organizations: Gogoa, Amnistiaren Aldeko Batzordeak, Senideak, Bakea Orain, Elkarri, Egizan, Herria 2000 Eliza, Gernika Batzordea, Autodeterminazioaren Biltzarrak.
   See *El País*, 13 September 1998.
94 See Paddy Woodworth's article ('Spanish divided on Irish model as way forward'), in *The Irish Times*, 17 September 1998; other statements in *El País* and *El Diario Vasco*, 14./15 September 1998.
95 *El País*, 16 September 1998.
96 Text in *Euskadi Información*, 17 September 1998.
97 Quotations from the article 'Basques expect a new impetus to peace process', by P. Woodworth in *The Irish Times*, 30 October 1998.
98 Results in *El Diario Vasco*, 26 October 1998.

9 The End of a Dream

1 The Spanish translation of these documents, as well as the document quoted further below, can be found in *El Diario Vasco*, 4 May 2000.
2 Statement by EA's president and former *Lehendakari* Carlos Garaikoetxea in *El Diario Vasco*, 19 May 1999. See here also the text of the agreement signed by Ibarretxe and leaders of the three parties.
3 'Mensajes contradictorios', *El País*, 19 May 1999.
4 Founding document and statements of the politicians in *El Diario Vasco*, 19 September 1999; figures concerning the regional origin of the delegates in J. L. De La Granja and S. De Pablo, 'La encrucijada vasca: entre Ermua y Estella', in: J. Tusell, *El gobierno de Aznar: Balance de una gestión, 1996–2000* (Barcelona: Crítica, 2000), pp. 153–79, figures p. 175.
5 *Gara*, 1 May 2000.
6 'Euzko Alderdi Jeltzalearen gutuna ETAri', *Gara*, 29 April 2000; for the information concerning the meeting between ETA, PNV and EA, see ibid.
7 See the Spanish version of the document in http://www.elpais.es/temas.
8 *Gara*, 30 April 2000.

9   See the web-site of the Ministry of the Interior (www.mir.es/policia) and www.elpais.es/temas/eta.

10   In January 2002, in a flat in France used by ETA militants, a list with 100 members of the PNV and details concerning their residence, jobs, etc. was found.

11   Waldmann, *Terrorismus*, p. 187.

12   W. Zartman (ed.), *Elusive Peace: Negotiations and End to Civil Wars* (Washington, DC: The Brookings Institution, 1995), p. 333.

13   'Declaración del Lehendakari', *El Diario Vasco*, 23 February 2000.

14   The other one was in May 2000, leaking the documents concerning the secret negotiations to newspapers close to the Liberation Movement.

15   See these declarations made by the PNV deputy and spokesman in the Spanish Cortes, Iñaki Anasagasti, the *Lehendakari* Ibarretxe and the PNV president Arzallus in *El País*, 28 July, 13 and 14 August 2000.

16   See the text of the document published in *El País*, 14 January 2000. See also the interesting comment by Alberto Surio in *El Diario Vasco*, 16 January 2000 ('El guión de Quebec'), comparing the programmes of 1977 and 2000. Surio traces the origin of the latter back to the book published by the PNV leader Ollora, *Una vía para la paz*, which I have commented on above as the first important and effective theoretical essay written by a leading nationalist favouring Basque sovereignty. According to this usually well-informed journalist, both Ollara's and the programme's principal ideas are rooted in the Québecois example of a democratic and negotiated struggle for self-determination including a referendum (or successive referenda).

17   Aznar's statements in *El Mundo*, 5 and 7 December 1999.

18   J. I. Ruiz Olabuenaga, *Opinión sin tregua: Visos y denuestos del nacionalismo vasco 1998–1999* (Bilbao: Fundación Sabino Arana, 2001), p. 27; A. Elorza, 'El lehendakari y la muerte', *El Diario Vasco*, 5 June 2000; Aznar's statement in *La Vanguardia*, 11 June 2000.

19   The PNV leader's declaration in *El País*, 9 December 1999.

20   M. Weber, 'Die rationale Staatsanstalt und die modernen politischen Parteien und Parlamente (Staatssoziologie)', in: M. Weber, *Wirtschaft und Gesellschaft*, pp. 815–68, especially p. 824.

21   J. Linz, *Breakdown of Democratic Regimes: Crisis, Breakdown and Equilibration* (Baltimore: Johns Hopkins, 1978), p. 20.

22   See a larger explanation of these points in 'Acuerdo de coalición que suscriben los partidos políticos Euzko Alderdi Jeltzalea–Partido Nacionalista Vasco (EAJ–PNV) y Eusko Alkartasuna (EA) para la formación del Gobierno Vasco (VII Legislatura)', Vitoria–Gasteiz, 6 July 2001, pp. 17–19.

23   I had the opportunity to discuss some of the issues raised here in two previous articles. See L. Mees, 'Between Votes and Bullets. Conflicting Ethnic Identities in the Basque Country', *Ethnic and Racial Studies*, XXIV, 5 (2001), pp. 798–827, and 'Nacionalismo y secularización en la España de entre siglos', in: M. Suárez Cortina (ed.), *Secularización y laicismo en la España contemporánea (III Encuentro de Historia de la Restauración)*, (Santander: Sociedad Menéndez Pelayo, 2001), pp. 223–53. I am grateful to Santiago de Pablo and José Luis de la Granja for their extensive comments and criticisms on these articles.

24   Darby and Mac Ginty, p. 254.

25   J. Navarro, *Buenos días Euskadi* (Madrid: Foca, 2000), p. 150.

26   J. Darby and R. Mac Ginty, 'Northern Ireland: Long, Cold Peace', in: Darby and Mac Ginty, pp. 61–106, especially pp. 62 and 75.

27   Information according to *Gara*, 30 January 2002.
28   See the text of the document in J. Darby, *Scorpions in a Bottle: Conflicting Cultures in Northern Ireland* (London: Minority Rights Publications, 1997), pp. 206–9.
29   This is the point made by the Spanish daily *El País* in an article, 'Why in Ireland and Why Not Here?' See *El País*, 28 October 2001.
30   The Palace of Moncloa is the residence of the Spanish President.
31   Darby and Mac Ginty, pp. 62 and 64.
32   Obviously, I am unable to check the veracity of the argument that Gorka Aguirre, one of the PNV leaders present during the contacts with ETA, made when I confronted him with this same question. Aguirre's answer consisted in explaining the return to arms as a consequence of a shift in the balance of power within ETA's Ruling Council, where the initially more political majority had been outnumbered by a more military and anti-ceasefire majority.
33   J. Villanueva, *Nacionalismos y conflicto nacional en la sociedad vasco–navarra 1997–2000* (San Sebastián: Tercera Prensa, 2000), pp. 170–1. Unlike Watson, I am completely unable to see in the Lizarra Agreement any kind of 'process of a move toward a postnational model of interdependence' nor a 'move toward postnational political identities'. See C. Watson, 'Imagining ETA', in W. Douglass *et al.* (eds), *Basque Politics and Nationalism on the Eve of the Millennium* (Reno: University of Nevada, 1999), pp. 94–114, especially pp. 110–11.
34   Quoted according to the Spanish version of the communiqué in http://www. elpais.es/temas/eta.
35   A. D. Smith, *Nationalism: Theory, Ideology, History* (Cambridge: Polity Press, 2001), pp. 40–1.
36   Since Ted W. Gurr's classic study *Why Men Rebel* (Princeton: Princeton University Press, 1970), the list of publications on the issue of violence has become very large and complex. Comprehensive overviews on the different theoretical and conceptual approaches can be found in Zimmermann, *Political Violence*; A. P. Schmid, *Political Terrorism: A Research Guide to Concepts, Theories, Data Bases and Literature* (Amsterdam: North Holland, 1983); P. H. Merkl (ed.), *Political Violence and Terror: Motifs and Motivations* (Berkeley: University of California Press, 1986), especially pp. 17–59; A. Rapoport, *The Origins of Violence: Approaches to the Study of Conflict* (New York: Paragon House, 1989).
37   Irvin, *Militant Nationalism*, p. 7.
38   J. S. Holmes, *Terrorism and Democratic Stability* (Manchester and New York: Manchester University Press, 2001), pp. 148 and 159.
39   E. Moxon-Browne, *Spain and the ETA: The Bid for Basque Autonomy* (London: Centre for Security and Conflict Studies, 1987), p. 52. This publication is nearly identical with the chapter 'The Basque Country' in Moxon-Browne's book *Political Change in Spain* (London and New York: Routledge 1989), pp. 50–63; Clark, *The Basque Insurgents*; Clark, *Negotiating with ETA*; Jáuregui, *Ideología*; A. Elorza *et al.*, *La historia de ETA*.
40   Zirakzadeh, *A Rebellious People*, p. 7; Conversi, *The Basques*; J. Díez Medrano, *Divided Nations: Class, Politics, and Nationalism in the Basque Country and Catalonia* (Ithaca and London: Cornell University Press, 1995); Waldmann, *Ethnischer Radikalismus*; Waldmann, *Terrorismus*.
41   Irvin, pp. 19 and 179.
42   Irvin, p. 196.
43   H. Van Amersfoort and J. Mansvelt Beck, 'Institutional Plurality: a Way Out of the Basque Conflict?', *Journal of Ethnic and Migration Studies*, XXVI, 3, 2000, pp. 449–67, quotation pp. 458, 461.

44 Information taken from *El País*, 31 March 2002 ('Es viable una Euskadi independiente?').

45 J. Mansvelt Beck, 'The Continuity of Basque Political Violence: a Geographical Perspective on the Legitimization of Violence', *GeoJournal*, 48, pp. 109–21.

46 'Attached to ETA, the nationalist left will commit political suicide'. See the interview with Aranzadi in *El Diario Vasco*, 4 January 2002.

47 On the contrary, we know that most of the Nazi officials who organized and executed the Holocaust were loving husbands and fathers, in short, very normal people. This is also one of the conclusions in a recent book on the biographies of ETA prisoners. See F. Reinares, *Patriotas de la muerte: Quiénes han militado en ETA y por qué* (Madrid: Taurus, 2001).

48 Waldmann, *Terrorismus*, p. 129.

49 J. Arregi, *La nación vasca posible: El nacionalismo democrático en la sociedad vasca* (Barcelona: Crítica, 2000).

50 Irvin, p. 42.

51 P. Heywood, *The Government and Politics of Spain* (London: Macmillan Press – now Palgrave Macmillan, 1995), p. 39.

52 M. Crenshaw, 'The Causes of Terrorism', in E. Moxon-Browne (ed.), *European Terrorism* (Aldershot: Dartmouth, 1993), pp. 379–99, quotation p. 394.

53 Crenshaw, p. 394.

54 Waldmann, *Terrorismus*, p. 92.

55 A. Guelke, *The Age of Terrorism and the International Political System* (London: Tauris Academic Studies, 1985).

56 E. Durkheim, *The Elementary Forms of the Religious Life* (London: George Allen, 1982) {first edn.: 1915}.

57 The pioneer was R. Aron, *L'âge des empires et l'avenir de la France* (Paris: Ed. Défense de la France, 1946), pp. 287–380; see also J. P. Sironneau, *Sécularisation et religions politiques* (Le Haye: Mouton, 1982); R. J. Wuthnow, 'Sociology of Religion', in: N. S. Smelser (ed.), *Handbook of Sociology* (London: Sage Publications, 1988), pp. 473–509; Th. Hanf (ed.), *Dealing with Difference: Religion, Ethnicity, and Politics: Comparing Cases and Concepts* (Opladen: Westdeutscher Verlag, 1999).

58 St Grosby, 'Nationality and Religion', in: M. Guibernau and J. Hutchinson (eds), *Understanding Nationalism* (Cambridge: Polity Press, 2001), pp. 97–119. As an example of an identification of nationalism and (political) religion, see the recent book of the German historian of society Hans-Ulrich Wehler, *Nationalismus: Geschichte, Formen, Folgen,*(München: C. H. Beck, 2001), especially chapter III ('Der Ideenfundus des Nationalismus – Die Steigerung zur "Politischen Religion"'), pp. 27–35.

59 Smith, *Nationalism*, especially pp. 82, 145, 146.

60 J. Zulaika, *Basque Violence*.

61 Mansvelt Beck, p. 118.

62 Sironneau, pp. 318–25 ('Les rassemblements comme cérémonies sacrées').

63 Sironneau, p. 583; a brief analysis of ETA's discourse as expressed in communiqués and interviews can be found in Mees, 'Nacionalismo y secularización', especially pp. 250–3.

64 I do not agree with the thesis that the roots of violent nationalism as a political religion should be traced back to the ideology of the PNV founder Sabino Arana. See A. Elorza, *La religión política: 'El nacionalismo sabiniano' y otros ensayos sobre nacionalismo e integrismo* (San Sebastián: R & B Ediciones, 1995), pp. 29–56; A. Elorza, *Un pueblo escogido: Génesis y desarrollo del nacionalismo vasco* (Barcelona: Crítica, 2001), pp. 179–89. For a discussion of Elorza's arguments, see L. Mees, 'Nacionalismo y secularización'.

65   I. Sáez de la Fuente Aldama, *El Movimiento de Liberación Nacional Vasco, una religión de sustitución* (Bilbao: Instituto Diocesano de Teología y Pastoral, 2002).
66   Waldmann, *Terrorismus*, p. 169.

10   Epilogue: the Basque Contention in the Age of Globalization: Old Problems, New Opportunities

1   Weber, *Peasants*, p. 99.
2   See M. Castells, *The Information Age: Economy, Society and Culture*, Vol. II, *The Power of Identity* (Cambridge, Mass.: Blackwell, 1997), especially chapter 1.
3   These groups, which define themselves as left-wing in favour of Basque sovereignty, but reject violence, are Aralar, Zutik, Batzarre and, in the French Basque Country, Abertzaleen Batasuna. They have already been severely criticized by ETA, who blames them for the loss of power suffered by the nationalist left and for being 'regionalists' instead of nationalists. See the clandestine bulletin 'Zutabe', n. 95, quoted in *El Diario Vasco*, 22 May 2002.
4   This is the official name adopted by HB/EH after an internal process of reorganization initiated in 1998.
5   Darby and Mac Ginty, p. 8.
6   M. Guibernau, *Nations without States: Political Communities in a Global Age* (Malden, Ma.: Polity Press, 2000), p. 181.
7   D. Miller, *Citizenship and National Identity* (Malden, Ma.: Blackwell, 2000), pp. 125–41 ('Nationalism in Divided Societies').
8   M. Keating, 'Nations without States: the Accommodation of Nationalism in the New State Order', in M. Keating and J. McGarry (eds), *Minority Nationalism and the Changing International Order* (Oxford: Oxford University Press, 2001), pp. 19–43, quotation on p. 34.
9   In September 2002, the Basque *Lehendakari* Ibarretxe presented his proposal for negotiating with the Spanish state a 'new status of free association' for the Basque Country, based upon the principle of co-sovereignty. This proposal has been severely criticized by the Spanish government and the non-nationalist parties as a badly disguised step towards independence.

Bibliography

1. Newspapers and journals

Cambio 16
Deia
Egin
El Correo Español
El Diario Vasco
El Mundo
El País
Euskadi Información
Gara
Hika
La Vanguardia
Landeia
The Irish Times

2. Websites

www.euskadi.net
www.avt.org/eta
www.contrast.org/mirrors/ehj
www.europa.eu.int/comm/eurostat
www.basque.red.net/tregua/lizarra/htm
www.elpais.es/temas
www.mir.es/policia

3. Tape documents

Interview with J.M. Korta and J.M. Ruiz Urchegui (ADEGI), 14 November 1997.
Interview with X. Azkarzibar (Gesto por la Paz), 9 June 1997.
Interview with J. Egibar (PNV), 15 May 1997.

4. Books and articles

Actitudes hacia la violencia en el País Vasco, Mayo 1997 (Ed.: Gobierno Vasco. Presidencia, Gabinete de Prospección Sociológico), Ms.
Acuerdo de coalición que suscriben los partidos políticos Euzko Alderdi Jeltzalea – Partido Nacionalista Vasco (EAJ-PNV) y Eusko Alkartasuna (EA) para la formación del Gobierno Vasco (VII Legislatura), Vitoria–Gasteiz, 6 July 2001, Ms.
Aguirre y Lecube, J.A. de, *Diario de Aguirre* (Tafalla: Editorial Txalaparta, 1998).
Aguirre y Lecube, J.A. de, *Escape via Berlin* (New York: Macmillan, 1944).
Aja, E., *El Estado Autonómico: Federalismo y hechos diferenciales* (Madrid: Alianza, 1999).
Alonso, R., *La paz de Belfast* (Madrid: Alianza, 2000).

Alonso, R., *Irlanda del Norte: una historia de guerra y la búsqueda de la paz* (Madrid: Editorial Complutense, 2001).

Alter, P., *Nationalismus* (Frankfurt a.M.: Suhrkamp, 1985).

Alvarez Junco, J. 'La nación en duda', in: J. Pan-Montojo (ed.), *Más se perdió en Cuba: España, 1898 y la crisis de fin de siglo* (Madrid: Alianza, 1998), pp. 405–75.

Alvarez Santa Cristina, J.L./ Pikabea Ugalde, K./ Pikabea Ugalde, R., *Abertzaleon estrategiaz*, 1997ko abuztua (Ms).

Anderson, B., *Imagined Communities: Reflections upon the Origin and Spread of Nationalism* (London / New York: Verso, 1991).

Aron, R., *L'âge des empires et l'avenir de la France* (Paris: Ed. Défense de la France, 1946).

Arregi, J. *La nación vasca possible: El nacionalismo democrático en la sociedad vasca*, (Barcelona: Crítica, 2000).

Arriaga, M., *Y nosotros que éramos de HB: sociología de una heterodoxia abertzale* (San Sebastián: Haranburu, 1997).

Arteta, A./ Velasco, D./ Zubero, I., *Razones contra la violencia: Por la convivencia democrática en el País Vasco*, Vol II (Bilbao: Bakeaz, 1998).

Aulestia, K., *HB. Crónica de un delirio* (Madrid: Temas de hoy, 1998).

Baeza, A., *GAL, crimen de Estado* (Madrid: ABL, 1996).

Balfour, S., *The End of the Spanish Empire (1898–1923)* (Oxford: Clarendon Press, 1996).

Blinkhorn, M., 'The Basque Ulster: Navarre and the Basque Autonomy Question under the Spanish Second Republic', *The Historical Journal*, 17/3 (1974), pp. 595–613.

Bonaparte, L.L., *Carta lingüística del Príncipe Louis-Lucien Bonaparte, publicada en el número 116 (tomo IX) de la revista bascongada 'Euskal-Erria'* (San Sebastián: J.R. Baroja, 1883) (first edn: London: 1863).

Castells, L., 'El nacionalismo vasco (1890–1923): ¿una ideología modernizadora?' *Ayer*, 28 (1997), pp. 127–62.

Castells, M., *The Information Age: Economy, Society and Culture*, Vol. I, *The Rise of the Network Society* (Cambridge, Mass.: Blackwell, 1996).

Castells, M., *The Information Age: Economy, Society and Culture*, Vol. II, *The Power of Identity* (Cambridge, Mass.: Blackwell, 1997).

Castro, R., *Juan María Bandrés, memorias para la paz* (Majadahonda: HMR, 1998).

Chueca, J., *El nacionalismo vasco en Navarra (1931–1936)* (Bilbao: Universidad del País Vasco, 1999).

Clark, R.P., *Negotiating with ETA: Obstacles to Peace in the Basque Country, 1975–1988* (Reno: University of Nevada Press, 1990).

Clark, R.P., *The Basque Insurgents: ETA, 1952–1980* (Madison: University of Wisconsin Press, 1984).

Clavero, B., *Fueros vascos: Historia en tiempo de Constitución* (Barcelona: Ariel, 1985).

Conversi, D., *The Basques, the Catalans, and Spain* (London: Hurst, 1997).

Coordinadora Gesto por La Paz de Euskal Herria, *El trabajo por la paz en Euskal Herria: Situación actual y propuestas de futuro*, 28 July 1995, Ms.

Corcuera, J., *La patria de los vascos. Orígenes, ideología y organización del nacionalismo vasco, 1876–1903* (Madrid: Taurus, 2001).

Corcuera, J., *Política y derecho: La construcción de la autonomía vasca* (Madrid: Centro de Estudios Constitucionales, 1991).

Crenshaw, M., 'The causes of terrorism', in E. Moxon-Browne (ed.), *European Terrorism* (Aldershot: Dartmouth, 1993), pp. 379–99.

Darby, J. and Mac Ginty, R. (eds), *The Management of Peace Processes* (London: Palgrave – now Palgrave Macmillan, 2000).

Darby, J., *Scorpions in a Bottle: Conflicting Cultures in Northern Ireland* (London: Minority Rights Publications, 1997).

Delgado Soto, B. and Mencía Gullón, A.J., *Diario de un secuestro: Ortega Lara, 532 días en un zulo* (Madrid: Alianza, 1998).

Díez Medrano, J., *Divided Nations. Class, Politics, and Nationalism in the Basque Country and Catalonia* (Ithaca and London: Cornell University Press, 1995).

Domínguez Iribarren, F., *De la negociación a la tregua. ¿El final de ETA?* (Madrid: Taurus, 1998).

Domínguez Iribarren, F., *ETA: Estrategia organizativa y actuaciones 1978–1992* (Bilbao: Universidad del País Vasco, 1998).

Durkheim, E., *The Elementary Forms of the Religious Life* (London: George Allen, 1982) {first edn.: 1915}.

Egaña, I. and Giacopucci, G., *Los días de Argel. Crónica de las conversaciones entre ETA y el Gobierno español* (Tafalla: Txalaparte, 1992).

Elkarri, 'Elkarri, el trayecto de una idea' (1997), Ms.

Elkarri, *The Basque Conflict* (1995), Ms.

Elorza, A. *et al.*, *La historia de ETA* (Madrid: Temas de Hoy, 2000).

Elorza, A., *La religión política. 'El nacionalismo sabiniano' y otros ensayos sobre nacionalismo e integrismo* (San Sebastián: R & B Ediciones, 1995).

Elorza, A., *Un pueblo escogido. Génesis y desarrollo del nacionalismo vasco* (Barcelona: Crítica, 2001).

Esenwein, G. and Shubert, A., *Spain at War: The Spanish Civil War in Context, 1931–1939* (London: Longman, 1995).

Etxeberria Balerdi, F., *Bilingüismo y educación en el País del Euskara* (San Sebastián: Erein, 1999).

Extramiana, J., *Historia de las Guerras Carlistas*, 2 vols (San Sebastián: Luis Haramburu, 1979).

Fernández Sebastián, J., *La génesis del fuerismo: Prensa e ideas políticas en la crisis del Antiguo Régimen (País Vasco, 1750–1840)* (Madrid: Siglo XXI, 1991).

Ferrer, M., *Elecciones y partidos políticos en Navarra durante la Segunda República* (Pamplona: Gobierno de Navarra, 1992).

Flynn, M.K., *Ideology, Mobilization, and the Nation: The Rise of Irish, Basque and Carlist National Movements in the Nineteenth and Early Twentieth Centuries* (New York: St. Martin's Press – now Palgrave Macmillan, 2000).

Fonseca, C., *Negociar con ETA: De Argel al Gobierno del PP* (Madrid: Temas de Hoy, 1996).

Funes, M.J., *La salida del silencio: Movilizaciones por la paz en Euskadi 1986–1998* (Madrid: Akal, 1998).

Fusi J.P. and Palafox, J., *España: 1808–1996: El desafío de la modernidad*, 4th edn (Madrid: Espasa-Calpe, 1998).

Fusi, J.P., *El problema vasco en la II República* (Madrid: Turner, 1979).

Gárate, M., *El proceso de desarrollo económico en Guipúzcoa* (San Sebastián: Cámara de Comercio de Guipúzcoa, 1976).

Garitaonaindia, C. and Granja, J.L. de la (eds), *La Guerra Civil en el País Vasco: 50 años después* (Bilbao: Universidad del País Vasco, 1987).

Garmendia, J.M. and Elordi, A., *La Resistencia vasca* (San Sebastián: Haranburu, 1982).

Garmendia, J.M., *Historia de ETA* (San Sebastián: Haranburu, 1995).

Garmendia, V., *La ideología carlista (1868–1876), En los orígenes del nacionalismo vasco* (San Sebastián: Diputación Foral de Guipúzcoa, 1984).

Giacopucci, G., *ETA-pm: el otro camino* (Tafalla: Txalaparta, 1997).

González Antón, L., *España y las Españas* (Madrid: Alianza, 1997).

González Portilla, M., *La formación de la sociedad capitalista en el País Vasco*, 2 vols (San Sebastián: Luis Haramburu, 1981).

Granja, J.L. de la and Pablo, S. de, 'La encrucijada vasca: entre Ermua y Estella', in: J. Tusell, *El gobierno de Aznar: Balance de una gestión, 1996–2000* (Barcelona: Crítica, 2000), pp. 153–79.

Granja, J.L. de la, 'La invención de la historia. Nación, mitos e historia en el pensamiento del fundador del nacionalismo vasco', in: J.G. Beramendi/R. Máiz/X.M. Nuñez Seixas (eds), *Nationalism in Europe: Past and Present*, Vol. II (Santiago de Compostela: Universidad de Santiago de Compostela, 1994), pp. 97–139.

Granja, J.L. de la, *Nacionalismo y II República en el País Vasco: Estatutos de Autonomía, partidos y elecciones. Historia de Acción Nacionalista Vasca: 1930–1936* (Madrid: CIS/ Siglo XXI, 1986).

Granja, J.L. de la, *Nacionalismo y Segunda República en el País Vasco* (Madrid: Centro de Investigaciones Sociológicas/Siglo XXI, 1986).

Granja, J.L. de la, *República y Guerra Civil en Euskadi* (Oñati: IVAP, 1990).

Granja, J.L. de la/ Beramendi, J./ Anguera, P., *La España de los nacionalismos y las autonomías* (Madrid: Síntesis, 2001).

Grosby, St, 'Nationality and Religion', in: M. Guibernau and J. Hutchinson (eds), *Understanding Nationalism* (Cambridge: Polity Press, 2001), pp. 97–119.

Guelke, A., *The Age of Terrorism and the International Political System* (London: Tauris Academic Studies, 1985).

Guibernau, M., *Nations without States: Political Communities in a Global Age* (Malden, Ma.: Polity Press, 2000).

Gunther, R./ Puhle, H.-J./ Nikiforos, P.N. (eds), *The Politics of Democratic Consolidation: Southern Europe in Comparative Perspective* (Baltimore/London: Johns Hopkins University Press, 1995).

Gunther, R./ Sani, G./ Shabad, G., *Spain after Franco: The Making of a Competitive Party System* (Berkeley: University of California Press, 1986).

Gurr, T. R. and Harff, B., *Ethnic Conflict in World Politics* (Boulder: Westview Press, 1994).

Gurr, T.W., *Why Men Rebel* (Princeton: Princeton University Press, 1970).

Gurruchaga, A., *El código nacionalista vasco durante el Franquismo* (Barcelona: Anthropos).

Gurruchaga, I., *El modelo irlandés: historia secreta de un proceso de paz* (Barcelona: Península, 1998).

Hanf, Th. (ed.), *Dealing with Difference: Religion, Ethnicity, and Politics: Comparing Cases and Concepts* (Opladen: Westdeutscher Verlag, 1999).

Heywood, P., *The Government and Politics of Spain* (London: Macmillan Press – now Palgrave Macmillan, 1995).

Hobsbawm, E.J. and Ranger, R. (eds), *The Invention of Tradition* (Cambridge: Cambridge University Press, 1983).

Hobsbawm, E.J., *Nations and Nationalism since 1780: Programme, Myth, Reality* (Cambridge: Cambridge University Press, 1990).

Holmes, J.S., *Terrorism and Democratic Stability* (Manchester and New York: Manchester University Press, 2001).

Horowitz, I.L., 'The Routinization of Terrorism and Its Unanticipated Consequences', in: M. Crenshaw (ed.), *Terrorism, Legitimacy, and Power: The Consequences of Political Violence* (Middletown, Connecticut: Wesleyan University Press, 1986), pp. 38–51.

Hroch, M., *Social Preconditions and National Revival in Europe: A Comparative Analysis of the Social Composition of the Smaller European Nations* (Cambridge: Cambridge University Press, 1985).

Humboldt, W. von, 'Ankündigung einer Schrift über die Vascische Sprache und Nation, nebst Angabe des Gesichtspunctes und Inhalt derselben', in: ibid., *Gesammelte Schriften*, Vol. III (Berlin: B. Behr, 1904), pp. 288–99.

Huntington, S.P., *The Third Wave: Democratization in the Late Twentieth Century* (Norman: University of Oklahoma Press, 1991).

Ibarra, P., *La evolución estratégica de ETA* (San Sebastián: Kriselu, 1987).

Iglesias, M.A. (ed.), *Ermua, 4 días de julio: 40 voces tras la muerte de Miguel Angel Blanco* (Madrid: El País–Aguilar, 1997).

Intxausti, J., *Euskera, la lengua de los vascos* (San Sebastián: Elkar, 1992).

Irujo, J.M. and Arques, R., *ETA: la derrota de las armas. Todas las sombras, secretos y contactos de la organización terrorista al descubierto* (Barcelona: Plaza & Janes, 1993).

Irujo, M., *Un vasco en el Ministerio de Justicia*, 3 vols (Buenos Aires: Ekin, 1976–79).

Irvin, C.L., *Militant Nationalism: Between Movement and Party in Ireland and the Basque Country* (Minneapolis and London: University of Minnesota Press, 1999).

Izu Belloso, M.J., *Navarra como problema: Nación y nacionalismo en Navarra* (Madrid: Biblioteca Nueva, 2001).

Jacob, J.E., *Hills of Conflict: Basque Nationalism in France* (Reno: Nevada University Press, 1994).

Jáuregui, G., 'La cuestión nacional vasca y el Estatuto de Autonomía', *Revista Vasca de Administración Pública*, 1 (1981), pp. 79–109.

Jáuregui, G., *Ideología y estrategia política de ETA: Análisis de su evolución entre 1959 y 1968* (Madrid: Siglo XXI, 1981).

Jenkins, B., *Nationalism in France. Class and Nation since 1789* (Savage-Maryland: Barnes & Noble, 1999).

Jiménez de Aberásturi, J.C. (ed.), *Los vascos en la II Guerra Mundial: El Consejo Nacional Vasco en Londres 1940–44 (Recopilación documental)* (San Sebastián: Sociedad de Estudios Vascos, 1991).

Jiménez de Aberásturi, J.C. and San Sebastián, K., *La huelga general del 1. de mayo de 1947 (Artículos y documentos)* (San Sebastián: Sociedad de Estudios Vascos, 1991).

Jiménez de Aberásturi, J.C., *De la derrota a la esperanza: políticas vascas durante la Segunda Guerra Mundial (1937–1947)* (Oñati: IVAP, 1999).

Jover Zamora, J.M., *La civilización española a mediados del siglo XIX* (Madrid: Espasa-Calpe, 1992).

Juaristi, J., *El bucle melancólico: Historias de nacionalistas vascos*, 5th edn (Madrid: Espasa Calpe, 1998).

Juaristi, J., *El linaje de Aitor: La invención de la tradición vasca* (Madrid: Taurus, 1987).

Keating, M., 'Nations without States: the Accommodation of Nationalism in the New State Order', in M. Keating and J. McGarry (eds), *Minority Nationalism and the Changing International Order* (Oxford: Oxford University Press, 2001), pp. 19–43.

Keating, M., 'Do Workers Really Have no Country? Peripheral Nationalism and Socialism in the United Kingdom, France, Italy and Spain', in: J. Coackley (ed.), *The Social Origins of Nationalist Movements: The Contemporary West European Experience* (London: Sage, 1992), pp. 62–80.

Larronde, J.-C., *El nacionalismo vasco: su origen y su ideología en la obra de Sabino Arana-Goiri* (San Sebastián: Txertoa, 1977).

Letamendia, F., *Historia del nacionalismo vasco y de ETA*, 3 vols (San Sebastián: R & B, 1994).

Linz, J. and Stepan, A., *Problems of Democratic Transition and Consolidation: Southern Europe, South Africa, and Post-Communist Europe* (Baltimore: Johns Hopkins University Press, 1996).

Linz, J. et al., *Atlas electoral del País Vasco y Navarra* (Madrid: Centro de Investigaciones Sociológicas, 1981), pp. 88–93.

Linz, J., *Breakdown of Democratic Regimes: Crisis, Breakdown and Equilibration* (Baltimore: Johns Hopkins University Press, 1978).

Linz, J., 'Early State-Building and Late Peripheral Nationalisms against the State: The Case of Spain', in: S.N. Eisenstadt and St Rokkan (eds): *Building States and Nations: Analyses by Regions*, Vol. II (Beverly Hills: Sage Publications, 1973), pp. 32–116.

Llera, F., *Los vascos y la política* (Bilbao: Universidad del País Vasco, 1994).

López de Juan Abad, J.M., *La autonomía vasca. Crónica del comienzo (El Consejo General del País Vasco)* (San Sebastián: Txertoa, 1998).

Majuelo, E., *LAB sindikatuaren historia: Langile Abertzaleen Batzordeak (1975–2000)* (Tafalla: Txalaparta, 2000).

Majuelo, E., *Lucha de clases en Navarra, 1931–1936* (Pamplona: Gobierno de Navarra, 1989).

Mansvelt Beck, J., 'The Continuity of Basque Political Violence: A Geographical Perspective on the Legitimization of Violence', *GeoJournal*, 48, pp. 109–21.

Maravall, J.M., *Regimes, Politics, and Markets: Democratization and Economic Change in Southern and Eastern Europe* (Oxford: Oxford University Press, 1997).

Mata, J.M., *El nacionalismo vasco radical: Discurso, organización y expresiones* (Bilbao: Universidad del País Vasco, 1993).

Meer, F. De, *El Partido Nacionalista Vasco ante la Guerra de España (1936–1937)*, (Pamplona: EUNSA, 1992).

Mees, L., 'Das baskische Labyrinth: Sozialgeschichtliche Implikationen, kulturelles Umfeld und politische Artikulation des baskischen Nationalismus 1876–1937', *Archiv für Sozialgeschichte*, 32 (1992), pp. 33–55.

Mees, L., 'Der spanische "Sonderweg": Staat und Nation(en) im Spanien des 19. und 20. Jahrhunderts', in: *Archiv für Sozialgeschichte*, 40, 2000, pp. 29–66.

Mees, L., 'El nacionalismo vasco y España: reflexiones en torno a un largo desencuentro', *Espacio, Tiempo y Forma. Historia Contemporánea*, Serie V, IX (1996), pp. 67–83.

Mees, L., 'Social Solidarity and National Identity in the Basque Country: The Case of the Nationalist Trade Union ELA/STV', in: P. Pasture and J. Verberckmoes (eds), *Working-Class Internationalism and the Appeal of National Identity: Historical Debates and Current Perspectives* (Oxford and New York: Berg, 1998), pp. 43–81.

Mees, L., 'Zwischen Mobilisierung und Institutionalisierung: Der baskische Nationalismus 1953–1995', in: H. Timmermann (ed.), *Nationalismus in Europa 1945–1995* (Berlin: Duncker & Humblot, 2001), pp. 221–62.

Mees, L., 'Between Votes and Bullets. Conflicting Ethnic Identities in the Basque Country', *Ethnic and Racial Studies*, XXIV, 5 (2001), pp. 798–827.

Mees, L., 'Nacionalismo y secularización en la España de entre siglos', in: M. Suárez Cortina (ed.), *Secularización y laicismo en la España contemporánea (III Encuentro de Historia de la Restauración)* (Santander: Sociedad Menéndez Pelayo, 2001), pp. 223–53.

Mees, L., *Entre nación y clase: El nacionalismo vasco y su base social en perspectiva comparativa* (Bilbao: Fundación Sabino Arana, 1991).

Mees, L., *Nacionalismo vasco, movimiento obrero y cuestión social (1903–1923)* (Bilbao: Fundación Sabino Arana, 1992).

Merkel, W. and Puhle, H.-J., *Von der Diktatur zur Demokratie: Transformationen, Erfolgsbedingungen, Entwicklungspfade* (Opladen: Westdeutscher Verlag, 1999).

Merkl, P.H. (ed.), *Political Violence and Terror: Motifs and Motivations* (Berkeley: University of California Press, 1986).

Miller, D., *Citizenship and National Identity* (Malden, Ma.: Blackwell, 2000).

Bibliography 215

Mina, M.C., *Fueros y revolución liberal en Navarra* (Madrid: Alianza, 1981).
Miralles, M. and Arques, R., *Amedo: el Estado contra ETA*, 3rd edn (Barcelona: Plaza & Janes, 1989).
Morales Moya, A., 'Los orígenes de la administración pública contemporánea', in: A. Morales Moya and M. Esteban de Vega (eds): *La historia contemporánea en España* (Salamanca: Universidad de Salamanca, 1996), pp. 53–72.
Morán Blanco, S., *ETA entre España y Francia* (Madrid: Editorial Complutense, 1997).
Mosse, G.L., *The Nationalization of the Masses: Political Symbolism and Mass Movements in Germany from the Napoleonic Wars through the Third Reich* (Ithaca, New York: Cornell University Press, 1977).
Moxon-Browne, E., 'La política étnica: estudio comparativo de los católicos norteirlandeses y los vascos españoles', *Revista de Estudios Políticos*, vol. 63, 1989, pp. 83–105.
Moxon-Browne, E., *Political Change in Spain* (London and New York: Routledge, 1989).
Moxon-Browne, E., *Spain and ETA: The Bid for Basque Autonomy* (London: Centre for Security and Conflict Studies, 1987).
Navarro, J., *Buenos días Euskadi* (Madrid: Foca, 2000).
Nieburg, H.L., *Political Violence: The Behavioral Process* (New York: St. Martin's Press, 1969).
Núñez Seixas, X.M., *Los nacionalismos en la España contemporánea (siglos XIX y XX)* (Barcelona: Hipòtesi, 1999).
Núñez Seixas, X.M., 'El espejo irlandés y los reflejos ibéricos', *Cuadernos de Alzate*, 18, 1998, pp. 169–90.
Núñez Seixas, X.M., 'El mito del nacionalismo irlandés y su influencia en los nacionalismos gallego, vasco y catalán (1880–1936)', *Spagna Contemporanea*, 2, 1992, pp. 25–58.
Núñez, L.C., *Clases sociales en Euskadi* (San Sebastián: Txertoa, 1977).
Núñez, L.C., *Opresión y defensa del euskera* (San Sebastián: Txertoa, 1977).
Oldartzen. Oinarrizko Txostena. Egoeraren azterketa eta ildo politikoa, December 1994, Ms.
Ollora, J.M., *Un futuro para Euskadi* (San Sebastián: Erein, 1994).
Pablo, S. de, *La Segunda República en Alava: Elecciones, partidos y vida política* (Bilbao: Universidad del País Vasco, 1989).
Pablo, S. de/ Granja, J.L. de la/ Mees, L., *Documentos para la historia del nacionalismo vasco: De los Fueros a nuestros días* (Barcelona: Ariel, 1998).
Pablo, S. de and Mees, L., 'Historia social del nacionalismo vasco (1876–1937). Teoría y práctica de un movimiento social interclasista', in: J. Beramendi/R. Máiz/ X.M. Núñez Seixas (eds), *Nationalism in Europe: Past and Present*, Vol. II (Santiago de Compostela: Universidad de Santiago de Compostela, 1994) pp. 247–74.
Pablo, S. de/ Mees, L./ Rodríguez Ranz, J.A., *El péndulo patriótico. Historia del Partido Nacionalista Vasco*, Vol. I (Barcelona: Crítica, 1999).
Pablo, S. de/ Mees, L./ Rodríguez Ranz, J.A., *El Péndulo Patriótico: Historia del Partido Nacionalista Vasco, vol. II: 1936–1979* (Barcelona: Crítica, 2001).
Para un acuerdo entre los Partidos de la Mesa sobre el 'final dialogado'. Documento de Trabajo, Ms, Vitoria-Gasteiz, 17 March 1998.
Payne, S., *Basque Nationalism* (Reno: University of Nevada Press, 1975).
Plan de Actuación del Gobierno para el desarrollo de los valores democráticos y fomento de actitudes de solidaridad, tolerancia y responsabilidad en los adolescentes y jóvenes vascos (ed. Gobierno Vasco), Vitoria (1997), Ms.
Powell, Ch. T., *El piloto del cambio: el rey, la monarquía y la transición a la democracia* (Barcelona: Planeta, 1991).

Pozas, A., *Las conversaciones secretas Gobierno–ETA* (Barcelona: Ediciones B, 1992).

Preston, P., *Franco* (London: HarperCollins, 1993).

Rapoport, A., *The Origins of Violence: Approaches to the Study of Conflict* (New York: Paragon House, 1989).

Reinares, F., *Patriotas de la muerte: Quiénes han militado en ETA y por qué* (Madrid: Taurus, 2001).

Rivera, A., 'La transición en el País Vasco: un caso particular', in: J. Ugarte (ed.), *La transición en el País Vasco y España: Historia y memoria* (Bilbao: Universidad del País Vasco, 1998), pp. 79–91.

Rodríguez Ranz, J.A., *Guipúzcoa y San Sebastián en las elecciones de la II República* (San Sebastián: Fundación Social y Cultural Kutxa, 1994).

Ross, J.I., 'Structural Causes of Oppositional Political Terrorism: Towards a Causal Model', *Journal of Peace Research*, Vol. 30, 3 (1993), pp. 317–29.

Rucht, D., *Modernisierung und neue soziale Bewegungen: Deutschland, Frankreich und USA im Vergleich* (Frankfurt a.M.: Campus, 1994).

Ruiz Olabuenaga, J. and Blanco, M. C., *La inmigración vasca: Análisis trigeneracional de 150 años de inmigración* (Bilbao: Universidad de Deusto, 1994).

Ruiz Olabuenaga, J.I., *Opinión sin tregua. Visos y denuestos del nacionalismo vasco 1998–1999* (Bilbao: Fundación Sabino Arana, 2001).

Sáez de la Fuente Aldama, I., *El Movimiento de Liberación Nacional Vasco, una religión de sustitución* (Bilbao: Instituto Diocesano de Teología y Pastoral, 2002).

San Sebastián, K., *Crónicas de postguerra 1937–1951* (Bilbao: Idatz Ekintza, 1985).

Sarrailh de Ihartza, F. (pseudonym: F. Krutwig), *Vasconia: Estudio dialéctico de una nacionalidad* (Buenos Aires: Norbait, 1973; first: 1963).

Schmid, A.P., *Political Terrorism: A Research Guide to Concepts, Theories, Data Bases and Literature* (Amsterdam: North Holland, 1983).

Schulze, H., *Staat und Nation in der europäischen Geschichte* (München: Beck, 1994).

Jenkins, B. and Sofos, S., 'Nation and Nationalism in Contemporary Europe: A Theoretical Perspective', in: B. Jenkins and S. Sofos (eds): *Nation and Identity in Contemporary Europe* (London: Routledge, 1996), pp. 9–32.

Seaton, J., 'Why Do We Think the Serbs Do It? The New "Ethnic" Wars and the Media', *Political Quarterly*, 70, 3 (1999), pp. 254–70.

Share, D. and S. Mainwaring, 'Transition through Transaction: Democratization in Brazil and Spain', in: W. Selcher (ed.), *Political Liberalization in Brazil* (Boulder: Westview Press, 1986), pp. 175–215.

Share, D., *The Making of Spanish Democracy* (New York: Praeger, 1986).

Sironneau, J.P., *Sécularisation et religions politiques* (Le Haye: Mouton, 1982).

Smith, A.D., *The Ethnic Origins of Nations* (Oxford: Blackwell, 1986).

Smith, A.D., *Nationalism: Theory, Ideology, History* (Cambridge: Polity Press, 2001).

Solé Tura, J., *Nacionalidades y nacionalismos en España. Autonomías, federalismo y autodeterminación* (Madrid: Alianza, 1985).

Solozabal, J.J., *El primer nacionalismo vasco: Industrialismo y conciencia nacional* (Madrid: Túcar, 1975).

Soto, A., *La transición a la democracia: España 1975–1982* (Madrid: Alianza, 1998).

Southworth, H., *Guernica! A Study of Journalism, Diplomacy, Propaganda, and History* (Berkeley: University of California Press, 1977).

Sullivan, J., *ETA and Basque Nationalism: The Fight for Euskadi 1890–1986* (London: Routledge, 1988).

Tarrow, S., *Democracy and Disorder: Protest and Politics in Italy 1965–1975* (Oxford: Clarendon Press, 1989).

Tarrow, S., *Power in Movement: Social Movements, Collective Action and Politics* (Cambridge: Cambridge University Press, 1994).

Tejerina, B./ Fernández Sobrado, J.M./ Aierdi, X., *Sociedad civil, protesta y movimientos sociales en el País Vasco: Los límites de la teoría de la movilización de recursos* (Vitoria: Gobierno Vasco, 1995).

Tejerina, B., *Nacionalismo y lengua* (Madrid: CIS/ Siglo XXI, 1992).

Texto del Plan de Acercamiento de Presos a Cárceles Próximas al País Vasco aprobado por el Parlamento Vasco, Vitoria-Gasteiz, Febrero de 1997, Ms.

Tilly, Ch. (ed.), *The Formation of National States in Western Europe* (Princeton: Princeton University Press, 1975).

Tilly, Ch., *From Mobilization to Revolution* (New York: McGraw-Hill, 1978).

Torrealdai, J.M., XX. *Mendeko Euskal Liburuen Katalogoa (1900–1992)* (Donostia: Gipuzkoako Foru Aldundia, 1993).

Tuñón de Lara, M. (ed.), *Gernika: 50 años después (1937–1987). Nacionalismo, República, Guerra Civil* (San Sebastián: Universidad del País Vasco, 1987).

Tusell, J. and Soto, A. (eds), *Historia de la transición 1975–1986* (Madrid: Alianza, 1996).

Tusell, J., *Juan Carlos I: La restauración de la monarquía* (Madrid: Temas de Hoy, 1995).

Ugalde Zubiri, A., *La acción exterior del nacionalismo vasco (1890–1939): Historia, pensamiento y relaciones internacionales* (Bilbao: Universidad del País Vasco, 1996).

Ugalde, M., *Mujeres y nacionalismo vasco: Génesis y desarrollo de Emakume Abertzale Batza. 1906–1936* (Bilbao: Universidad del País Vasco, 1993).

Unamuno, M. de, *Obras Completas*, Vol. IV (Madrid: Escelier, 1968).

Universidad del País Vasco, Vicerectorado de *Euskara, Situación actual de la docencia bilingüe en la UPV* (Bilbao: Universidad del País Vasco, 1998).

Urkijo, I.B., *Galíndez: la tumba abierta. Los vascos y los Estados Unidos* (Vitoria-Gasteiz: Gobierno Vasco, 1993).

Van Amersfoort, H. and Mansvelt Beck, J., 'Institutional Plurality: A Way Out of the Basque Conflict?', *Journal of Ethnic and Migration Studies*, XXVI, 3, 2000, pp. 449–67.

Velasco y Fernández de la Fuente, L., *Los Euskaros en Alava, Guipúzcoa y Vizcaya: Sus orígenes, historia, lengua, leyes, costumbres y tradiciones* (Bilbao: Amigos del Libro Vasco, 1983) (first edn: Barcelona, 1879).

Villanueva, J., *Nacionalismos y conflicto nacional en la sociedad vasco-navarra 1997–2000* (San Sebastián: Tercera Prensa, 2000).

Von Tangen Page, M., *Prisons, Peace and Terrorism. Penal Policy in the Reduction of Political Violence in Northern Ireland, Italy and the Spanish Basque Country, 1968–97* (London: Macmillan Press – now Palgrave Macmillan, 1998).

Waldmann, P., *Militanter Nationalismus im Baskenland* (Frankfurt: Vervuert, 1990).

Waldmann, P., *Ethnischer Radikalismus: Ursachen und Folgen gewaltsamer Minderheitenkonflikte am Beispiel des Baskenlandes, Nordirlands und Quebecs* (Opladen: Westdeutscher Verlag, 1984).

Waldmann, P., *Terrorismus: Provokation der Macht*, 2nd edn (München: Gerling Akademie Verlag, 2001).

Watson, C., 'Imagining ETA', in W. Douglass *et al.* (eds), *Basque Politics and Nationalism on the Eve of the Millennium* (Reno: University of Nevada, 1999), pp. 94–114.

Watson, C.J., *Sacred Earth, Symbolic Blood: A Cultural History of Basque Political Violence from Arana to ETA* (Ann Arbor: UMJ, 1996).

Weber, E., *Peasants into Frenchmen: The Modernization of Rural France 1870–1914* (Stanford: Stanford University Press, 1976).

Weber, M., *Wirtschaft und Gesellschaft*, 5th edn (Tübingen: Mohr, 1980).

Wehler, H.-U., *Nationalismus: Geschichte, Formen, Folgen* (München: C.H. Beck, 2001).

Wuthnow, R.J., 'Sociology of Religion', in: N.S. Smelser (ed.), *Handbook of Sociology* (London: Sage Publications, 1988), pp. 473–509.

Zald, M.N. and McCarthy, J.D., *Social Movements in an Organizational Society* (New Brunswick: Transaction, 1987).

Zallo, R., *Euskadi o la Segunda Transición: Nación, cultura, ideologías y paz en un cambio de época* (San Sebastián: Erein, 1997).

Zartman, W. (ed.), *Elusive Peace: Negotiations and End to Civil Wars* (Washington, DC: The Brookings Institution, 1995).

Zimmermann, E., *Political Violence, Crises, and Revolutions: Theories and Research* (Boston, MA: G.K. Hall, 1983).

Zirakzadeh, C.E., *A Rebellious People: Basques, Protests, and Politics* (Reno: Nevada University Press, 1991).

Zulaika, J., *Basque Violence: Metaphor and Sacrament* (Reno: Nevada University Press, 1988).

Index